264 BC

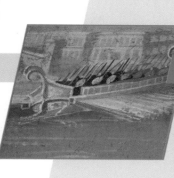

The beginning of the first of the Punic Wars, in which Rome fought Carthage for supremacy in the Mediterranean world.

from 200 BC

The Nazca culture evolves in Peru, not far from the Paracas. The Nazca are best-known today for the mysterious Nazca lines and their colourful pottery.

300 BC

216 BC

In the Second Punic War, Hannibal, a military commander from New Carthage in Spain, crosses the Pyrenees then the Alps with his army and challenges Rome.

from 300 BC

In Japan, the clan of Jimmu Tenno rises to power and founds the Yamato Kingdom.

221 BC

The ruler of the Qin clan, Ying Shen, unifies the separate kingdoms of China into a single state. He becomes its first emperor, taking the name Shihuangdi.

202 BC

Kao-Ti becomes emperor of China and establishes the Han dynasty, building a new capital at Xian.

EUROPE

113 BC

The Celtic Germanic tribes known as the Cimbri and Teutones inflict a series of defeats on the Romans.

60 BC

Pompeius, Crassus and Julius Caesar take power as Rome's First Triumvirate.

44 BC

Gaius Julius Ca[...] murdered. His [...] marks the end o[...] Roman republic. [...] ensuing civil war [...] for 17 years.

AMERICA

100 BC

The Hopewell culture, which had been gradually superseding the Adena culture in the Ohio region, reached its peak.

100 BC

AFRICA

146 BC

The Third Punic War ends with the complete destruction of Carthage by its enemy, Rome. In 27 BC, on the orders of Emperor Augustus, the city will be rebuilt as a colony of Rome.

The death of Queen [...] Egypt brings the who[...] Africa under Roman [...] region becomes an im[...] pillar of the Roman er[...]

30 BC

ASIA

63 BC

A Roman army under Pompey invades Judea and annexes the Jewish kingdom to the newly created province of Syria.

c.6 BC

Jesus is born in Roman-controlled Palestine.

OCEANIA

27 BC

Octavius becomes Rome's first emperor, receiving the honorary title 'Augustus'. Over the following centuries, the Roman Empire flourishes.

AD 44

The Romans conquer most of Britain. The Celts hold out in the northern and western fringes. Ireland and Scotland remain independent.

AD

Empero
power i
others: t
Maximiar
Galerius a

AD 100

The Pyramid of the Sun is built at Teotihuacan. Over the following centuries, Teotihuacan developed into the largest pre-Columbian city of the Americas.

AD 1

...sar is
...ath
...he
...e
...sts

Cleopatra of
e of North
le. The
portant
pire.

AD 193

Septimius Severus becomes the first African-born emperor of Rome.

AD 70

A Roman army conquers Jerusalem and destroys the Temple, the Jews' most sacred site.

from AD 100

The kingdom of Funan flourishes in Southeast Asia, centred on what is now south Cambodia but extending into Vietnam, Thailand and the Malay peninsular.

to 461 BC

Athens emerges from the wars with Persia as the leading power not just in Greece but in the Ancient World.

387 BC

Plato opens his Academy, a school of philosophy, in Athens. The institution retains its dominant position until the 6th century AD.

about 500 BC

The Maya culture experiences its first flowering. The Maya city of Kaminaljuyu (today's Guatemala City) is founded in Central America.

400 BC

C

e emerges
ok are
y for
ds of
try.

c.400 BC

The Carthaginians succeed in dislodging the Greeks from Sicily, cementing their position as the major maritime power of the western Mediterranean.

from 334 BC

Alexander the Great invades and conquers the Persian Empire. Over the next decade his military campaigns will take him and his army into Egypt and then India.

from 321 BC

The Maurya dynasty founds an empire in India in which Buddhism becomes the leading religion.

xpel
and
a
onsul,
tus

from 750 BC

The Greeks begin to found colonies around the Mediterranean.

540 BC

The Etruscans attain the peak of their power in Italy, when their fleet defeats the Greeks near Corsica.

509 BC

The Romans e their last king Rome becomes republic with a Lucius Junius Br (left), at the heli

from 700 BC

The Adena culture, one of the early Native North American civilisations, emerges in the Ohio basin.

from 600 BC

The Paracas culture flourishes in southern Peru. The Paracas people are masters of colourful textiles and intricate embroidery.

600 BC

c.760 BC

Kashata becomes the first of the black pharaohs of Egypt, as ancient Egypt is conquered by its former colony of Nubia, now the ingdom of Kush.

500 B

The Nok cultu in Nigeria. The best-known to sculpting clay h considerable art

from 770 BC

ou dynasty its power hina. The ge comes in China nset of e.

from 600 BC

Under Darius I the great Persian Empire, founded by Darius's father Cyrus II, rises to become the dominant power in the Middle East.

560 BC

Prince Siddharta is born a small kingdom in the Himalayas, in what is now Nepal. He will later experience enlightenment and become the Buddha.

283

Diocletian shares Rome with three e co-emperor and two caesars, d Constantine.

AD 313

Emperor Constantine ends the persecution of Christians in the Roman Empire. Constantine himself converted to Christianity shortly before his death in 337.

AD 380

By decree of the Emperor Theodosius, Christianity becomes the official religion of the Roman Empire.

AD 395

The Roman Empire is officially divided in two. The eastern half is ruled from Constantinople, which had been made an imperial capital by Constantine

from AD 350

The Nazca civilisation of Peru reaches its cultural zenith.

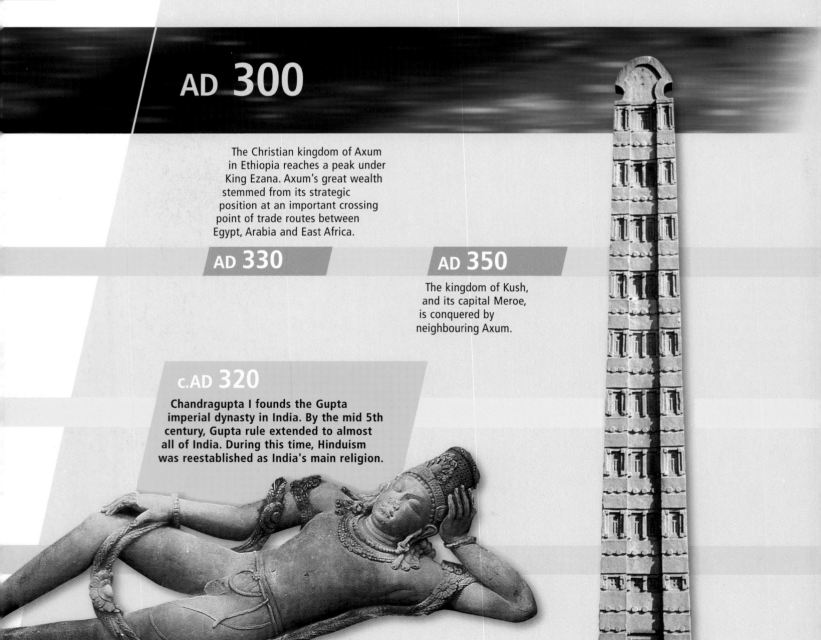

AD 300

The Christian kingdom of Axum in Ethiopia reaches a peak under King Ezana. Axum's great wealth stemmed from its strategic position at an important crossing point of trade routes between Egypt, Arabia and East Africa.

AD 330

AD 350

The kingdom of Kush, and its capital Meroe, is conquered by neighbouring Axum.

c.AD 320

Chandragupta I founds the Gupta imperial dynasty in India. By the mid 5th century, Gupta rule extended to almost all of India. During this time, Hinduism was reestablished as India's main religion.

THE
ANCIENT WORLD

900 BC – AD 430

PUBLISHED BY THE READER'S DIGEST ASSOCIATION LIMITED
LONDON • NEW YORK • SYDNEY • MONTREAL

A classic view From its position on top of the Acropolis, the Parthenon still dominates the city of Athens. It was built in the time of Pericles, now thought of as the classic age of Ancient Greece: the artistic principles established at this time are still a golden mean of perfection.

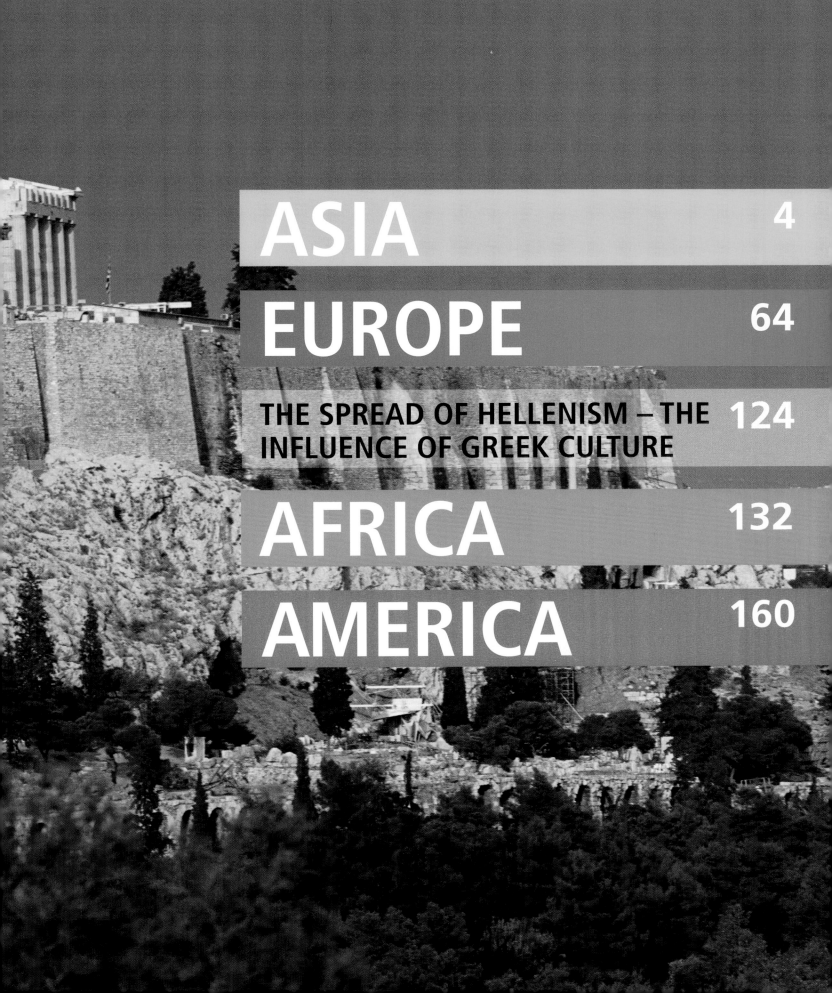

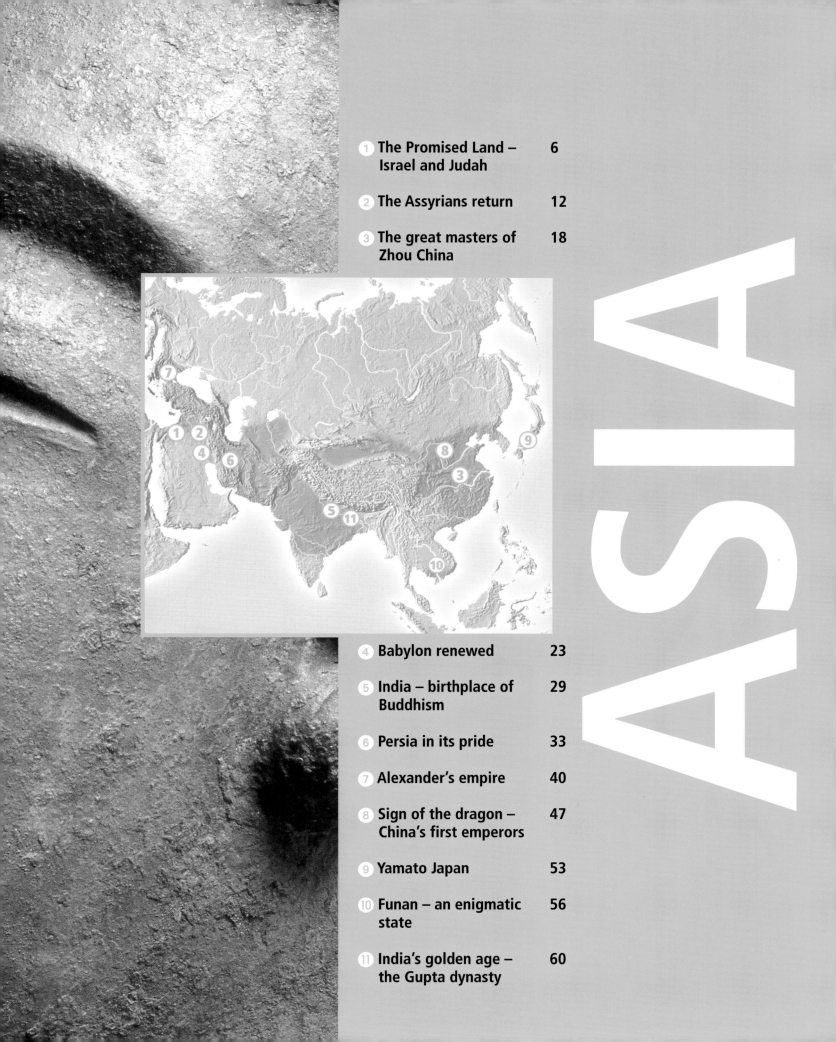

ASIA

The Promised Land – Israel and Judah

Two hundred years after Solomon's Kingdom was split in two, Jewish independence came to an end. From that time forward, Palestine was ruled by foreign masters.

Canaanite cult
This female figure from Palestine is holding a dove, a sacred animal of the Canaanite goddess Astarte, which suggests that older religious traditions survived after the Israelites had colonised the region.

King Solomon died in 926 BC, having built a major state, but the price for his achievements had been paid by the people of Palestine in crippling taxes and enforced labour. His son and successor Rehoboam persisted in the same policies, despite the impassioned pleas of his people, especially those in the north. The result, before long, was violent rebellion. The northern tribes seceded, proclaiming Jeroboam I as their king. Solomon's kingdom was effectively broken in two: the southern state of Judah and this new northern state which took the name of Israel. Conflict between the two was never far away. Jeroboam I emphasised his independence by having two shrines constructed on the northern and southern borders of his realm. In each the graven image of a bull was set up for veneration, underlining the Canaanite influence long evident in northern Palestine.

In 878 King Omri came to power in Israel and established a new royal capital at Samaria. His son Ahab oversaw the completion of the magnificent palace buildings his father had inaugurated – a match for anything in Solomon's Jerusalem. Ahab's wife was a princess from Tyre, and close ties developed with this Phoenician trading city.

Over time, the alliance with Tyre contributed greatly to Israel's wealth. There were obvious cultural influences, too, not only in the palace, which was decorated with Phoenician ivory, but in the adoption of the cult of the deity Baal. Around the same time, a rapprochement with Judah normalised relations between the two kingdoms, and they even undertook a joint campaign against the Kingdom of Moab.

Yet many Israelites felt threatened by the increasing influence of an alien culture and religion. Their feelings are echoed in words from the Book of the Prophet Amos: 'I shall tear down both the Winter and Summer Palaces, and the Houses of Ivory shall be no more, says the Lord.' Led by the warlord Jehu, followers of the Prophet Elijah deposed Omri's last descendant, King Joram, murdering both him and his hated mother Isabel. Jehu then became the new king. Ahasja, then King of Judah, also perished in the coup.

Despite a short spell of hostilities which broke out later, the uprising did not sow serious discord between Israel and Judah. Up till now, Israel had been constantly in conflict with the neighbouring Aramaic kingdom of Damascus, but that state was now fully occupied with a serious threat from the mighty Assyrian Empire. Both Judah and Israel flourished during the first half of the 8th century BC. Yet Assyrian encroachment into Syria was already casting a long shadow.

The end of the northern kingdom

By 738 BC, Israel was being threatened by Tiglathpileser III's Assyrian armies, and King Menachem was forced to pay a huge tribute of 1000 silver talents. His successor engaged in

The Dead Sea Scrolls
Found in these caves at Qumran, the famous Dead Sea Scrolls contain the oldest extant manuscripts of books of the Hebrew Bible. The text in the scroll below is written in Aramaic.

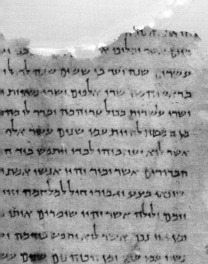

secret negotiations with Egypt, but even this could not prevent the Assyrians from invading. In 722 BC, Sargon II captured Samaria and deported its surviving inhabitants to Mesopotamia. In his victory inscription, Sargon boasts: 'At the beginning of my reign…I overran Samaria and carried off 17,290 people who were living there!'

So the fate of Israel was sealed, and time was rapidly running out for Judah. King Hezekiah of Judah joined in a coalition with Egypt and a group of small Syrian states, all of whom lived in fear of Assyrian military might. The onslaught was not long in coming. King Sennacherib launched a massive attack on Judah, and in 701 BC the city of Lachish fell. These dramatic events are vividly depicted on a relief in the Assyrian royal palace at Nineveh. It shows the battle

raging round the city's walls; mobile siege towers run up against the walls under covering fire from archers; and, finally, terrified inhabitants are escorted from the captured city.

The Prophet Isaiah described the attacking Assyrians: 'Their arrows are sharpened and their bows drawn…and their chariot wheels spin like a whirlwind.' Soon Jerusalem itself was under siege, but, after payment of a tribute, the Assyrians withdrew. Henceforth, the kings of Judah would be vassals of the Assyrian king.

Assyria, though, was generally content to allow its subject states a fair degree of autonomy, and in most respects Judah was allowed to go its own way. So it was that, under King Josiah (639–609 BC), the cult of Yahweh was revived and the old Canaanite religion was as far as possible eradicated. Yahweh became the kingdom's

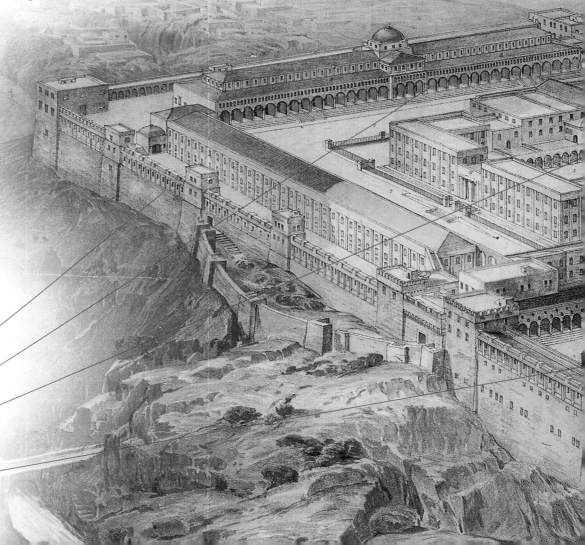

The Second Temple at Jerusalem
This 19th-century illustration re-creates the Temple of Solomon in the Byzantine style of late Antiquity. As such, it is anachronistic – it could not have existed in this form at the time – but the reconstruction does convey the huge extent and imposing nature of the complex. The renovation of the temple undertaken by Herod in 20 BC was, in part, in the Graeco-Roman style.

The remains of the massive enclosing wall now form the Western (Wailing) Wall.

Colonnades surrounded the extensive forecourts.

The temple itself was modelled on that of Solomon.

The Fortress of Antonia built by Herod to protect the shrine from attack.

one and only official god, and the Temple at Jerusalem his sole shrine.

Changing power-relations in the wider region had meanwhile seen Babylon gain renewed ascendancy over Assyria, and King Jehoiakim became subjugated to the Babylonian king Nebuchadnezzar II. The relationship would be short-lived: before long Jehoiakim broke with the Babylonians, but it was his son Jehoiachin who had to bear the consequences.

In 597 BC, Nebuchadnezzar captured and sacked Jerusalem and Jehoiachin was deported to Babylon along with much of Judah's ruling elite. The Babylonian king installed Zedekiah, a relative of Jehoiachin, in the ousted ruler's place, but he too ultimately proved wayward. Disregarding impassioned warnings by the Prophet Jeremiah, Zedekiah opened negotiations with Egypt in an attempt to form an alliance against Babylonian power. Inevitably, in 590 BC, Nebuchadnezzar II launched an attack. 'A lion has arisen from its lair,' lamented Jeremiah, 'to make your land a desert…and lay waste to your cities….' His predictions proved true.

The Babylonian exile

Jerusalem fell to the invaders in 587 BC after a punishing three-year siege. Nebuchadnezzar razed the city to the ground and his vengeance did not stop there. The unfortunate Zedekiah was forced to watch the execution of his sons, then his eyes were put out and he was led off to Babylon together with the entire population of Jerusalem.

Thus began the episode which has become known as the 'Babylonian Captivity'. The expression is, however, in certain respects misleading. What the deportees had to endure was more an involuntary exile than the imprisonment

BACKGROUND

The Diaspora – the fate of the Jews

The Greek word 'Diaspora' literally means 'dispersal', the destiny of the Jewish people through so many centuries. It began as early as the 6th century BC with the Babylonian Captivity, but there were also diasporas in the 2nd and 1st centuries BC in Alexandria. At that time, the population of the Egyptian seaport was some 40 per cent Jewish; by the 1st century AD the number of Jews living scattered around the Roman Empire far exceeded those living in Palestine itself. Following major Jewish uprisings in AD 70 and 135 – both savagely suppressed by the Romans – those who survived were deported and sold off as slaves. However, Jews living in the Diaspora constantly turned their gaze towards Jerusalem, the symbolic centre of their traditions and identity.

The farmers' calendar
This stone from 9th-century BC Gezer is inscribed with Ancient Hebrew script that records the activities of the agricultural year.

Early reflections
These two bronze mirrors are from 1st century AD Palestine. They would have been polished to a sheen to give a clear reflection.

that the term 'captivity' implies. They were allowed to move around freely in Babylon; they built houses, laid out gardens, and could worship together and convene meetings. However, they still felt a long way from home and very out of place, especially as the practice of their religion was rooted so firmly in Jerusalem. By observing particular sacred customs, they developed a special sense of unity which helped to reinforce their shared Jewish identity. These customs included strict observance of the Sabbath on the seventh day of the week and circumcision of young boys. Their enforced contact with Babylonian culture also introduced them to Mesopotamian creation myths; this was where they heard the story of the Flood, as it has come down to us in the Bible. The impact of the 'Babylonian Captivity' on Jewish consciousness was profound and enduring, but the captivity itself did not actually last all that long. The Persian king Cyrus II overran Babylon, and he allowed the Jews to return to Palestine in 538 BC.

A new temple in Jerusalem

The period of Persian rule over Palestine that followed was notable for religious tolerance. Cyrus expressly

ordered that the Temple in Jerusalem be rebuilt with public funding and that plundered artefacts be restored. Economic difficulties meant that work on the new building was repeatedly delayed, however, and the Temple was not finally dedicated until 515 BC. The loss of political independence in Palestine led to greater prominence being accorded to the office of High Priest of the Temple of Jerusalem, whose influence as a secular leader accordingly grew.

In 332 BC, Alexander the Great passed this way with his army of conquest *en route* to Egypt: for the most part Palestine surrendered without a fight to become part of Alexander's empire. Under Alexander's successors, the land was first ruled as part of the Ptolemaic kingdom of Egypt, but then it was overrun by the Seleucid king, Antiochus III, in 198 BC. The population of Jerusalem appear to have been content with this change of leadership – they enthusiastically greeted the Seleucid troops as they rode into the city on their war elephants. In return, the Seleucid king lowered taxation and granted special privileges to the Temple.

Yet tensions soon arose over the growing influence of Hellenistic culture and lifestyle, between traditional and 'modern-minded' Jews. Antiochus IV made the mistake of plundering the Temple and interfering in Jewish religious practice. When, in 166 BC, he staged Greek rituals of worship in the Temple, open revolt broke out.

The Hasmoneans

A traditionalist family, the Hasmoneans were prominent in the revolt. One member, Judas, nicknamed Maccabeus or 'the Hammer', ultimately became the leader of the uprising. The revolt of the Maccabees spread and, in 142 BC, Simeon Maccabeus

was finally able to gain independence from the Seleucids. He promptly took on the offices of both High Priest and ruler of the land, with the privilege of minting his own coins.

In 104 BC, Aristobolus I assumed the title of king, which then passed to his successors. During this period, a large number of religious-political movements formed, most notably the Pharisees and the Sadducees. These groups differed from each other in their interpretation of Biblical law, the Torah, but there were also other sects who looked to sources outside Jewish tradition for inspiration, drawing on a wide range of Egyptian, Greek and Near Eastern religious influences. Some sects even anticipated the coming of the Messiah, or Saviour.

The Romans in Jerusalem

Perhaps inevitably, these religious differences gave rise first to political tensions and then to violent strife. In 64 BC the Roman general Pompey intervened to impose a peace, at the invitation of a number of different factions, each of which hoped to gain

something to their advantage. But Roman conquest was a disaster for the Jews. In 63 BC, Jerusalem was taken, the Temple sacked and over 12,000 people killed. Stability followed when Hyrcanus II was installed as High Priest, albeit without the title of King, and Hyrcanus' rival Antipater was shrewd enough to back Julius Caesar in his struggle with Pompey. Antipater himself was assassinated in the same year as Caesar, 44 BC, but four years later his son Herod was recognised by the Roman Senate as King of Judea.

Herod's successors ruled until AD 44, when the kingdom was brought under direct Roman rule as the province of Judea. In exercising their authority, the Roman administration committed many errors that enraged devout Jews. The spark of revolt was finally ignited in AD 66, when the Roman procurator, Florus, took 17 talents from the coffers of the Temple in Jerusalem. The Romans were forced to deploy a large part of their armed forces to bring the country under control again. Only with the capture of Jerusalem by Titus in AD 70 did they successfully re-establish their authority.

The victor's spoils
This relief from the Arch of Titus in Rome depicts the triumphal procession of the victorious general. The treasures being paraded, including the seven-branched menorah, were looted from Jerusalem's Temple.

The Assyrians return

The Assyrians returned to the ascendant in the 1st millennium BC and built an empire extending from the Mediterranean to the Persian Gulf. Their warlike ferocity masked a remarkably sophisticated culture.

In 612 BC, the well-armed forces of a coalition of Babylonians and Iranian Medes were massed outside the walls of Nineveh. The city was convulsed with fear, provisions were exhausted and the supply network close to collapse. Yet resistance remained bitter and obdurate, surrender out of the question, for everyone remembered the fate of Assur just two years before. In 614 BC, this same enemy razed Assur to the ground, massacring men, women and children in an orgy of bloodletting. Why expect a kinder fate this time? But three months of desperate struggle only postponed the inevitable: the enemy finally forced entry and the inhabitants' worst terrors were realised. Only a handful managed to escape the slaughter – anyone caught was instantly put to death.

The fall of Nineveh was more than a human tragedy, it was a turning point in ancient history, marking the end of some 270 years of the Assyrian Empire. Nineveh was the last capital city of the Assyrians, a warrior people who at their height controlled an empire stretching from Egypt to Persia. Now, that power passed to the Babylonians.

Cruel conquerors

There was a hideous irony about the brutal way in which the Assyrians met their end: they had themselves shown little mercy towards conquered foes. For the vanquished, Assyrian occupation had meant despoliation, deportation, torture and, all too often, death. Nor had the Assyrians been shy about such atrocities, which were routinely recorded in official inscriptions and bas-reliefs without a hint of remorse – in fact, quite the reverse, as with the proclamation of one Assyrian king after an especially bloody campaign: 'One month ago, I reduced the land of Elam to rubble. The voices of the people, the stamping of buffalo, every cry of joy – all these I reduced to silence.' Dreadful scenes are shown on the reliefs, such as prisoners being impaled on stakes, flayed alive and blinded.

The Babylonians, in particular, were not likely to look sympathetically on Assyrian suffering. It was not so many years since the Assyrian siege of Babylon, during which the Assyrians had completely cut off the food supply to the city. It was rumoured that the besieged inhabitants had been forced to resort to cannibalism. Few in Mesopotamia or the wider Middle East had reason to mourn the end of Assyrian ascendancy – on the contrary, it was greeted with immense relief.

In the Biblical account, in the Book of the Prophet Nahum, the destruction of Nineveh is presented as just retribution for the evil deeds of the Assyrians: 'Woe to the city which has spilt so much blood, which is a master of lies and deceit! It is full of stolen goods, and yet cannot desist from plundering. Its downfall draws near, with the sound of cracking whips and

Royal wreath
Adorned with pomegranates and surmounted by four-winged protective spirits, this elaborate diadem was found during archaeological excavations at the end of the 20th century in the Iraqi city of Nimrud, the splendid new capital of Assyria in the 9th century BC.

rattling wheels, galloping horses, racing chariots, and riders dashing around. Swords flash like fire and spears like lightning! There will be heaps of the fallen dead; people will stumble over the innumerable corpses. All this shall come to pass in Nineveh – the whore, which, with its allures and magical arts, has held the people captive in thrall.'

Tactics of terror

It would be wrong to assume, however, that the Assyrians were in some deep psychological sense a cruel or sadistic people: their atrocities were part of a programme of tactical terror. That their crimes were committed in a spirit of cold calculation rather than in an explosion of insane bloodlust hardly diminishes their guilt, yet it is important to understand their motivations and the times in which they lived. For the Assyrians, the cruel and humiliating treatment of conquered peoples and prisoners was first and foremost a means of forcing their subjects into obedience and discipline. The deterrent effect was paramount and this was why, far from concealing what we would call their 'war crimes', the Assyrians

proclaimed them far and wide: their reputation for ruthlessness discouraged opposition. Practical considerations also lay behind the practice of carrying off prisoners of war into slavery, and settling them on home territory. Not only did this provide the Assyrians with an abundance of labour for their lands, but it also depleted the vanquished enemies' fighting strength, keeping them in their place.

The rise of the Assyrians from the 9th century BC onwards was not their first irruption into the history of Mesopotamia. During the 2nd millennium BC, Assyrian rulers had time and again played a prominent role among the peoples and cities between the Tigris and Euphrates – then, too, they had been notorious for warlike prowess and ruthless savagery. That first Assyrian state had eventually foundered, however, and by around 1000 BC, the once-feared race of warriors had largely subsided into passivity. The former sackers of cities now

Lion hunt
Hunting was primarily about status for Assyrian kings. The killing of a lion, the king of beasts, was an assertion of power and strength by 'the kings of the world'.

Warrior king
Ashurnasirpal II did more than anyone to rebuild Assyrian military power. He appears here in full armour, attended by a slave who shields him from the sun with a parasol.

made a meek living as small-scale farmers and pastoralists; only the emptiest shell of Assyrian statehood remained. All that changed in 883 BC with the accession of Ashurnasirpal II to the throne in what was then the royal capital of Assur.

Portraits of Ashurnasirpal which have survived show a king of haughty bearing, and stern features, a penetrating stare and aquiline nose. He appears to have had much of the cruel charisma of the Assyrian kings of old – yet a fierce expression would clearly only have taken him so far. Ashurnasirpal's real achievement was in reconstructing the Assyrian military machine, which he did with such skill and on such a grand scale that the old aura of invincibility was soon revived.

EVERYDAY LIFE

Life in Assyria for farmers, city dwellers and women

The Assyrians were a warlike people, yet the splendours of Nineveh and Assur make it clear that their cultural horizons extended far beyond the battlefield. Moreover, Assyrian civilisation was neither solely, nor even pre-eminently, urban: most Assyrians lived in small scattered rural communities and worked the land.

As elsewhere in the Middle East, houses were simply built and sparsely furnished. Poverty was not widespread, however. The lands between the Tigris and Euphrates rivers were so fertile even the poorest peasant could hope to make a reasonable living.

Life in the cities moved at a more bustling tempo, especially in the royal capitals. The atmosphere here was cosmopolitan, an impression underlined by the presence of so many foreigners carried off from their homelands into slavery.

Since the cities were centres of business and trade, an astonishing

variety of professions developed here. Architects and skilled craftsmen were in especially high demand, thanks not only to the numerous royal construction projects, but also to competition between status-conscious aristocratic families who wished to surround themselves with the most impressive show of magnificence.

Despite the sophistication of the society, even the highest-born women had little influence: a wife was regarded as her husband's chattel and governed by laws in existence since the Middle Assyrian period. One unyielding statute proclaimed: 'A man may beat his wife, he may tear out her hair, and twist and injure her ears. There is nothing unlawful in this.'

The Assyrian way of dealing with women who had an abortion did full justice to their reputation for cruelty: as punishment for this crime, a woman might be impaled on a stake and then her body denied a proper burial.

Assyrians on the march

The sheer number of warriors the Assyrians could call upon was impressive in itself: the king could field 20,000 foot soldiers armed with iron daggers and swords, plus 12,000 horsemen, equipped with bows and arrows. The Assyrian attack had an extra cutting-edge thanks to the skilled deployment of war chariots, each crewed by a team of three men.

Assyrian forces were admirably well prepared for besieging and storming cities. Scarcely a wall had been built that could withstand their heavy siege engines, which included six-wheeled battering rams and scaling ladders. Up these swarmed intrepid fighters equipped with pickaxes and crowbars, to open up breaches through which their comrades could pour unchecked. Soon the state coffers were once again filled with war booty and overflowing with the tributes exacted from conquered peoples and cities.

Ashurnasirpal was anxious to assert both his authority and that of the Assyrian state. Accordingly, at Kalach (modern Nimrud), to the north of the city of Assur, he set about the construction of a spectacular new capital. Thousands of forced labourers – mostly prisoners of war – were pressed into work on this awesomely ambitious project.

At the centre of the new metropolis stood a magnificent palace complex, surrounded on every side by spacious grounds. Among other attractions, there was a zoological garden where the public could come to marvel at exotic animals such as lions, ostriches and monkeys.

Ashurnasirpal celebrated the official dedication of his royal residence in 879 BC with a banquet that put all previous functions in the shade. It is reported that some 70,000 invited guests ate and drank for a full ten days, entirely at the king's expense.

By the time Ashurnasirpal II died, in 859 BC, the Assyrians ruled over the whole of northern and central Mesopotamia, and they had mounted exploratory forays further west. In the reigns of succeeding kings they extended their sphere of influence a great deal further, with major campaigns in Syria and Palestine. The kings hoped to gain control of the lucrative commercial corridor linking the valleys of the Tigris and Euphrates rivers with the Mediterranean. To a large extent they succeeded, making vassals of leading rulers in the region, though Damascus was never to be subjugated.

Consolidating power

Yet along with military successes came administrative problems. As the empire grew larger, the governors appointed in the occupied territories to represent the interests of their Assyrian masters became more important. The loyalty that such officials showed to whichever Assyrian king was in power at the time depended crucially upon how strong that particular ruler was.

The royal title conferred no authority in itself and weakness at the imperial centre was quickly exploited, whatever oracular utterances or magical formulae the king could produce to show divine approval. Ashurnasirpal's successors were to learn the hard way that if they neglected the wider empire, leading governors would begin to carve out all but autonomous territories of their own. The inevitable results were civil wars within the Assyrian Empire, which spiralled slowly out of control until the accession of Tiglathpileser III (745–727 BC).

Tiglathpileser was one of the great rulers of the ancient near East. He not only restored royal rule but extended Assyrian dominions so far that he was in a position to style himself, with a fair amount of justification, as 'King of the Four Corners of the Earth'.

By the time Tiglathpileser died, in 727 BC, the Assyrians ruled not only northern Syria, Damascus and Gaza, but also the southern part of Mesopotamia. In 729 BC, under the name of Pulu,

Tiglathpileser had even had himself crowned king of Babylon.

Such sustained expansionism was principally made possible by a round of reforms through which Tiglathpileser created the most advanced army the world had ever seen. Military technology was brought to a new pitch of perfection and a sophisticated system of fortresses was built across the empire. Still more important was the establishment of a standing army whose full-time soldiers could be deployed wherever and whenever they were needed.

But innovation extended far beyond the immediate military sphere: Tiglathpileser undertook wide-ranging economic reforms to ensure that significant forces could be spared for action at any given moment; no longer did military campaigning have to fit in with the rhythms of the farming calendar. The result was an unprecedented freedom of military action: unencumbered by economic and agrarian concerns, the king could confidently consider any military undertaking, from a large invasion to a three-year siege. Such

Lion tamer
With a lion slung across his shoulders, and gripping a ram by its horns, this figure proclaims the strength of the Assyrians – and the virtuosity of their craftsmen. The background image shows the palace of Dur-Sharrukin.

The glory of Nineveh
This artist's impression conveys something of the splendour of King Sennacherib's capital. Today, the ruins of this once-great city can be seen near Mosul, in Iraq.

measures left Tiglathpileser's successors well equipped to continue his policy of further conquest, bringing the Assyrians to the very zenith of their power.

This was a time when every king seemed to bring new conquests. Sargon II (722–705 BC), for instance, captured the kingdom of Urartu, fought the Medes and defeated the Egyptians. Following the example of Ashurnasirpal, he founded a new royal capital called Dur-Sharrukin ('City of Sargon'), an architectural monument to the majesty of his rule. Inscriptions here tell of his great deeds, enumerating massacres and deportations with a bookkeeper's aplomb: 'I had 27,290 people, who lived in this city, led away,' he boasts of one campaign.

Sargon's son Sennacherib (704–641 BC) conquered Judah and its capital Jerusalem, and destroyed the insubordinate Babylon. The bloodbath there was appalling even by Assyrian standards. Under Sennacherib, Nineveh was renewed and enlarged to become a magnificent royal capital: the city was reconceived on a splendid scale. Sennacherib wished to make this old city a jewel that would put

all others in the shade. Like other Assyrian capitals, the renovated Nineveh was dominated by its royal palace complex. And, in the tradition established by Ashurnasirpal, Sennacherib made sure his city put on a stunning show, with wonderful parks and gardens within its walls, and orchards, olive groves and vineyards without.

After the assassination of Sennacherib (the exact reasons for which have never been satisfactorily explained), his son Esarhaddon ascended the Assyrian throne. His reign saw another round of expansion, with Assyria's forces once again undertaking a series of large-scale military campaigns. Following the conquest of Egypt and Nubia, the empire was at its greatest extent.

Fostering culture

'I am Ashurbanipal, the King of the World, the King of Assyria. My princely fancy led me to grab a desert lion by the tail and at the behest of my masters, the gods Ninib and Nergal, I split its skull open with my double-headed axe.' So reads one inscription in which

Esarhaddon's successor introduces himself: military prowess was central not only to Assyrian self-esteem but to the image the state promoted to the world at large. In this manner Ashurbanipal, who succeeded Esarhaddon in 669 BC, placed himself firmly in the tradition of his forebears, all of whom had proudly proclaimed their strength and their courage – and their ruthlessness.

Yet another inscription, just as vain-glorious, reveals a very different side to this same Ashurbanipal, and gives us a far more three-dimensional sense of what it meant to be an Assyrian: 'I am solving the most complex problems of division and multiplication,' it announces. 'I have read the elaborate written tablets from Sumer and obscure Akkadian, which is difficult to learn. I can understand the text inscribed on stones that predate the Great Flood.'

Here, Ashurbanipal presents himself not as a mighty ruler, but as a scholar. Two very different pronouncements, then, but they reflect the split personality he showed in a reign which lasted until 626 BC, and point to a wider paradox in the Assyrian character. On the one hand, he was the ruler of a state whose existence revolved around war: this was how the empire had been built, and only in this way could it be held together. On the other hand, Ashurbanipal personified an aspect of Assyrian culture too often eclipsed by reports of military might and fearful cruelty. Such testimony is true, but it does not tell the whole story: the Assyrians were not the uncultured barbarians that they may have seemed.

The library at Nineveh

For evidence of this, one need look no further than the great library Ashurbanipal founded at Nineveh: archaeologists have discovered more than 25,000 clay tablets in the ruins of the royal palace. On these an incredible diversity of texts were recorded, ranging from myths and legends to astronomical treatises, from medical theory to sacred hymns and prayers. Also in Ashurbanipal's library was the most complete edition yet found of the most famous epic poem of ancient Near Eastern literature. Comprising some 3000 verses carved onto 12 tablets, this is the most extensive version known of the *Epic of Gilgamesh*, which tells of a quest for everlasting renown pursued by a legendary ruler of Uruk.

Busy as he would have been with his affairs of state, Ashurbanipal would hardly have been able to read every book in his library, yet he would certainly have been familiar with the deeds of Gilgamesh. He resembled the fabled king in many respects: like him he was striving for lasting fame, yet his name is now associated with the beginnings of imperial decline. Egypt was lost during his reign, and though a resurgent Babylon was successfully – and savagely – put down in 648 BC, Assyria was weakened in the struggle to reassert its supremacy. On Ashurbanipal's death in 626 BC, civil war broke out as his sons fought over the succession, presenting a golden opportunity to Assyria's subject peoples. A newly emboldened Babylon joined forces with the Medes to lead a coalition of the discontented against their old oppressor. After so many decades of domination, one concerted heave was all it ultimately took: with the destruction of Nineveh, the history of the Assyrians reached its end.

A noble lady
Phoenician craftsmen made this woman's head of ivory for Assyria's Sargon II. It formed part of the decoration for a piece of furniture.

The great masters of Zhou China

The Bronze Age in China saw a descent into disorder as the hold of the Zhou dynasty grew ever weaker. Local warlords fought incessantly, yet despite the chaotic conditions, there was an extraordinary flowering of Chinese culture.

Bronze mirror
A tigress chases her tail around this delightful mirror from the 8th–6th centuries BC: a closer look reveals that she is pregnant with cubs.

The Huang He is officially the world's muddiest river. Its heavy load of sediment – some 2.2g per litre – gives the river is distinctive colour and led to its name in English of 'Yellow River'. It also accounts for the extraordinary fertility of the floodplain that lines the river's oozing course through the heart of Central China. For centuries, this rich mud had been the basis of a thriving agricultural economy: millet and barley needed no encouragement to grow here. Mud built a civilisation in more ways than one: local farmers built their settlements of mud huts encircled by high mud walls.

The larger settlements had workshops where craftsmen laboured to produce bronze vessels and weaponry, and busy markets to which merchants flocked from far and wide. Lording it over this bustling activity were the kings of the Zhou dynasty, who bore the title Tianzi, or 'Son of Heaven', and those members of the aristocratic warrior-class whose ancestors were worshipped along with the gods in the community's temples. The Zhou had replaced the rulers of the Shang dynasty in the 11th century BC and made their capital at Qishan, but their hold on their kingdom had been

weakening ever since. Under a system similar to the feudalism of medieval Europe, the leading aristocrats had grown rich on the produce of the peasantry, which was provided to them in return for protection. These nobles had become accustomed to being little kings at local level – and increasingly wayward in their relationship with the ruling dynasty.

By the beginning of the 8th century BC local warlords were actively scheming to seize power themselves, and in 771 BC they made common cause with the Quan Rong, nomadic raiders from the steppes to the north. Rising up in revolt against their Zhou rulers, they captured Qishan, bringing to an end what has come to be known as the Western Zhou dynasty.

The royal household fled to safety and established a new capital farther east at Luoyang. But although the Eastern Zhou dynasty endured 500 years (770–256 BC), its rulers were no more than figureheads: real power was held – and fiercely fought over – by the leading nobles.

Barbarian values

By 700 BC, the Eastern Zhou Empire comprised more than a hundred separate statelets, each with an urban centre from which a local king or warlord wielded power. Many of these kingdoms were tiny (even at their most extensive, Zhou dominions never covered anything like

This coloured woodcut shows Confucius, one of the great masters and teachers of the Zhou period. His philosophy still influences Chinese thought and society today.

For whom the bell tolls
Bronze bells were rung in honour of the ancestors. The ritual, performed as part of the cult of the ancestors, is recorded here on a metal jar.

what we now think of as China), but their rulers prized their independence just the same. Collectively, these kingdoms referred to themselves as the *Zhongguo* – literally, 'the states of the Middle', more familiar as the Middle Kingdom – a name said to stem from their inhabitants' comfortable assumption that their homeland lay at the centre of the earth.

To the north, they knew, was an endless arid expanse across which nomadic herding peoples roamed. All too often, these nomads struck southward, invading and pillaging border regions. To the south lay tropical forests whose tribes seemed alien to the Chinese, though they valued many of the products the jungles yielded.

The Middle Kingdom traded with the southern tribes, offering fabrics, tools and weapons of bronze (and increasingly from around 500 BC, iron), and receiving gemstones, bamboo and rhinoceros hides in return. Along with merchandise came cultural influences: the growing of rice in submerged paddy fields, for example,

probably came from southern farmers. Relations between the Chinese and the northern nomads, though more fraught, were also fruitful. The Chinese copied riding gear and weaponry from the raiders (notably, the short bow), along with many of the artistic motifs of the 'animal style'.

Slowly but surely, a recognisably Chinese culture began to emerge in the Middle Kingdom – yet political coherence was a distant dream. Quarrels erupted and alliances shifted with bewildering speed: war was the only constant. Gradually, by the start of the 5th century BC, seven larger states emerged from the confusion: the Han, Wei, Zhao, Qi, Yan, Chu and Qin. Though they dwarfed the diminished Zhou kingdom, the Zhou remained nominal overlords. But no equilibrium had been reached: the conflict intensified between these larger kingdoms in what Chinese history calls *Zhanguo*, the Period of the Warring States (475–221 BC).

Courts of culture

It may seem paradoxical that an age of such instability and widespread war should also have been a time of magnificent achievements in philosophy, science and the arts, but in fact the rivalry of these kingdoms and their royal courts was pivotal. The kings of the warring states knew the dangers of an over-powerful aristocracy – they themselves had achieved regal power at the expense of their Zhou overlords. So it made sense for them to concentrate power and status around themselves, making their courts the splendid centres of their kingdoms.

The Zhou dynasty had sought to ensure the loyalty of its nobility with generous grants of land, but this had merely encouraged the powerful lords in their arrogance. The new rulers opted to employ advisers and officials drawn from the lower ranks of the aristocracy – an early example of a civil service. In order to train up this cohort of bureaucrats, and instil in them the virtues of orderliness and obedience, academies were established to teach religion and philosophy. Writings by leading scholars of the time have endured to offer us a fascinating window on the life and thought of Bronze Age China.

Scientific study was also fostered because any technological advance might bestow an edge in economic prowess – or, of course, a much-needed advantage on the battlefield. The demotion of the old elite extended into the realm of the military. At one time, war had been the business of a few great warriors, heroic figures in their mighty chariots, their clashes a chivalrous, almost ritualised affair. Now this knightly class was sidelined and the work of warfare fell instead to vast armies of low-born – and expendable – infantry, who fought to the death, under the direction of a new breed of ruthless and resourceful generals.

BACKGROUND

The hundred schools of the great masters

The 'schools of thought' of Zhou period China provided an environment of scientific and philosophical enquiry in which 'great masters' produced works of eternal value. The greatest master of all was Kong Fuzi, better known as Confucius, who lived from 551 to 479 BC. He set out an ethic of public duty and deference to authority that has held ever since, even under communism. Xun Zi's 'Legalism' was a philosophical justification of state authority over wilful, selfish individuals. Taoism was a more inward-looking, even mystic belief that offered a bit more personal, private and spiritual space. Mo Zi preached a vision of equality and brotherly love.

From bronze to iron

Not surprisingly, a time of almost permanent war was also a time of innovation in the military sphere. As armies fought back and forth across each other's territories, they acquired new skills in siege warfare and fortification, and the advent of the crossbow transformed the battlefield. Even allowing for exaggeration on the part of the chroniclers, armies may have been many tens of thousand strong, suggesting an impressive degree of organisation, not only in the field but in logistical support. The supply of everything from weapons to cooking utensils would have meant industrial production on a considerable scale.

The advent of iron-working helped. Chinese metalworking evolved independently of advances farther west. For some time Chinese smiths had been making bronze with high iron content for extra durability; now iron became the catalyst of an industrial revolution. The addition of carbon in the form of charcoal allowed iron to be cast from molten ore, using high-temperature techniques originally developed for the manufacture of specialised bronze and ceramic products. Cast-iron items had the advantage that they could be mass-produced, but they were too brittle to make effective

Mastery of metal
A Mongolian boy showing off his birds is beautifully captured in this bronze from the late 4th century BC.

tools, so a new process was developed to produce useable working tools. However, they never managed to attain the high quality of wrought steel needed for weapons, so traditional forging methods still had to be used for these.

The skills and labour required to construct the huge fortifications that were a feature of this period were as much a triumph of organisation as of engineering. Giant walls of compacted mud, sun-dried brick and sometimes stone snaked for miles across vulnerable border areas. At a time when each state lived in suspicion of its neighbours – and all dreaded the periodic onslaught of nomadic raiders from the north – the need for fortified frontiers was undisputed.

Arms or adornment?
Zhou craftsmen lavished attention and imagination on the weapons they made. The haft of this dagger is an intricate creation of gold and turquoise.

Science leads the way

Organisation combined with technological developments and new ideas were key to advances in other areas, too. The idea that crops should be planted in rows originated at this time – it would not occur to farmers in Europe for another 2000 years. Another Chinese innovation of the 6th century BC was the iron ploughshare, which allowed far more efficient cultivation. Iron hoes boosted productivity and enabled peasants to weed that much more precisely, which reduced the loss of moisture through evaporation. Previously uncultivable land was brought into use through draining marshes and the irrigation of arid tracts. The development of scientific principles also led to the use of manure: even the best soils could benefit from the use of fertiliser. With the administrations of the larger states taking over from feudal masters, economic activity could be conceived on a far larger scale. Mines were dug for metal ores and salt, and government administrators rationalised everything from fishing to horse-breeding. Domestic prosperity gave rise to a growing export trade. The development of coinage made commerce much easier, but it was also absolutely crucial to the conduct of the public finances, as the peasants now paid taxes to the government rather than taking produce to the local lord.

Towns and cities grew in size: the largest, Yanxiadu, may have been home to as many as 320,000 people. Cities were increasingly orderly in their construction. In order to maintain an aura of mystique, the king with his court and officials remained aloof from the general life of the city. Royal palaces and administrative areas were raised on rammed-earth platforms and marked off as secret cities-within-cities. The richer the kingdom, the more splendid the palace: the image of the ruler and the magnificence in which he lived became a proclamation of his power.

Immediately adjacent to the palace complex was the artisans' quarter. Here the treasures of the court were created, from exquisite jewellery to weaponry embellished with bone and jade, from lacquered ornaments to elegant ceramics. Beautiful vessels, decorated with animal motifs, were created in bronze, now superseded as a material for weapons. These luxuries were also traded abroad, not only a lucrative export for these kingdoms but a sign of their prosperity and success.

The seven warring states were certainly successful, even if the good economic fortune of the people must have been tempered by the chronic insecurity under which they lived. Over time, however, the position of the individual kings would be called into question by the same centralising logic which had originally assured their power. Eventually, the Qin state began a campaign of conquest over its neighbours: in 221 BC, Qin Shihuangdi made himself the first Emperor of China.

Babylon renewed

Babylon had long been a spent force, but that was all about to change. Under King Nebuchadnezzar II the Babylonian Empire recovered and even surpassed its former glory. The city itself was fortified and its buildings reconstructed in the greatest splendour imaginable.

The lions of Babylon
One of 120 lions made of glazed bricks which adorn the great triumphal avenue in Babylon.

O n 7 September, 605 BC, a new era dawned for Mesopotamia, when Nebuchadnezzar II became the King of Babylon. Succeeding his father Nabopolassar, he was to reign in power and prosperity for 43 years. By the time he died in 562 BC, he had brought Babylon back to pre-eminence in Mesopotamia, and restored the city to the glory it had enjoyed almost 1500 years earlier under the leadership of the great King Hammurabi.

Nebuchadnezzar was fortunate in the legacy that came from his father. Nabopolassar was a highly energetic man and an effective ruler, and he did much to lay the foundations for Babylon's rise. Crucially, he forged a grand coalition of peoples to oppose the warlike Assyrians, at that time still the undisputed superpower in the region. Together with the Medes from Iran, Nabopolassar's Babylonian armies conquered the Assyrian royal city of Assur in 614 BC, then destroyed the imperial capital, Nineveh, in 612 BC.

The fall of the Assyrians from power left a vacuum – which the Babylonians were perfectly placed to fill. Yet the road to regional supremacy would be a long and arduous one. Nebuchadnezzar had first to consolidate the gains his father had made. This was no easy feat, for welcome though the Assyrian fall was in principle, it destabilised the entire Middle East.

The Egyptian Pharaoh in particular looked on events in Mesopotamia with a

distrustful eye. He had vied constantly with the Assyrians for control of Syria, and he knew it would be no different now with the Babylonians. King Nebuchadnezzar would inevitably direct his attentions towards a country of such vital economic and

Jerusalem. In 597 BC, after a three-month siege, the Jewish capital fell, and some 3000 people were deported to Babylon – a portent of things to come.

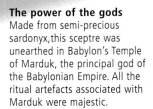

The power of the gods
Made from semi-precious sardonyx, this sceptre was unearthed in Babylon's Temple of Marduk, the principal god of the Babylonian Empire. All the ritual artefacts associated with Marduk were majestic.

strategic interest.
Conflict between Babylon and Egypt would flare often, punctuating the long decades of Babylonian ascendancy, and ultimately costing the kingdom on the Euphrates dear.

The Babylonian exile

Trouble flared first in Palestine. Jehoiakim, the king of Israel, was weak but prided himself on political cunning. Sensing in the enmity between the Pharaoh and Nebuchadnezzar a chance to free himself from dependence on the Babylonians, he refused to pay the tribute promised to his masters. Nebuchadnezzar reacted with swift and characteristic decisiveness, sending an army to lay siege to the city of

Ten years later, the Jews fared still worse when, as unrest flared up once more, Nebuchadnezzar sent another punitive expedition to Jerusalem. In 587 BC, the Babylonians destroyed the Temple, the spiritual home of Judaism since its construction by King Solomon. This time the entire population of Jews were deported *en masse* to Mesopotamia and thus began what became known in Jewish history as the 'Babylonian Captivity'. It would be almost half a century before Babylon fell to the Persians and King Cyrus II allowed the Jews to return home.

Not surprisingly, Babylon became associated in Jewish tradition with despotism and sin. At home, however, Nebuchadnezzar was celebrated as a military commander and architect of the new Babylonian superpower.

TIME WITNESS

The King is dead – long live the King

Writing in the 4th–3rd century BC, a Babylonian priest called Berossos described the accession of Nebuchadnezzar in 605 BC:

'Now, it came to pass that Nabopolassar fell ill at this time, and expired in the city of the Babylonians, after having ruled for 21 years. On learning of his father's death shortly thereafter, Nebuchadnezzar brought his affairs concerning Egypt and the other regions to a conclusion and ordered...the Jewish, Phoenician and Syrian prisoners, together with those from Egypt, and along with his heavily armed soldiers and his retinue, to accompany him on his return to Babylon. There, the Chaldeans had been looking after his interests

in the interim. On his arrival, Nebuchadnezzar immediately took control of all these affairs, and with them the entire empire that had belonged to his father. Then he arranged that the prisoners, once they had arrived, should be settled in the most suitable parts of Babylon. For his own part, the king made generous donations from his war booty to the Temple of Baal and those of other deities, and also added a whole new quarter to the venerable city of Babylon.'

Berossos goes on to report that King Nebuchadnezzar had a double defensive wall built right around the city, with magnificent gates and a glorious palace.

Babylon – the city between Heaven and Earth

Nebuchadnezzar did not just want to go down in history as a great warrior prince and political operator. Little by little, as the situation on his borders became calmer, he was able to turn his attention to other matters – above all, to his vision for rebuilding Babylon. He was determined to transform his capital into the most magnificent metropolis in the region, thereby creating a permanent monument to himself and to his people. In Babylonian geography, the city was traditionally placed at the very centre of the world, and Nebuchadnezzar planned to rebuild it in appropriate splendour.

The financial conditions for realising his dream could hardly have been more favourable. Tribute was now flowing in fast from the four corners of his growing empire. In addition, the Babylonians were endowed with real economic acumen – a fact borne out by the cuneiform texts of Nebuchadnezzar's time. As analysed by modern archaeologists, these testify to a cleverly organised and abundantly productive system of slave-based agriculture supported by a sophisticated network of irrigation ditches which diverted water from the Euphrates. The state's extensive trade relations were another important source of income.

The priesthood played a key economic role as well as a spiritual one, holding and administering almost half the land on Babylonian territory. The number of different trades and professions recorded in the cuneiform texts – ranging from bakers and coppersmiths to bird-catchers and brewers of beer – bears witness to the extremely flourishing state of Babylonian business at this time.

Money was accordingly no object when the King embarked upon 'Project Babylon'. The ancient city already had much to recommend it. Its first ruler Hammurabi (*c*.1792–1750 BC) had thought big from the start. When he established his capital on the Euphrates he

The Ishtar Gate
A reconstruction of the famous ceremonial gate can be seen in Berlin's Pergamon Museum. This artist's impression shows how it might have looked in Nebuchadnezzar's time

had consecrated it to the god Marduk and erected a splendid temple in his honour. Standing 92m (just over 300ft) tall, the ziggurat of this shrine was the historical model for the Biblical 'Tower of Babel'. In the Babylonian language, the temple tower was called *Etemenanki*, which translates as 'foundation of heaven and earth', a phrase that reflects the Babylonian belief that their city was the axis by which the world and sky were joined.

A wall for eternity

The most ambitious part of King Nebuchadnezzar's plans for the city was the construction of a massive city wall.

The weather god
The dignitary shown on the right is venerating the weather god Adad, who holds symbols of lightning in his hands. For the civilisations of Mesopotamia, which relied so heavily on irrigation, the favour of the weather god was all-important.

Even though the Babylonian Empire had no serious external enemies to fear at the time, the potential practical value of such a fortification was incalculable. Nebuchadnezzar knew all too well how swiftly the political and military situation could change: the city had been overrun several times by the Assyrians in the past.

Yet over and above the defensive role of the wall, the King's plans undoubtedly contained at least an element of self-aggrandisement – he was creating something that would demand the admiration of all who saw it. Some of the greatest architects and tens of thousands of labourers, were mobilised and set to work, and Nebuchadnezzar had inscriptions made that proudly record his personal involvement in the project: 'I did what no other king before me had done, and had Babylon surrounded by a strong defensive wall measuring 4000 cubits in length…so that the city could not be attacked from afar. I dug its ditches and built its embankments…as high as mountains. I added its broad gates, and equipped them with doors of cedar wood clad with bronze.'

Excavations undertaken by the German archaeologist Richard Koldewey between 1899 and 1917 provided essential insights into the appearance and scale of this mighty fortification, built in a spirit of defensive utility and vainglory. Once complete, the city was protected by a massive double wall of clay bricks some 7m (23ft) wide. The external walls stretched 18km (11 miles) in length. To give a better view of the surrounding area, towers were set into the wall at regular intervals, and moats provided an additional layer of protection. When the installations were finished, the citizens of Babylon had every reason to regard their city as effectively impregnable.

The Ishtar Gate

The King decreed that the main northern gate should be the showpiece ceremonial entrance into the city. Now reconstructed in Berlin's Pergamon Museum, the Ishtar Gate was a mighty double-tower complex that stood 15m (almost 50ft) high and bestrode a tunnel-like entrance-way some 50m (165ft) long. Ishtar, after whom the gate was named, was worshipped by the Babylonians as a goddess both of love and war. Contemporary observers were fascinated by the lavish decoration: against a dark blue background, a total of 575 bulls and dragons were depicted, all of them redolent with symbolism – the bull was sacred to the weather god Adad, the dragon to Marduk, Lord of Heaven and Earth and chief tutelary deity of the city.

The Ishtar Gate formed a spectacular backdrop for the city's ritual life. The New Year celebrations were held there and it seems likely that the King himself was the centre of an imperial and civic cult. Certainly, Nebuchadnezzar seemed keen to leave no doubt about the central part he had played in constructing the ceremonial complex. In one inscription, for instance, he notes: 'For the procession of the great Lord Marduk, I had a huge earth bank thrown up on the road to Babylon.'

The hanging gardens of Babylon

As a ruler with an astute political sense, Nebuchadnezzar would clearly have been conscious of the impact the Ishtar Gate must have made upon visitors from foreign courts. Such walls as these could only have been built to surround the richest, most powerful city in the world. Once through the gate, moreover, the visitor would have found much to back up this impression. Where else in the world were there such broad boulevards, so many temples and markets, such a hubbub of activity, or so much luxury?

According to conservative estimates, some 200,000 people lived in Babylon at this time. No other city on Earth approached this size.

Visitors would have been eager to see one attraction in particular – the hanging gardens which later came to be counted among the Seven Wonders of the Ancient World. Contemporary witnesses do not agree on all points, but there is agreement on the overwhelming spectacle that these gardens presented: they seem to have been built on an airy elevation in a square, terraced arrangement set on several levels and supported on arched vaults. Water was drawn from the nearby Euphrates by ingenious mechanical means.

Amazing stories spread far and wide about the gardens, which were often referred to at the time as the 'hanging gardens of Semiramis'. Semiramis was an Assyrian queen who had ruled in Nineveh in around 800 BC. She was rumoured to have undertaken grandiose building projects both in Babylon and Iran. It was naturally assumed, therefore, that she was

The ruins of Babylon
All that remains of the proud city of Babylon, where the Tower of Babel once soared high into the sky, are a few ruins (top). As in many ancient cultures, the Babylonians believed it was important to be able to divine the will of the gods. A favoured method was to read the entrails of a sacrificed bull (bottom).

The Babylonian worldview
As well as written records, this tablet contains an early Babylonian map. It shows the world as a disc, with their city at the centre and the River Euphrates running through it. The rest of the world is pushed to the outer edges.

the guiding hand behind the astonishing garden complex near Nebuchadnezzar's palace. Ancient visitors would perhaps have been disappointed to learn that the gardens had nothing to do with Semiramis. Reliable reports suggest they were yet another of Nebuchadnezzar's projects. There is abundant evidence of both the King's taste for extravagance and his liking for technological ingenuity, so it seems perfectly likely that this wonder was a work of his.

The priest Berossos, a native of Babylon writing in the 4th-3rd centuries BC, was certainly of this opinion. His writings also offer an original and plausible explanation for the King's garden commission: 'In the palace, he constructed stone heights, gave them a form strongly resembling the mountains, planted them with all sorts of trees and in so doing contrived to complete the so-called "Hanging Park", all because his wife hankered after a mountainous environment, having been brought up in the region of Medea.'

A mishandled inheritance

Nebuchadnezzar had good reason to expect the empire he had built to endure for generations, but after his death, in 562 BC, its glory quickly passed. With hindsight it is clear that it had been his own towering personality that had given the state of Babylon its cohesion. His authority had masked deep divisions, and these soon resurfaced after he was gone. Various powerful interest groups in Babylonian society – the aristocracy, the army, the priesthood of Marduk – now vied with one another for influence. The result was a rapid and unstoppable

decline. In the space of little more than 20 years, Nebuchadnezzar's powerful realm was reduced to insignificance.

In accordance with the prevailing dynastic principle in Babylon, Nebuchadnezzar had named his son Awil-Marduk as his successor, yet he ruled for only two years. A military commander and major landowner called Neriglissar then took over the reins of power. When he died, his son seized power, but found himself immediately embroiled in civil war and was murdered. The victors in the ensuing conflict put their own candidate, Nabonid, on the throne. In order to bolster his authority, Nabonid named his son Belshazzar as co-regent. But then he committed a fateful error: he devoted himself to the cult of the moon god Sin, and thus made bitter enemies of the influential Marduk priests.

The internal crisis was compounded by a rapidly mounting external threat. To the east, Cyrus II had ascended the Persian throne. An insatiably ambitious ruler, this new Persian king set out to achieve undisputed hegemony over the entire Middle East.

Cyrus's powerful, disciplined army made short work of the feuding Babylonians. When he dispatched one of his generals to take their capital city, the citizens opened the gates to him without any resistance and handed over King Nabonid as a prisoner. Just 23 years after Nebuchadnezzar's death, Babylon was the property of the Persian kings, bringing to a close a glorious chapter in the history of Mesopotamia.

Yet fame and near-mythic renown attaches to Babylon to this day: to that extent at least Nebuchadnezzar's yearning for lasting fame has been fulfilled. Certainly, Alexander the Great could think of no better capital for his mighty empire than the city on the Euphrates. The only thing that prevented him from carrying out this plan was his untimely death in 323 BC – which occurred, of all places, in Babylon itself.

India – birthplace of Buddhism

The Buddha, it is said, taught 84,000 ways to enlightenment, not one of which was political power. Yet this unworldly creed became the basis of an empire that embraced almost all of India.

The valleys of the Ganges and Indus rivers form a clear corridor across northern India. The rivers meander across a broad plain, India's most fertile and densely populated region, hemmed in by the mountains of the Hindu Kush to the northwest, the Himalayas to the northeast, and the rugged Deccan Plateau to the south. These lowlands have been a bustling centre of economic and cultural life for millennia, while the ever-flowing waters of the rivers are a symbol of Indian life itself: dramatic change has always come down from higher ground. It was over the Khyber Pass from the western steppes that the nomadic Aryans first

The Sanchi stupa
The oldest surviving Buddhist site, this temple in central India was built by Emperor Asoka in the late 3rd century BC.

Meditating Buddhas
This fresco is one of many paintings that have survived on the walls of the Ajanta caves, an ancient Buddhist complex northeast of Aurangabad in Maharashtra. Under Asoka's rule, however, the Buddhist message was emblazoned just about everywhere.

swept down around 1500 BC; Darius I followed with his conquering army a thousand years later. And in 327 BC, Alexander marched his men across the mountains.

Another force for change emerged from high in the Himalayan foothills around 560 BC, when a son was born to the leader of the Sakya clan in the Terai district of modern-day Nepal. Named Siddhartha Gauthama, he was marked out for a high destiny, the soothsayers said, either as a great warrior or as an important spiritual leader. His father asked the advisers how he could ensure his son followed the path to royal power and military glory. The answer was clear: as long as Siddhartha saw no sign of suffering, sadness or evil, he would accept his princely vocation.

So Siddhartha was brought up in the utmost luxury, surrounded by servants who anticipated his every desire. Even in adulthood he was protected: his beautiful wife Yasodhara, who joined him in his opulent seclusion, helped to perpetuate her husband's world of innocence.

A reality of woes

But Siddhartha was a man of natural compassion and intelligence, and his curiosity could not be contained. One day he slipped out of the palatial prison in which his father kept him to see what life was like outside. His father, anticipating that his son would one day make an escape, had ensured that the illusion of perfection was maintained in the area

around the royal palace. The streets were swept, the buildings magnificent, their inhabitants well clothed and fed – a picture of contentment. Yet imperfection could not be abolished altogether. To his astonishment, Siddhartha saw a stooped and wrinkled old man: all men came to this, his charioteer told him.

He made further forays into the city, seeing more sights that opened his eyes to the human condition: a man racked by disease, and then a lifeless corpse. Siddhartha's Fourth Sight offered him some hope: a prayerful ascetic who possessed nothing but his robe and a begging bowl, yet radiated inner peace and contentment. Inspired by this example, Siddhartha left his wife and child and his life as prince to wander the world seeking spiritual enlightenment.

The birth of the Buddha

Although attracted by asceticism, the bodhisattva, or Buddha-to-be, came to believe that forsaking all the pleasures of the world was no better than being shielded from all its ills. Six years as a wandering beggar failed to yield the inner peace he had been searching for. What was needed, he realised, was not to punish the physical body but to transcend it: the journey to enlightenment was an inward one. So it was that, one night in May at the full moon, the 35-year-old Siddhartha sat down beneath a tree to meditate, gradually divesting himself of all earthly attachments. All night long he remained in a trance, and before dawn he found that ecstatic self-transcendence known to his followers as nirvana. The Buddha – the 'Enlightened One' – had found a new way to spiritual fulfilment which offered hope to all the people of India.

The path to peace

It had been a long time since religion had been any sort of liberating force in India. The beliefs brought by the Aryans had hardened into a harsh and unforgiving form of Hinduism. Their descendants, the

Brahmanic priests, had set themselves at the top of a rigid structure of social castes which condemned the vast majority to toil all their lives for minimal reward. Key to their creed was the doctrine of *samsara*, or reincarnation – the belief that all beings lived countless lives in an eternal, swirling cycle of death and rebirth. Those in the lower castes had been placed there in punishment for sins committed in former lives, every act bringing its consequences by the principle of karma. Since virtue would be rewarded, it was an optimistic doctrine in theory, but the reality was that life condemned most of the population to wretched poverty. The idea that this existence would be endlessly repeated was a source not of hope but of despair.

Buddha believed in reincarnation too, but for those pure enough to reach the spiritual condition of bodhisattva, his teachings offered a way of escaping the loop. The soul, arriving at this blessed state, escaped into stillness and calm, released for ever from the stresses and anxieties of everyday life. People in their thousands turned to the teachings of the holy man as he trudged the dusty Indian roads and attempted to embrace the code for living that he called the Dharma. Finally, at the age of 80, after 45 years of preaching, he felt his work was done, lay down in an enchanted grove and died.

An India divided
Northern India at that time was in the grip of tumultuous change. The invasions by Persians and Greeks destabilised northwestern districts, especially because neither had been able to establish a firm hold. The Persian presence was still quite new when it was swept away by Alexander, yet the Macedonian king was

operating at the end of an impossibly long supply line. Faced with the mutiny of his exhausted troops, he was forced to turn back in 325 BC, and the regime he left behind never seemed secure. Farther east in the valley of the Ganges, untouched by foreign invasion, there was endemic conflict among 16 separate kingdoms, who squabbled and fought one another. Yet none could hope to thrive as the generations came and went in a mutually draining struggle.

The Mauryan Empire
With historical hindsight it is clear that there was a power vacuum in the region as a whole – until Chandragupta Maurya emerged with the vision, the will and the ability to fill the gap. Ambitious, resourceful and by some accounts ruthless, Chandragupta was ruler of the north-eastern kingdom of Magadha from 321 to 297 BC. Its influence had been growing at the expense of its neighbours for a century or more: under Chandragupta it embarked on a campaign of expansion.

Pushing westward, he conquered territories extending well into what is now Pakistan, as well as south across the uplands of the Deccan Plateau. Chandragupta's rule in these new dominions was

A mythical beast
Myths of monsters and demons from earlier times persisted in the Buddhist Mauryan Empire. This sculpture dates from around the 3rd century BC

Asoka's column
In this column-capital from the reign of the Emperor Asoka, four lions face the cardinal points of the compass, standing on a wheel symbolising the cycle of birth and death.

tough, even tyrannical, but it did bring stability. The consolidation of what had been a confusion of little kingdoms, all jostling and vying for supremacy, into a single giant state also increased prosperity across the whole of northern India. The wealthiest place was Chandragupta's capital at Pataliputra, near present-day Patna, the commercial and governing centre of the empire. Its markets boomed and its population soared. As Chandragupta's son extended the empire, Pataliputra grew in importance. It reached its peak in the reign of his grandson, Asoka (ruled 272–232 BC).

By now, the empire included Afghanistan and Beluchistan, and stretched south to include all except the far south of the subcontinent. From the port of Tamluk, at the mouth of the Ganges, a thriving trade with southeast Asia opened up, and vessels plied from other ports to eastern outposts of the Roman world. Ivory, textiles and spices were much in demand in the Mediterranean: the remains of a Roman trading colony have been uncovered at Arikamedu on the east coast of the Deccan. At the other end of the empire, in the mountains of the far northwest, Taxila became the seat of a university famed throughout Asia.

A royal convert

Asoka was to prove Buddhism's most influential convert. Sickened by the carnage involved in his conquest of Kalinga in 269 BC, he turned to Buddhism in search of a better way. Asoka did not make Buddhism an 'official' religion – he tolerated other faiths – but he did make it the main religion of the Mauryan Empire and gave it all the moral support he could. He constructed a network of richly endowed Buddhist temples, monasteries and many monuments, from impressive columns to wayside boulders inscribed with religious mottos. Most characteristic was the stupa, a hemispherical structure conceived as a mountain straining upward from material existence toward heavenly nirvana.

Cynics note the convenience of Asoka's conversion, which came just as the Mauryan Empire reached its largest extent, its work of conquest done, and when a redirection of efforts towards peaceful trade was most obviously called for. There can be no doubt that the new mood of peace and piety suited Asoka politically. His institutionalisation of what had been a highly personal, even mystic religion helped to strengthen his own authority across the empire, as all his subjects became united in a common creed. But whatever his intention in adopting Buddhism, he certainly did what he could to promote it, whilst giving it the coherence it would need to become one of the great world religions.

All is transient

In the end, Asoka overreached himself, all but bankrupting his empire with his lavish programmes of public works. Discontent grew – especially among the Brahman elite who had a vested interest in the restoration of older Hindu ways. Some scholars have suggested that the cultivation of Buddhist piety and pacifism, conducive as it may have been to social unity, left the Mauryan regime ill-equipped to defend itself against either external aggression or internal threats. Whatever the precise reasons, the Mauryan heyday ended with Asoka's death: decline and disintegration quickly followed. By about 180 BC, the Mauryan Empire was no more, and northern India was once again an unruly collection of warring kingdoms.

Persia in its pride

From the middle of the 6th century BC, a small tribe from southwestern Iran acquired a mighty empire through military conquest. At their height, the Persians ruled territories from the Aegean to the Indus and from the Nile to the Caspian Sea.

The Persian guard
Picked out in glazed brick, these soldiers patrol the walls of Darius's palace at Susa. Their robes and headbands mark them out as members of the elite royal guard, the 'ten thousand immortals'.

‘I, Darius, the Great King, King of Kings, King on this Earth, Son of Hystaspes, the Achaeminid. Thus speaks Darius the King: Ahura Mazda, who is the mightiest of the gods, created me, and has made me King. He has given me this kingdom, possessed of good horses, possessed of good men.’

This inscription, found among the stones at the site of the emperor's winter palace at Susa in Khuzestan, southwestern Iran, proclaims the enormous pride of the Achaemenid Empire in Persia. Named after their legendary founder, the great warrior-hero Achaemenes, this dynasty emerged in the 6th century BC and embarked on a campaign of conquest, gaining territories which ultimately covered the whole of the Middle East, if not, as Darius claimed, the entire world.

A tale of two palaces

How far Persian dominions extended is clear from the far-flung provenance of the materials used in the construction of Darius' new palace, and of the craftsmen summoned to Susa to undertake the task. Cedar wood for the roof came from the Lebanon; gold from wealthy Lydia in what is now southwestern Turkey; semi-precious stones like lapis lazuli, carnelian and turquoise were carried overland from Afghanistan and Uzbekistan; and ivory was imported from Nubia. The finished palace was intended as a splendid mirror of the world ruled by Darius, the Great King.

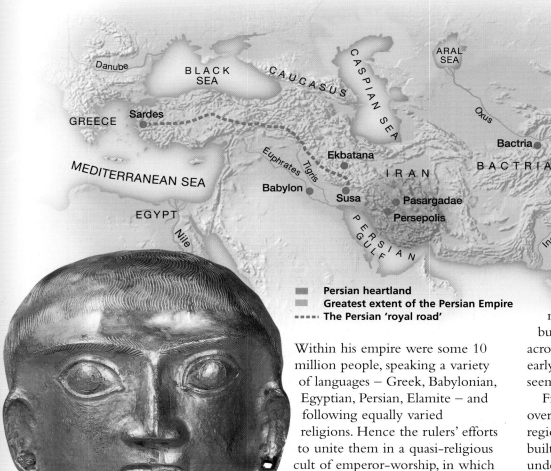

Danube
BLACK SEA
CAUCASUS
ARAL SEA
CASPIAN SEA
Oxus
GREECE Sardes
Ekbatana
Bactria
BACTRIA
Euphrates Tigris IRAN
MEDITERRANEAN SEA
Babylon
Susa Pasargadae
Persepolis
EGYPT
Nile
P E R S I A N G U L F
Indus

■ **Persian heartland**
■ **Greatest extent of the Persian Empire**
∎∎∎∎ **The Persian 'royal road'**

Carving out a world empire

Comparative newcomers to the region, the Persians had until the 2nd millennium BC roamed the central Asian steppes as nomadic herders. They belonged to the Aryan group of peoples (hence the name they gave to their adoptive land – Iran), and joined in the general dispersal that began around 1500 BC. They were related, therefore, to the Aryans who made themselves masters of northern India, but to begin with their fortunes could hardly have been more different. Far from being empire-builders, the tribes that moved south across the Iranian Plateau through the early centuries of the 1st millennium BC seemed fated to be ruled by others.

From 700 BC, the Elamites were their overlords, allowing them to settle in the region of Parsa to the east, where they built their own city. Then as Elam fell under Assyrian sway, the 'Persians' were doubly subjected. Even when Assyrian power imploded in the late 7th century BC, they did not benefit. Instead, they were dominated by the Medes, whose homeland lay between the Zagros Mountains and the Caspian coast. Then in 559 BC Cyrus II became the Persian king, and all that changed.

Cunning in conspiracy, adept in diplomacy and ruthless in war, Cyrus encouraged the Medes in a revolt against their hated king, Astyages, in 550 BC. He could then present his own invasion as a friendly intervention on behalf of the Medes people, though the result was that their country became a province of Persia. He built his own new capital, Pasargadae, on the site of his victory over Astyages, but allowed the former Median capital, Ekbatana, to keep much of its old autonomy. Cyrus used the same basic formula when he conquered Babylon in 539, playing on local rivalries so as to cast himself in the role of liberator.

Within his empire were some 10 million people, speaking a variety of languages – Greek, Babylonian, Egyptian, Persian, Elamite – and following equally varied religions. Hence the rulers' efforts to unite them in a quasi-religious cult of emperor-worship, in which the splendid Achaemenid palaces and tombs played an important part.

Darius's words at Susa did not simply reflect personal pride: Achaemenid arrogance was central to the ethos of the empire. It was never more eloquently expressed than in the audience-hall, the *apadana*, in the emperor's palace at Persepolis. It was said that ten horsemen could ride abreast up the giant, gently sloping staircases which led up to this vast hall – they may well have done so in procession.

The apadana itself could accommodate 10,000 people. Reliefs on the ruined walls still show the supplicants who flocked here each year, bearing precious gifts from every corner of the empire, to pay homage or seek favour from the King of Kings. The sheer diversity of people who came has been captured in stone by consummate craftsmen; an astonishing range of hairstyles, costumes and offerings is displayed – no fewer than 23 distinct ethnic groups have been identified.

Portrait in gold
This golden head of a young man with pierced ears was part of a huge hoard of Persian treasures found near the River Oxus in the far northeast of the empire.

Triumph through tolerance

Cyrus was so successful in turning popular discontent to his own advantage that he frequently prevailed without having to fight at all. In Babylon, for instance, by promoting the worship of Marduk, the city's patron deity, and restoring the city's temples, he gained the genuine admiration and affection of the people. The origins of the later cult of emperor-worship can be seen in Cyrus's policies: as long as he could rely on obedience and respect for his rule, he took an easy-going attitude to local loyalties and religious beliefs.

The beauty of the imperial cult was that it could be superimposed onto any existing religious structure, allowing traditional rites to flourish under Persian rule. On taking Babylon, Cyrus allowed the Jews to end almost half a century's 'captivity' in the city and return home – he even ordered the reconstruction of their temple in Jerusalem.

On the other hand, he could be tough when he wanted, as King Croesus of Lydia had learned when he marched an army into Media to avenge Astyages, his brother-in-law, in 547 BC. All the legendary wealth of Croesus was worthless in the face of the Persian assault. Resistance was brutally put down, including that of the Greek cities of Asia Minor, a move that would later have lasting repercussions for the Persian Empire. And by now, with the addition of Asia Minor to its territories, it really was an empire. Cyrus's successor, Cambyses II (ruled 529–522 BC), continued the expansion by taking Egypt. The empire reached its full extent, however, under

An imperial resting place
With an eye on the authority he would pass on to his successors, Cyrus II – 'The Great' – had this austere yet imposing tomb built during his own lifetime.

The conquering chariot
A Persian warrior surveys the battlefield from the platform behind his charioteer, in this exquisite gold model, just 10cm (4in) high.

Making an entrance
Winged bulls with bearded human heads stand guard at this imposing gateway into the Persepolis palace complex. The gate was built by Xerxes (ruled 486–465 BC), Darius I's son and successor.

both sides – massively enriching rulers on the Asian side like King Croesus – but the advent of Persia produced a culture-shock of seismic proportions.

The full flowering of Athenian democracy was still to come when Cyrus II came to power in Persia, and other Greek cities never quite matched the steps towards representative government taken in Athens. Yet the general tendency in Greece was towards the extension of autonomy – for communities, for households, even for individuals. The idea that the Persian emperor should have authority over so many different peoples with so many different traditions seemed utterly alien to Greek ways of thinking.

The tolerance actually shown towards local traditions did not mollify the outraged Greeks. From the first, a state of 'cold war' existed between the Greeks and the Persians, with much of the animosity originating on the Greek side. Persia became much more than a conventional enemy for the Greeks, with far-reaching implications for western culture in the centuries since.

Persian rule: the realities

The Persian way of doing things differed from that of the Greeks, but what seems most striking now about the Achaemenid Empire is the way in which its centralised structure accommodated an enormous ethnic and cultural diversity, allowing a

Darius I (ruled 522–486 BC), whose dominions stretched from the Balkans to the Indus Valley, but who would face an implacable enemy in the Greeks.

A clash of civilisations

It is ironic that the prevailing modern image of Achaemenid Persia should be one of barbaric cruelty and autocracy, for there was much that was enlightened about its rule. The reason for the slur is clear: Cyrus's imperial expansion brought him into direct conflict with the people of classical Greece, so many of whose values – and prejudices – have been absorbed into western tradition.

Since the 8th century BC, the city-states of Greece had been establishing colonies around the coasts of Asia Minor. The resulting trade had been beneficial to

degree of local independence to coexist with overall stability. The empire as a whole comprised 20 provinces known as satrapies. These were obliged to pay tribute to the emperor, and provide a steady flow of conscripts to the imperial armies. Under Cyrus, tribute was paid in kind: gold from India; ivory from Ethiopia; camels from Arabia; horses from Scythia, and so forth. Manufactured items were also acceptable, including weaponry (swords, battle-axes, armour, chariots) and luxuries like jewellery and ceramics.

Transporting cumbersome commodities and uncooperative livestock across the empire – and keeping track of who had paid what and where it all was at any given time – must have been a massive logistical and administrative challenge for imperial officials. It made sense, then, when Darius moved towards a more flexible and efficient system of taxation in the form of gold and silver.

The satraps ('protectors of power') who ruled the satrapies on the emperor's behalf were drawn from the inner circle of the royal family: they were like little kings. But the 'civil service' of scribes, officials and messengers who assisted them were responsible to the emperor himself, ensuring that the interests of the empire as a whole were served. The nobility enjoyed considerable privileges, receiving generous grants of land from the emperor, but

A residence fit for emperors
The palace at Persepolis – some 40km (25 miles) southeast of Cyrus II's capital at Pasargadae – was built by Darius I, but his successors continued to make additions.

absolute loyalty was expected in return. Thus the Persian system struck a balance between allowing independence on the one hand and enforcing unquestionable authority on the other.

The imperial centre and the provinces were kept in close touch by a superb system of communications: the empire was criss-crossed by well-kept highways. The 'royal road', a metalled highway that ran from Susa to Sardes in the far west of Asia Minor, covered a distance of almost 2300km (1400 miles). A system of way-stations, equipped with water, provisions and changes of horses, enabled messages to be carried with incredible speed: a courier could make the whole journey in just five days. It was also under Darius that an early version of the Suez Canal was dug, a continuous waterway connecting the Red Sea with the Mediterranean via the lower Nile.

Royal sun screen
This stone relief from the Hall of a Hundred columns at Persepolis shows the Emperor Xerxes leaving the hall, with two servants in attendance.

Eternal fire

Darius I and his Achaemenid successors were laid to rest in the Valley of Naqsh-i Rustam, near to Persepolis. Carved out of the solid rock, their splendid tombs proclaim the importance of a dynasty whose rule was divinely ordained by the highest of the gods, Ahura Mazda. The great creator had made the universe, but he fought a constant battle in order for his life and truth to prevail against the evil conspiracies of Angra Mainyu, the spirit of darkness, death and destruction.

Such was the cosmic struggle between good and evil envisioned by a 7th-century BC priest, Zoroaster, and outlined in a series of 17 *gathas* or hymns. These, claimed the Persian prophet, were directly inspired by Ahura Mazda; more sceptical scholars see them as a systematisation of a number of earlier, polytheistic faiths. In practice, ancestral deities often endured as good or evil spirits after the Persian court adopted Zoroastrianism, but their images were replaced as objects of worship by the Atas, the sacred fire whose light and energy symbolised Ahura Mazda. The emperor, as Darius's inscription at Susa made clear, was Ahura Mazda's representative on earth: to defy his authority was to upset the eternal order.

Force of arms

The emperor's authority was backed up more tangibly by a truly formidable fighting force, at whose heart was the emperor's own elite division: the 10,000 *Amrtaka* or 'Immortals'. These men were immediately replaced if incapacitated, giving the impression of an immortal unit, forever strong. The size of the Persian army cannot be estimated accurately: it would have varied from campaign to campaign.

Greek commentators spoke of enormous forces — three million and upwards — but even though they had an obvious interest in talking up the threat, it seems likely that the Persians could put armies of over 300,000 men into the field at any given time.

At its core, the army was Persian: all males between the ages of 15 to 50 were eligible to serve if called upon and they were trained as infantrymen with spears and bows. The army's relative lack of cavalry was a problem Persia's rulers were well aware of, so starting with Cyrus II, emperors encouraged Persian nobles to make skill in horsemanship and cavalry fighting a mark of status. Persia's gift for balancing local autonomy against centralised organisation paid off in the military sphere, as different nations brought different skills and equipment to the field of war. While Persia's own infantry was lightly armed and flexible, the Babylonians were heavily armed, as were soldiers drawn from Syria and Egypt. Units from the empire's Indian territories brought fighting elephants which could be deployed in the field like modern tanks.

A vulnerable foe

Although the Persian army was vast, in practice it was unwieldy. With such a mass of men to be marshalled, such a babel of languages, its immense size could turn from a strength to a source of weakness. Such enormous armies were uncomfortable in confined spaces and upland country. And despite the best efforts of the emperors, Persian cavalry could never quite match the saddle-skills of the steppe nomads living along their northern and eastern frontiers.

Cool discipline was often key: an opponent who could conquer his fear had a realistic hope of prevailing against the Persians, even when they advanced in overwhelming numbers. There was a certain inevitability about the fact that, when the might of Persia was humbled, it was at the hands of the ancient Greeks. The same solidarity of citizens that even then was providing the first impulse towards democracy in Athens provided the basis for the dogged discipline of the hoplite phalanx.

First, in 490 BC, Darius I was defeated at Marathon, the unshakeable solidity of the Athenian hoplites seeing them through against the odds. His son, Xerxes I, seemed at first to fare better. In 480 BC he succeeded in taking the city of Athens – only to find that he had failed to break the will of the people. The comprehensive naval defeat that followed at Salamis saw Persia's credibility as a threat almost completely destroyed. The event sparked revolts the length and breadth of Asia Minor. The despotic harshness with which the Persians put down unrest only confirmed the Greek caricature of Persia's rule as cruel tyranny. His imperial rule unravelling, Xerxes was assassinated in 465 BC, but none of his successors was able to check Persia's decline. Inevitably, perhaps, it was the Greeks who saw to the empire's final downfall under the leadership of the Macedonian, Alexander the Great.

Fantasy and flair
A prancing billy goat with wings makes an extravagantly improbable handle for a jug or drinking cup, fashioned with amazing skill by a Persian goldsmith.

and language, and even into the minds and thoughts of his subjects. He had a deep distrust of intellectual subversion, so books were burned at public ceremonies – many of them the classic Confucian texts, distrusted as possible sources of nostalgia for the old ways. In fact, when it came to protecting the imperial order he had constructed, Shihuangdi had no scruples: in 212 BC, he had 460 scholars buried alive. Yet whatever his faults, Ying Sheng had conceived a great nation and forced it into being: without him, there would have been no China.

The descent into chaos

The empire that Shihuangdi had built did not survive his passing. His son Hu Hai was not his father's equal. A usurper himself, urged on to oust his elder brother by scheming counsellors, 'Er Shuangdi', the second emperor, would never feel secure. Within months, rebellion was spreading across the empire like wildfire, with local leaders fighting one another as well as what remained of the imperial government's forces. In 206 BC, an unknown rebel group forced its way into Hsienyang, and sacked the city. Hu Hai committed suicide, leaving Qin 'rule' to be briefly represented by one of Ying Sheng's grandsons, the unfortunate Tzuying: his execution brought the Qin dynasty and its empire to an end.

The crisis deepened further as Tzuying's killers were forced to battle for supremacy with a rival rebel force led by Liu Pang. A former imperial policeman of peasant origins, Liu Pang emerged as a charismatic and clever leader, and by 202 BC he had claimed the role of emperor. Ruling under the title of Kao-Ti, he established the Han dynasty that was to dominate Chinese life for the next 400 years.

A difference in tone

Kao-Ti began by building his own new capital, Xian. Although this represented a break with the past, Xian was only a stone's throw from the old Qin capital of Hsienyang. This seems fitting, for Kao-Ti would not stray all that far from the imperial agenda worked out by Shihuangdi. Most of the first emperor's centralised institutional structures stayed in place, but the style of government changed. Under Kao-Ti the law was applied more leniently, censorship was relaxed, and the civil service was allowed more autonomy. Where Shihuangdi had been a highly visible and autocratic ruler, Kao-Ti was content to withdraw into the background and leave the job of running the empire to his bureaucrats. These officials became China's dominant class.

As it turned out, this was no bad thing: schooled in Confucian philosophy, with its strong ethic of public service, they ran the country well and conscientiously. Educated in special schools and colleges, they were assessed through rigorous exams: merit, rather than birth, was the criterion. This was a recipe for stability rather than for radical change, despite the new social mobility it allowed. In complete contrast to Shihuangdi's bid to wipe out all memory of the past by suppressing scholarship, Han officialdom

BACKGROUND

The divine dragon – symbol of the emperor

In European Christian culture the dragon has always been feared – a ferocious, fire-breathing monster, associated with everything that is darkest and most disturbing. Its breath recalls the flames of hell; its serpentine coils in religious images as it battles with St George suggest the snake form taken by the Devil in the Garden of Eden; it takes on phallic overtones as an abductor of princesses in fairy tales.

None of these associations bears any relevance to the role of the dragon in oriental myth: here its function could hardly be more different.

For the Chinese, in the first place, the dragon represents not infernal fire but life-giving water; its sinuous form suggests the flow of rivers and the course of the clouds across the sky. It is a symbol of heavenly beneficence, and occurs as an image of divine favour on artefacts dating from as far back as

bronze age times. It was only natural that it should be adopted as the emblem of the emperor, whose reign on Earth was said to be at the behest of Heaven.

Jade dragon
With its endless coils the dragon lent itself to all sorts of stylised, abstract artistic forms.

risked exalting it above both present and future, but after so much turmoil, their dull conservatism was reassuring.

Threat from the north

Like all Chinese emperors, Kao-Ti had to deal with the threat from the nomadic tribes who roamed the open steppe to the north. Known to the Chinese as the Hsiung-nu, they were forebears of the Huns who would later terrorise Roman Europe. For now they terrorised China, and the empire – worn out by the years of civil conflict before

China's Great Wall
Built by the First Emperor to keep out nomadic raiders from the north, the wall was also a symbol of the empire's unity.

EVERYDAY LIFE

The great work

The building of the Great Wall of China involved a workforce of more than 300,000 soldiers, peasants and convicts serving sentences of hard-labour – as well as thousands of engineers and supervisors to direct operations.

The wall joined up pre-existing fortifications. Parts of it were built of packed earth, others were made of stone, and it was a minimum of 4m (13ft) tall. Watch-towers and forts were placed at regular intervals, so danger-signals could be sent quickly along the wall by lighting beacon fires. Though built in the time of the First Emperor, the wall was much repaired and rebuilt over the years. The present structure dates largely from the time of the Ming dynasty in the 16th century.

Kao-Ti succeeded in winning power – was in no state to resist them. Kao-Ti decided to buy them off with tribute, even sending a princess to marry the Hsiung-nu leader, and the policy seemed to work.

After Kao-Ti's death, in battle in 195 BC, his widow the empress Lü held sway: three of her sons in turn reigned as puppets in her power. She is alleged to have schemed and murdered to assure the succession of her sons over those of the emperor's other wives, and she placed her own relations in key positions. However she gained her power, the empire went from strength to strength: these were times of peace and prosperity and so, too, were the reigns of those who followed her death in 180 BC: the emperors Wen-ti (180–157 BC) and Ching-ti (157–141 BC).

A time of splendour

In 141 BC, Wu-ti succeeded his father at the age of only 15. A reign of 54 years lay before him, in which time a significant state would become a superpower.

Wu-ti consciously cultivated an air of mystery – the very mention of his name was banned by law. Around him, Xian was fast becoming one of the world's great capitals, a bustling centre of commerce and craftsmanship, but he shut himself away in a complex of palaces, parks and pavilions the size of a small city. While Wu-ti stayed at home, his armies travelled

Ceramic watchtower
Two-storey towers resembling this ceramic one were built at regular intervals along China's fortified frontier.

far and wide on his behalf in a period of aggressive expansionism for Han China. First, the policy of appeasement towards the Hsiung-nu nomads was dropped: an eight-year campaign succeeded in driving them north and westward. Protected by garrisons and regular patrols, over 100,000 colonists were then settled in what had been the frontier zone. Other armies marched north into Korea and Manchuria and south into Vietnam and Burma (now Myanmar).

The road to prosperity

China's conquests in the north not only brought greater security, they opened up access to that great overland trade-route known as the 'Silk Road'. Almost 1500 years before Marco Polo traversed the

Bowl and spoon
In their grace and simplicity many artefacts from the Han period have an extraordinarily modern look.

Camping in comfort
With a portable stove like this one, the Chinese traveller of the Han period could be sure of keeping warm anywhere.

route from west to east, Wu-ti's ambassador Chiang Chien covered much of it in the opposite direction. He was sent out to establish alliances against the Hsiung-nu with tribes in Bactria, northern Afghanistan: he failed in his mission, but he opened Chinese eyes to other possibilities.

In the 1st century BC, China took control of the eastern sections of the Silk Road. The oasis towns of the Tarim Basin were taken as a base for camel caravans on what became an important commercial artery. Links were established with Roman settlements in Parthia and beyond. The Han rulers now had enormous domains to govern, but their vast army of trusted civil servants stood them in good stead, and this system was readily adaptable to new conditions. New clerks and counsellors had to be trained to take charge: more colleges were established, and the arts and all forms of learning flourished. An outward-looking empire was trading not just commodities but cultural influences in an age of great accomplishment and innovation in China.

Return to anarchy

Despite increases in trade and agricultural productivity, the costs of sustaining Han expansionism were crippling. The tax burden on the people grew steadily heavier. To make matters worse, the population had grown rapidly during the decades of prosperity, with the result that China was running out of cultivable land. So many peasants were left landless, agrarian unrest was almost inevitable. Big landowners became emboldened to withhold their taxes, compounding the chaos. In AD 9 an adviser called Wang Mang, appointed regent over a one-year-old emperor, seized control himself. He tried to break the power of the big landowners, but the weather conspired against him causing massive floods along the Huang He in AD 11. Famine followed, and Wang Mang found himself an enemy not just of the aristocracy but also of the peasants, his forces struggling to suppress a revolt by the 'Red Eyebrows' (its adherents painted their eyebrows red as a mark of membership). A growing range of rebels included a faction supporting Liu Hsiu, a descendant of the Han. In AD 25 he achieved power, restored the Han dynasty and reigned under the name Kuang-wu-Ti.

The later Han

Kuang-wu-Ti revived the old eastern Zhou capital at Luoyang. His 'later Han' dynasty would reign for almost 200 years, but its achievements cannot compare with those of the 'former Han'. The economic problems of the former Han had not been resolved, and the ferment in which Kuang-wu-Ti seized power rumbled on: weakened emperors found themselves tools of their advisers.

As the 2nd century unfolded, the ruling dynasty became irrelevant. In AD 184 the 'Yellow Turbans', a hitherto marginal Taoist sect, rose in rebellion in Shandong province. The unrest was put down by the imperial general Cao Cao, but this merely made the Han more dependent on their military strongman. Even that was not enough for Cao Cao's son, who seized power himself in 220, finally ending the Han dynasty. The country now split into three separate kingdoms, which set about warring with one another. China was reduced to anarchy once again.

Yamato Japan

Korean immigrants to Kyushu brought the equipment needed to establish Japan's first bronze-age agricultural society. Despite its foreign origins, the culture that took hold became a distinctively Japanese civilisation.

The islands of Japan were first settled around 30,000 BC, when immigrants arrived from eastern Asia. The stone-age lifestyle they established is known to archaeologists as the *Jomon* period and it survived undisturbed until the middle of the 1st millennium BC, when a wave of Korean immigrants arrived on Kyushu, the more southerly of Japan's main islands. They brought with them techniques for working bronze and iron; for creating superior, wheel-made ceramics fired at high temperatures for extra strength; and above all for growing crops – in particular, the 'wet' cultivation of rice in paddy fields. There were less obvious innovations, too: more complex ritual traditions and social structures, including ideas of hierarchy, would replace the easy egalitarianism of the old *Jomon* era hunter-gatherer ways.

Archaeological evidence, though vague, suggests a gradual dispersal of the new techniques from around 300 BC, first in Kyushu, then through much of Honshu, its neighbour to the north. The resulting culture is known as 'Yayoi', after the Tokyo suburb where artefacts relating to it were first found. Rather than the conquest of one people by another, however, the spread was more likely a matter of *Jomon* communities taking up the new lifestyle.

From culture to kingdom

An echo of this early episode endures in accounts written by Japanese chroniclers of the mythical first emperor, Jimmo Tenno. Tenno's father Ninigi, grandson of Amaterasu, the great sun goddess, was sent down to Kyushu to rule the Earth on her behalf. Ninigi sent Jimmu Tenno to Honshu to enforce his rule. According to tradition, this happened in 660 BC, and marked the start of the Japanese kingdom and imperial dynasty.

In practice, it is not clear exactly how or when Yayoi culture spread, but by the 1st century BC it was in place across almost the whole of Japan. Only in the far north of Honshu and Hokkaido did earlier hunter-gatherer ways prevail, kept alive by Japan's earliest inhabitants, the Ainu. The record is equally unclear on when Yayoi society came to constitute a 'kingdom'. The earliest written confirmation is an entry in the annals of the Han dynasty describing the visit, in AD 57, of an ambassador from a Japanese kingdom that the chronicler calls 'Nu Wo'. A later Chinese author, writing during the Wei

Grave watchers
Ceramic figures like this woman and warrior, known as *haniwa* figures, were left to watch over burial mounds.

dynasty (AD 220–265), left reports of a mysterious queen called Himiko who lived in a closely guarded palace and ruled through intermediaries. Her kingdom, known as Yamatai or Yamato, paid tribute to the Chinese emperor, which is why it appeared in the official annals. Within Japan, Yamato was said to have authority over 30 smaller kingdoms.

To this day, no-one is certain where the kingdom of Yamato was. It was long assumed to have been centred on Honshu, near modern Osaka, but more recent research has led to the suggestion that the kingdom arose on Kyushu where the Yayoi culture first arrived. A site at Yoshinogari, near the city of Saga, has produced particular excitement among archaeologists. Here the remains of a moat have been found surrounding a large settlement covering some 400,000m²; two inner moats surround separate groups of buildings. The sheer scale of the burial mound at the northern end of the settlement would have been evidence enough of its importance, even if archaeologists had not also recovered beautiful clothing and artefacts from its inner chamber.

Was this the capital of Yamato Japan? We will probably never know. Only the huge scale and obvious wealth of the site sets it apart from other settlements of similar age and layout in Kyushu and southern Honshu. The burial mound or *kofun* in particular is typical of the structures built as tombs for members of the ruling classes. Over 100,000 such mounds have been found in

Clay horse
This simple *haniwa* horse is one of many varied figures – warriors, ships, even models of houses – created for Yamato grave mounds. Together, these figures have offered archaeologists invaluable insights into the lifestyle.

Japan, many of them built to a distinctive keyhole-shaped groundplan. Some are enormous; the most impressive is believed to have been built in the 5th century AD for Nintoku, the 15th emperor, at Mozu in the Nara Valley, central Honshu – the region that became the Yamato heartland around the 5th century. Nintoku's *kofun* is 485m long (almost a third of a mile) and contains 15 million cubic metres of earth. It bristled with hundreds of *haniwas*, the ornamental ceramic figures that were placed on top of all such burial mounds. Sometimes these ceramics were simple cylinders; sometimes elaborately shaped houses, ships or warriors. It is thought that they were good luck charms intended to ward off evil spirits and accompany the tomb's occupant into the next life, and they offered information about the person's earthly life and family.

The roots of tradition

Excavations of Japan's *kofun* have uncovered a sophisticated culture. Korean and Chinese influences are unmistakeable: many imported goods have been found, from bronze mirrors to weapons; others appear to have been made in the Yamato kingdom by immigrants from those countries. Yet there are clear indications of a developing Japanese consciousness. It was about this time that the first *dotaku* seem to have been made. These large, extravagantly ornamented bronze bells were rung at religious ceremonies to invoke the protection of gods and spirits for the community.

Very little is known today about the ritual life of the Yamato kingdom: a great deal of diversity probably still existed at local level, with people offering sacrifices to the spirits of their nearby mountains, woods and streams. Shinto, when it later appeared, would organise these local cults into a state-wide scheme. The need to reconcile the traditions of grassroots communities and the overarching state was an influential factor in Japanese history for many centuries.

Despite a growing sense of nationhood, for now Japan was still very much a collection of extended families or tribes with their own identities. However, one deity – Amaterasu, the sun goddess – was acknowledged by all, so it was from her that the Yamato kings claimed their descent when they started to assume the more exalted status of emperors. The imperial house claimed a direct lineage, through Jimmu Tenno and Ninigi, to the sun goddess: the emperors were thus divinities themselves.

According to the legend, Ninigi was given a mirror, a sword and a special curved jewel as parting gifts before his journey to Earth. To this day, these are the the most sacred items of Japan's imperial regalia. To judge by the frequency with which these special symbols appear in Yamato burials, the cult of the emperors dates right back to the Yamato era.

The tables turned, and turned again

By the end of the 2nd century AD, the Yamato kingdom controlled most of the archipelago now known as Japan. By the middle of the 4th century, it was seeking conquests farther afield. In 366, the state founded by Korean immigrants invaded its ancestral homeland and established a military presence there that would last 200 years. At the time, Korea was divided into the rival kingdoms of Koguryo, Paekche and Shilla, and Japan ruled by playing them off against one another.

On the cultural front, however, Japan itself was being invaded by two lasting foreign influences: Buddhism and the Chinese script. Buddhism had almost certainly been brought in by Chinese and Korean settlers long before it officially arrived, in AD 522, when the king of Paekche sent the emperor a statue of the Buddha and some religious writings. The powerful Soga clan backed Buddhism for political reasons. They supported the imperial prince, Shotoku, who promoted the new religion. With the election of a Soga emperor, Yomei (ruled 585–587),

Buddhism was briefly the kingdom's official religion, and even when replaced by Shinto, it retained favoured status.

Chinese characters were used for Japanese writing from about the 4th century AD, but the new script opened up a window on Chinese civilisation as a whole: its law and poetry, its philosophy and science. A fashion for all things Chinese gripped Japan in the middle of the 1st millennium AD, affecting not only clothes and crafts but attitudes and thought. Many of these imported styles and customs became so deeply embedded they came to be quintessentially Japanese.

Tendai temple
Prince Shotuku, patron of Buddhism in Japan, had this fine temple built at Kyoto in AD 594. It is just one of the 46 temples he had constructed across the country.

Funan – an enigmatic state

To Indian chroniclers in the 2nd century AD, Southeast Asia was a 'Land of Gold', with trading links stretching as far as the Mediterranean. But little is known of mysterious Funan.

Hindu symbols in stone
The centrepiece of this carved stone from the 7th century AD shows Brahma's birth from a lotus-flower (left) beside the trident of Shiva (centre). On the right is the discus and club of Vishnu, his equipment as creator, completing this Funan representation of the Trimurti, or Hindu trinity.

An Indian prince in a Chinese myth seems an appropriate starting point for the story of Indochinese culture. A Brahman called Kaundinya, sailing eastward in his ship, found himself off a foreign coast with another vessel heading towards him. Understandably nervous, he grabbed his javelin and hurled it at the oncoming craft with all his force.

Fortunately he missed, for the only occupant of the boat was a beautiful young woman, daughter of the king of the unknown land, in a state of distress and undress. Smitten by the princess's beauty, Kaundinya resolved to stay. His first act was to cover her nakedness. His spear landed harmlessly on the shore nearby, so he decided to build his capital there. What might so easily have been a tragedy turned out to have a happy ending: the two married and lived happily ever after.

In some versions of the tale, Kaundinya is a descendant of the sun and his bride belongs to the dynasty of the moon. Other accounts tell how the Nagi Soma – the 'snake princess' – is the daughter of the king of the sea-serpents or nagas: her father drinks up the seawater so that they can have a country – Kambuja, or Cambodia.

An India in the East

There is no doubt that a real civilisation flourished in Southeast Asia from about the 1st century AD. An exploratory mission sent out by the Chinese Wei emperor around AD 245 reported on their travels in a country they called Funan. (Why they gave this name to a country centred on the Mekong Delta is far from clear, since the word Funan has tradition-ally been interpreted to mean 'mountain'. A more plausible explanation is that the word actually means 'port of the thousand rivers', although there is no conclusive proof of this etymology.)

Funan was ruled, the Chinese recorded, by King Fan-hsun who received offerings of bananas, sugar cane, turtles and birds from his subjects and foreign visitors. Their description of the people of Funan does not attempt to conceal their ingrained attitude, that all non-Chinese were barbarians: 'The men are all ugly and black, their hair is frizzy, and they go about naked and barefoot.' They are kinder, if condescending, about the Funan moral character: 'Their nature is simple and they are not at all inclined toward thievery.' Perhaps they are most reliable in their comments about Funan life:

'There are walled villages, palaces, and dwellings. ... They devote themselves to agriculture. They sow one year and harvest for three. Moreover, they like to engrave ornaments and to chisel. Many of their eating utensils are silver. Taxes are paid in

Ganesh, the elephant-headed god, is believed by Hindus to bring luck and wealth.

gold, silver, pearls or perfumes. There are books and depositories of archives and other things. Their characters resemble those of Hu.'

This last remark is especially revealing: the Hu were a people of central Asia whose writing was similar to Sanskrit, the ancient sacred script of Indian Hinduism. Strange as it may sound, therefore, there is an important germ of truth in the legend of Kaundinya's voyage: Indian immigration seems to have been key to the development

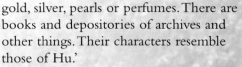

The Buddha
Buddhism was brought to Southeast Asia by Indian missionaries, and was taken up enthusiastically among the Khmer people. This head of the Buddha comes from the 2nd-century-AD period of Khmer art.

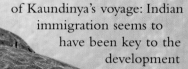

of Funan culture. A later Chinese report, written in the early part of the 6th century AD, describes a culture with unmistakeable signs of Indian influence:

'Where they live, they do not dig wells. By tens of families, they have a basin in common where they get water. The custom is to adore the spirits of the sky. Of these spirits they make images in bronze; those which have two faces, have four arms; those which have four faces, have eight arms. ... The King, when he travels, rides an elephant.'

The basins for water, the multi-armed gods, the royal elephants – all these are marks of Indian influence. But other traditions mark Funan firmly as Southeast Asian. The Funanese built bamboo houses, roofed with leaves and raised up on piles above floodwater level; they made canoes said to be up to 25m (80ft) long. 'For amusements, the people have cockfights and hog-fights', noted another Chinese visitor. Neither of these would have been pursued in the India of the time.

An elusive reality

The accounts of Funan add up to a fusion of Indian and more easterly traditions – a fusion that has been evident in aspects of Khmer culture ever since. That such a civilisation existed seems certain, but was there ever actually a state of Funan? Modern scholarship is inclined to be sceptical: a great many Khmer inscriptions from the time have now been recovered by archaeologists and what they suggest is a multiplicity of small kingdoms and communities – not a single state. The distinctions would have mattered little to the Chinese visitors, but they would have been of singular importance to the local chiefs reigning in the trading settlements clustered along the muddy channels of the Mekong Delta.

Some of these settlements were the size of cities. Oc Eo, for example, covered around 450 hectares (nearly 2 square miles), with possibly many thousands of inhabitants, and could have made a credible capital city. At first glance it seems surprisingly sited for a port, for it lies as far away from the sea as any place could realistically be in the south of Vietnam – about 15km (9 miles) east and inland from the Gulf of Thailand, and 30km (18 miles) west of the Mekong Delta. But this was actually an ideal situation, allowing Oc Eo to be connected by canals (another Indian introduction) to the sea in both directions, and to the emerging urban centre of Angkor Borei farther up the Mekong. Smaller canals served as streets, as they do still in many Southeast Asian cities, and houses were lifted up to safety on wooden piles. The rectangular plan suggests Indian influence, as does the use of rectangular reservoirs for capturing water.

There is evidence that the fields around Oc Eo were drained for cultivation, and artefacts that have been uncovered suggest the existence of a thriving crafts industry, with glass workers, potters, jewellers, engravers, goldsmiths and workers in bronze, iron and tin. The link with India is further attested to by an abundance of objects inscribed with Hindu and Buddhist motifs and sanskrit lettering. Chinese artefacts also abound, as do products from other parts of Southeast Asia and even from Persia. The most intriguing find, however, is a medallion of the Roman emperor Antoninus Pius, struck in AD 152. While no-one is suggesting that Roman merchants actually came to Funan, it underlines the distance over which items were traded at this time.

'Funan' history has to be speculative, though certain general suggestions may be made. Small trading states like Oc Eo appear to have grown up out of smaller villages, each with its own local deity, of whom the poñ, the village chief, was the acknowledged representative. When a chief died, his title passed not to his own son but to the son of his sister: authority was wielded by the male, but in a certain sense 'belonged' to womankind.

The assumption is that over time (and certainly by the 5th century AD) some of these chieftains were rising above others in a clear hierarchy, and claiming the status of kingship, with power over their fellows. The adoption of Indian names and titles may have been a means of setting themselves apart, though Hinduism and Buddhism do seem to have been embraced with genuine enthusiasm. With hindsight, the appeal of the Indian way is not difficult to understand. At this time the Gupta Empire was enjoying its 'golden age', and whilst rulers in the Delta could look to China for a 'role model' of successful statehood, the expansionist tendencies of the Middle Kingdom, and the oppressiveness of its bureaucratic rule, would have held little attraction for its smaller neighbours.

By the 6th century the focus of civilisation on the Mekong was already shifting farther upriver. There the state of Zhenla was on the rise: it would soon subsume the smaller states of the Delta, only to be swallowed up in its turn by the kingdom of Angkor in the 9th century.

BACKGROUND

The linga – a popular symbol of Shiva

To the western eye, the overtly phallic linga is a curious object to have religious status, but it is almost ubiquitous in Hindu statuary and art as a representation of the god Shiva. It originated among the agricultural people of ancient India, for whom such a frank fertility symbol was a perfectly apt object of devotion. The agricultural connection also explains how the term 'linga' came to be applied to the digging stick that farmers used for breaking up the soil.

Over time, the worship of the phallus came to be regarded as obscene, but the linga retained its popularity among the ordinary people who still saw Shiva primarily as a god of fertility. The linga's form changed, however, from the naturalistic phallus of early cult images to a more stylised design. Usually it is a carved and highly polished stone, rounded-off at the top and sometimes decorated with the face of Shiva. In the temple, it is often set up in a socket base which represents the female generative organ or yoni, thus combining the two functions of fertility.

The linga seems to have been adopted as enthusiastically by the farmers of Funan as it had been by those of India: innumerable examples have been excavated by archaeologists.

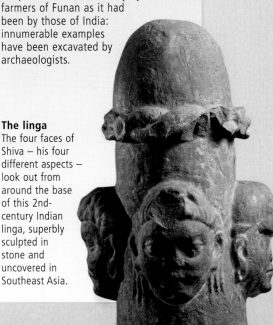

The linga
The four faces of Shiva – his four different aspects – look out from around the base of this 2nd-century Indian linga, superbly sculpted in stone and uncovered in Southeast Asia.

India's golden age – the Gupta dynasty

The Gupta dynasty unified most of the Indian subcontinent, bringing unprecedented stability and economic growth. Peace and prosperity – and a revitalised Hinduism – inspired a renaissance of the arts, sciences and learning.

I n Magadha, northeastern India, where Chandragupta Maurya had established his empire from around 320 BC, yet another Chandragupta embarked on an imperial enterprise in AD 320. This chronological coincidence is curious to the western eye, but has no real significance as it depends on a Christian calendar which had no relevance to the India of the time. Neither is there any great significance in the two men sharing a name, as there is no proof of a line of genealogical descent between the two. The second Chandragupta came to power after

nearly 500 years of anarchy following the Mauryan collapse in the 2nd century BC. The empire he established was Hindu, not Buddhist, and his dynasty is widely regarded as bringing India a 'golden age'.

An advantageous marriage

The heir to a small and impoverished kingdom, Chandragupta I ascended the throne of Magadha in AD 320 after the death of his father, King Ghatotkacha. The new king had big ideas, awarding himself a new title Maharajadhiraja, 'Great Rajah of Rajahs', or 'King of Kings'. It was an empty vaunt to begin with, but Chandragupta was determined to live up to it, and by the time of his death in AD 335 it would not sound so hollow.

He made a good start with his marriage to Kumaradevi, his first queen. Kumaradevi was a wealthy woman and one of the Licchavis, an ancient, powerful clan with territories extending north and west across the lower

Vishnu's temple
The square severity of the great Gupta temples, like this one at Deogarh, was beautifully counterpoised by the sumptuous, swirling carvings which adorned the stone.

Vishnu, the great creator, reclines on the coils of Ananta, the endless serpent of eternity, in this 5th-century relief from the Dasavara temple.

Life in Gupta India: a traveller's report

Fa Hsien, a Buddhist monk from China, spent several years in India around AD 400 and kept a record of his time there. He seems to have come in search of better editions of the Buddhist religious texts than were available in his own homeland.

Inevitably, he spent much of his time with people who shared his religion: his claim that 'Nobody in the whole land will kill a living thing, drink wine, or eat onions and garlic' probably stems from eating, most often, with other Buddhists.

Fa Hsien was touched by the tolerance extended to Buddhism and other creeds. There was great respect for religion and scholarship, he enthused, and he was impressed by the number of students at the universities. He was full of admiration for Indian life in general.

There was an air of peace and prosperity; the people seemed both 'numerous and happy'; and there were hospitals throughout the land for 'the poor and helpless, orphans, widows and cripples', where treatment could be had without charge.

Chandragupta II was a wise and humane ruler, according to Fa Hsien, 'resorting to physical punishment only in exceptional cases'.

Ganges Valley and into the Himalayan foothills of Nepal. Her dowry of estates strengthened Chandragupta's position, and his conquest of neighbouring countries created the basis for later development.

It was under their son Samudragupta that the kingdom really came into its own. He conquered the whole of the Ganges Valley, creating an empire that embraced the entire modern state of Uttar Pradesh, extended into western Punjab and took in a vast tranche of eastern India. Samudragupta's authority was recognised from Nepal in the north to Sri Lanka in the south, and kings across the Deccan plateau paid him homage.

'A god dwelling on Earth'

Samudragupta wielded power with a light hand, accepting the loyalty and obedience of local kings and chiefs, rather than building the sort of intrusive imperial bureaucracy found at the time in China – or even, 500 years earlier, in Mauryan India. All of India looked up to him: he was, one inscription states simply, 'a god on Earth'. A famous eulogy is carved into a pillar at Allahabad, Uttar Pradesh. It recounts that he was 'always striving to ease the sufferings of the poor, the destitute and the afflicted.' He 'reigned supreme as the king of poets', and his skills as a musician were admired by all.

Under the patronage of Samudragupta and his son Chandragupta II (ruled 380–415), Indian culture exploded into life after several centuries of stagnation. The Gupta dynasty has been regarded ever since as the classical period for Sanskrit poetry and drama, with magnificent achievements in painting, sculpture and architecture too. It helped that the Gupta kings had money to spend on lavish projects – taxes and tribute poured in from every corner of India – but there was more to this resurgence than affluence. Hinduism was flourishing, both encouraged and exploited by the Gupta kings, who placed their political status at the spiritual heart of Indian life.

Samudragupta fostered an identification between himself as king and Vishnu, the creator-god, which his successors took up with enthusiasm. The Hindu mythology provided endless inspiration for artistic endeavour; the building and decorating of temples offered enormous possibilities to architects, sculptors and painters.

A time of tolerance and learning

Chandragupta II consolidated his father's conquests in western India, and continued his work as patron of the arts and sciences. During his reign, the mathematicians and astronomers in India's seats of learning were far ahead of their time. The work of Kalidasa, India's most distinguished poet and dramatist, dates from this period, as does the Kamasutra, often caricatured as a sex-manual but in reality a wide-ranging work examining the place of pleasure in the spiritual scheme of things. The Gupta age saw no reason why religious devotion should preclude pleasure. Their faith was tolerant: if Buddhism began to decline, this was largely due to the rival attractions of a resurgent Hinduism.

A hardening of attitudes

Gradually, though, things started to change and by Chandragupta's death in 414 the difference could clearly be discerned. The peasantry had land to cultivate but they never really shared in the *dolce vita*, and the rent on their lands – payable to the king – had steadily grown. The old Hindu caste system was reintroduced, rigidly allocating Indians their place. At the top came the kshatriyas – the king and his warrior-class; next, the Brahman priest-hood; then the vaishyas, wealthy farmers and traders, followed by the shudras, the servants and labourers. The 'out-castes' at the bottom of the social pile were known as the chandalas or 'untouchables'; they carried out such tasks as burying the dead. This hierarchy was fixed by a person's birth, which in turn was determined by good or bad conduct in a previous life, under the divine rules of karma.

Decline and fall

The Gupta glory appeared undiminished through the reign of Kumaragupta I, Chandragupta II's son, which lasted from 415 to 454. But his heir, Skandagupta (ruled 454–467), had to fend off repeated raids and invasions from central Asia. The attackers were Huns – ferocious steppe nomads and kinsfolk of the warriors who, under Attila, were terrorising the Roman Empire far to the west. Resisting the incursions was a draining task for Skandagupta and his successors. By the end of the 5th century the Huns were rampaging across northern India, and though they did not succeed in conquering the country, the great Gupta kingdom fell apart into squabbling, rival states.

A Buddhist mural
Prince Nanda spurns the advances of his wife, Sundari, turning his back upon the pleasures of the world (top). This work was painted in a later period of creativity in the Ajanta Caves, between the 5th and 7th centuries, and was influenced by Gupta culture.

Gupta gold coins
The superb quality of coinage minted in the days of the Gupta dynasty proclaims both the wealth and artistic aspirations of India's 'golden age'.

EUROPE

Greece – birthplace of democracy

In the 8th to 6th centuries BC, a new culture arose in Greece that would fundamentally shape the attitudes of the western world – culturally, economically and politically.

Fight to the death
Two naked warriors do battle over a fallen body in this scene painted as decoration on a vase. The style is typical of Athenian ceramics and was popular all over the Mediterranean region from the 7th century BC.

In the Athens of 594 BC, the mighty cowered in their mansions in fear for their lives, as angry mobs roamed the city streets. The relationship between the wealthy aristocrats and the poor who worked their lands were reasonably stable when times were good, but agricultural incomes were down and Attica, the region around Athens, was in crisis. With cheap grain flooding in from Greek colonies in Egypt and around the Black Sea, there was no obvious economic solution in sight.

Fearing outright revolution, the nobles nominated a mediator. His name was Solon and his appointment to the office of archon – chief magistrate of Athens – was at first welcomed by aristocracy and people alike. The rich and powerful hoped he would protect their privileges while finding some way to pacify the poor; the poor hoped he would deliver them from their present state. Solon's speeches and verses are among the earliest examples of political argument in existence. In making them he invented a new social role – that of the politician, one who tries to direct society by the powers of his persuasion.

Democracy was thus born in Athens, in the late 6th century BC, out of hunger, fear, suspicion, inequality, class-hatred and violence: it was a toxic social brew, and democracy was the political antidote. Though afterwards exalted as a noble, even idealistic, principle, it came about as a compromise – a pragmatic response to a difficult situation. Rediscovered in modernity, the democratic system has proved durable, successfully negotiating the difficulties of an imperfect world.

The rise of the city-state

Around 1000 BC, the world of the Greeks could hardly have looked less promising as a potential birthplace of democracy. Its two great civilisations – Minoan Crete and Mycenaen Greece – had collapsed. Most people lived on the coasts, where their communities were vulnerable to raids from the sea, while nomadic Dorians invaded from the north. It was an unruly time, in which local warlords presided over scattered communities from hilltop strongholds, raiding one another's settlements for livestock and slaves. Eventually, however, as some lords or *basileis* grew

The Temple of Hera at Paestum on the Gulf of Salerno, Italy, was built by Greek colonists around 540 BC.

Sport and religion
Olympia (above) was more than a centre for sport – there were many temples there, too, as well as treasuries where offerings were stored. In Sparta athleticism was not confined to men: girls were also encouraged to develop strength and speed (below).

stronger, a degree of stability settled on the country and communities began to feel more secure. The growing wealth of leading warlords meant they could trade for fine clothes and fabrics, weaponry and jewels. Local craft industries arose, and demand grew for imported items and materials to be brought across the Aegean Sea from the islands, and from Asia beyond. Soon successful craftsmen and entrepreneurs commanded resources and lands to match those of the *basileis*: statehood quietly crept up on what had been autocratic kingdoms.

The typical polis, or city-state, was a form of republic, ruled not by a single man but by a wealthy elite. Within the polis there was a shift in focus from the hilltop citadel, or acropolis, around which the early settle-ments had formed,

to the agora, or open marketplace. There was a cultural benefit in this shift, too. Increased wealth not only fostered a taste for beautiful possessions, but also created time for leisure, education – and to talk. The agora became an arena for political and philosophical discussion.

The Greeks were open to ideas: trade was broadening their horizons, revealing other ways of thinking and of living. Indeed, it was from Phoenician merchants that they had acquired the symbols of their alphabet, the starting-point for all subsequent systems of writing in western Europe. But the Greeks were putting their ideas into practice in ways that were distinctively their own. Though their exact origins are unclear, the works of Homer are believed to date from this period. In ceramics, the 'geometric' style of the time was recognisably 'Greek': a collective consciousness was gradually forming.

Warlike relations

One of the great paradoxes of Greek civilisation is how it emerged from a large number of separate, autonomous states which were always in competition with one another – and often as not at war. Conflict between a polis and its neighbours was the norm, with military campaigns being mounted almost every year, although most were often little more than skirmishes. To a great extent, war affirmed the identity of the polis and built up a civic sense among the city-states. In time, the old warrior elites dwindled, and battle was waged by what were essentially citizen armies.

The Greek hoplite of the time has a vital place in military history: his appearance marks the displacement of the individual hero by the disciplined corps of fighting men. Armed with long spears they thrust at the enemy through a virtually impenetrable wall made by their round shields, pushing forward in a densely-packed square or phalanx.

The political significance of the hoplite is even greater, because his military service made him a stakeholder in his city-state. He provided his own armour and weaponry; he stood shoulder to shoulder with his fellow-citizens – the men of the polis, all for one, and one for all. War between the city-states reinforced local identities and fostered patriotism, but it also brought Greeks together, affirming the fact that they shared a language, culture and religion. It encouraged, if not affection, at least grudging respect.

Olympic ideals

Other customs and traditions also brought Greeks together, transcending local loyalties. These included the great shrines of the oracles. People travelled huge distances to visit the shrine of Zeus at Epiros in northern Greece, while the cities themselves made contributions to the

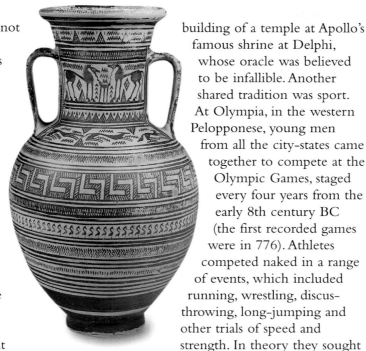

Austere beauty
The severe regimentation of the Greek 'geometric' style was also beautiful, as this elaborately decorated amphora shows.

building of a temple at Apollo's famous shrine at Delphi, whose oracle was believed to be infallible. Another shared tradition was sport. At Olympia, in the western Pelopponese, young men from all the city-states came together to compete at the Olympic Games, staged every four years from the early 8th century BC (the first recorded games were in 776). Athletes competed naked in a range of events, which included running, wrestling, discus-throwing, long-jumping and other trials of speed and strength. In theory they sought only the honour of the winner's laurel wreath, but competition between the city-states was fierce. Victors were showered with gifts on their return home: cheating and bribery were not unknown.

Other sporting festivals were held at Nemea, Isthmia and Delphi. The four were held in turn, at either two or four-year intervals, in what amounted to a continuous cycle. Such was the respect accorded to these festivals that in times of war a sacred truce was entered into, suspending hostilities, to allow safe passage to athletes. The Greeks were united by their spirit of mutual competition.

Outward expansion

Beyond the sphere of the games, competition between the city-states intensified as their populations grew, creating a severe shortage both of land and resources. Over a period of some 200 years, starting in about 750 BC, different cities sent out expeditions to found colonies abroad. The first of these colonies were established just across the Aegean on the western coast of Asia Minor – at Ephesus and Miletus, for example. Over time, more adventurous

Different forms of government

The Greeks were great experimenters and tried many forms of government.

One system was the oligarchy; the name comes from the Greek word *oligoi*, meaning 'the few', and refers to the exercise of power by a small circle of nobles – the *aristoi* (from which comes our modern word 'aristocracy').

Tyranny – rule by a single strongman – is from a Lydian term, not a Greek word, but the concept was operating in Greece in the 7th and 6th centuries BC.

Democracy – rule by the demos or 'people' – was an Athenian invention, but by modern standards their system was both far-reaching and restricted. It allowed genuine everyday participation in government, rather than just a vote for a representative every few years, but on the other hand whole sections of the city's population – women, immigrants, slaves – were excluded entirely.

Athenian voting system
Inscribed tallies like this one were placed in an urn to record a vote.

colonists spread along the northern coast of Turkey and crossed the Black Sea to Tanais in southern Ukraine and to Cheronesus in Crimea. Cities in western Greece sent parties across the Adriatic to southern Italy: Naples was established in this way, as was Syracuse in Sicily. There were colonies across the Mediterranean, at Naucratis in the Nile Delta, for example, and at Massilia, the site of modern Marseilles in southern France. From here the River Rhone became a thoroughfare along which a busy two-way traffic opened up with the Celtic peoples of the European interior. Broadly speaking, local people were glad of an outlet for surplus agricultural produce or raw materials, which they traded for fine pottery and manufactured luxuries of every kind. The contact stimulated new styles in Greek ceramic-ware and sculpture of the time, which began to show signs of Asiatic or Egyptian influence.

The introduction of coinage from Lydia, in western Asia Minor, in the early 7th century BC transformed trading relations, freeing them from the constraints of barter: a sum of money could be exchanged for anything the purchaser required. The effect appears to have been dramatic: the Greek economy boomed at this time – but it would continue to have its ups and downs.

The time of the tyrants

The money-economy brought new opportunities, but it also brought new risks: life seemed less safe, less predictable than it had in former times. Peasants who got into difficulties could sell their small patches of land to local landowners; if they had no land they could sell their labour effectively as bondslaves – but both were simply storing up trouble for later.

Even the rich had their insecurities. They were now exposed to the fluctuations of a volatile international market. Instability seemed built into the system, and by the late 7th century unrest was widespread. Tyrants seized power in several cities; they were not necessarily the monsters that the modern word implies – Corinth seems to have thrived under 'tyrannical' rule – but they were what we

Banquet scene
This detail from a 5th-century-BC fresco, painted in a tomb at Paestum in Italy, underlines the importance of socialising and hospitality for the Greeks. Great emphasis was placed on the giving and sharing of food and drink.

would think of as dictators. The appointment of Draco as the archon in Athens in 621 BC seems to have been an attempt by leading Athenians to pre-empt tyranny. He set out a system of laws with admirable impartiality, but with punishments so savage the term 'draconian' is still with us today – even minor crimes were punishable by death. But the root causes of public unrest remained and intensified in the decades that followed: the stage was set for Solon and his reforms.

Stumbling towards democracy

Solon's actions were nothing less than revolutionary. He abolished all existing debts, relieving the poor of a crippling burden. He outlawed the practice by which peasants used themselves as surety for loans, thus prohibiting slavery through debt, and steered the unemployed towards the urban trades. He urged diversification of crops on landowners and set a top limit on the amount of land one person could own. He also divided Athenians into four classes according to income, each with distinct social rights and responsibilities.

The reforms outraged the rich, but left the poor dissatisfied too. Solon's rhetoric had led them to expect far more. Athens was still hierarchical, its high offices reserved for the wealthy, whilst the lower orders felt as powerless as ever. Amid such continuing discontent it was inevitable that a tyrant would see his chance.

Peisistratos seized power in 560 BC. Though dislodged and driven into exile in 552 BC, he fought his way back to power by 541. His rule, though dictatorial, was on the whole benign. He did a great deal to improve the city with fine buildings and public spaces. His less popular sons, Hippias and Hipparchus, succeeded him in 528 and ruled in partnership. Not until 510 BC did the Athenians get their city back from the Peisistratids.

Two years later, the reforms that Solon had started were completed by an aristocrat called Cleisthenes, who revised the administrative system and broke the power of the aristocracy completely. Cleisthenes divided the population along broadly geographical lines into 10 groups. All Athenians would have a voice in the *Ekklesia*, or People's Assembly, at which policy decisions were made. A smaller council, or *boule*, was responsible for day-to-day matters of state: this had 500 members, 50 from each group. Citizens would serve on the *boule* by rota, a month at a time, meaning that all men should have a meaningful share in the government of their city.

The Spartan way

Athens' great rival among the Greek cities was Sparta, which emerged as the dominant power in the Pelopponese in about 700 BC. From the first a warlike people, the Spartans had won freedom and economic security for their citizens by enslaving the local population and that of neighbouring Messenia. The Helots, as they were called, were made to work the land on the Spartans' behalf. The Spartans did no work, but concentrated on perfecting warrior skills. Boys were taken from their mothers at the age of seven and brought up in all-male 'packs' which hardened them for the fighting life by hunger and hardship. Girls were also trained in toughness and athleticism. In effect, Sparta was a military camp, headed by two army 'kings', which kept itself at a pitch of military preparedness and prowess, not least to prevent rebellion by its underclass of slaves.

Although it had an assembly of adult males, democracy could never have developed in Sparta. With Athens taking the lead, however, Greece was about to step into a new and exciting era. A golden age was just around the corner.

Hoplite helmet
Pressing forward against the enemy in a tightly packed phalanx, the Greek foot soldier, or hoplite, needed effective protection. In addition to a sturdy bronze helmet, like this one, he wore heavy armour to cover his body and greaves over his legs. He carried a shield, sword and lance.

The Etruscans – cities of the dead

Extraordinary tomb-complexes left behind by Italy's first advanced culture offer tantalising glimpses into their long-vanished lives.

River spirit
An Etruscan goldsmith fashioned this bearded face, symbolising the River Acheloos, in the 6th century BC. It was made using the granulation technique, which involves affixing small balls of gold to the relevant surface of the artefact, then covering it with sand before consigning it to the smelting furnace.

When the first Greek colonists arrived on the west coast of central Italy in the 8th century BC, they encountered a people who called themselves the Rasena. They were soon to become the Greeks' greatest trading rivals in the western Mediterranean. Having written off the Rasena as savages to start with, the Greeks were disconcerted to find them such formidable competitors in the mercantile arena: they called them Tyrrhenoi and for a long time slandered them as pirates. The reality was that these supposed barbarians were destined to build one of Italy's most important early civilisations: we know them now by the name the Romans gave them, the Tusci or Etrusci.

> ### VIEWPOINT
>
> #### The first Italians?
>
> Even the ancient Greeks could not agree on the origins of the Etruscans. According to Herodotus, they had migrated to Europe from Asia Minor long before, but Dionysius of Halicarnassus described them as Italy's aboriginal inhabitants.
> In the 18th century it was thought that the Etruscans had come to Italy from across the Alps. Modern archaeologists side with Dionysius and generally assume that the Etruscans developed from the Villanova civilisation, an early, indigenous culture.

Eventually, the Greeks had no alternative but to come to terms with a people who controlled some of the most sought-after raw materials of the age. The Etruscans were sitting on a fortune: the Colline Metallifere between Volterra and Populonia contained immense quantities of copper, silver and iron, while tin, lead, copper and iron were mined in the Monti di Tolfa of southern Etruria, between Tarquinia and Cerveteri.

These resources financed the rise of the Etruscans into a power to match the Phoenicians and Greeks, but they were not the only basis for their prosperity. There were also the famously fertile soils and kindly climate of Etruria, which encompassed modern Tuscany along with parts of Umbria and Lazio. Cereals, olive oil, wine and hazelnuts all flourished here, while the forests had wood for smelting and shipbuilding.

On this economic foundation, in the 8th century BC, a number of villages of the pre-Etruscan Villanova civilisation grew into larger urban centres. The typical Etruscan town was surrounded by a defensive wall and equipped with an efficient drainage system, a paved forum, a stadium and a temple, usually dedicated to their principal deity, Tinia.

Luxury in the afterlife

The concentration of the population into towns and cities was accompanied by the gradual division of society into a class system. An aristocratic class emerged, enriched by its ownership of land and mines, and assumed political and religious leadership. Craftsmen, traders and sailors comprised a middle class of sorts, whilst the lowest class included peasants, mineworkers and slaves.

These trends were reflected in the funeral culture of the Etruscans. From the 7th century BC onwards, burial took place in often magnificently appointed necropolises – literally, 'cities of the dead'. Egypt apart, these Etruscan tombs were the largest and most elaborate of the ancient world. In the south of Etruria, the deceased were placed in ornate caves cut into the region's tufa rock, while farther to the north, ashes were interred in urns in imposingly constructed vaults. The Etruscans tried to ensure

that their ancestors were given familiar and comfortable surroundings, and so built their vaults along the same lines as their houses. As grave architecture developed over time, it reflected changing fashions in the houses of the living. The longhouse of the 7th century BC gave way, over time, to a broader three-roomed building, and then, from the 5th to the 3rd century BC, an early form of the atrium dwelling appeared, built around a courtyard.

So that the dead might want for nothing in the afterlife, their tombs were equipped like their houses with all the appropriate doors and windows, and all the requisite furnishings, carved life-sized out of stone. Interior walls were often

United in death
Sculptures of the dead – like this life-size terracotta couple from a sarcophagus in Caere – were often a feature of Etruscan funerary culture, as were frescoes and inscriptions recounting their virtues and deeds. Married couples were buried in the same tomb, though usually in separate chambers.

Slim style
Elongated bronze sculptures such as this startlingly modern-looking figure were a speciality of Etruscan bronze founders. This one is known as *l'ombra della sera* – 'The Evening Shadow'.

painted with frescoes, and splendid grave goods were placed in the vault. Status was every bit as important for the dead as for the living. In death as in life, a rich Etruscan woman would need her full dinner service, and it went without saying that she would have her jewellery. This was often of great beauty, including intricately worked pieces in repoussé or granulated metal – techniques in which Etruscan smiths excelled.

A woman's place

One striking aspect of Etruscan society was the equality accorded to women. This was widely remarked on in antiquity, exciting amazement (when it did not cause utter outrage) among Greek observers. Etruscan women were not restricted to the domestic sphere, but owned property, were often highly educated and participated fully in public life. What most scandalised the Greeks, however, was when Etruscan women danced alongside their menfolk at feasts, drank and even reclined with them on their banqueting benches.

The Greeks managed to overcome their indignation sufficiently to trade with the Etruscans, even settling as traders or craftsmen in their towns. The Etruscans' openness actually favoured this, allowing outsiders to be assimilated. One return benefit was that new knowledge and skills were adopted quickly. Etruscan artisans learned from Greek potters how to throw earthen vessels on a wheel, and their scholars devised a script based on the Greek alphabet. And while the Etruscans craved Greek luxury goods, their own black Bucchero ceramics and their expertly forged, cast or engraved bronze

artefacts were exported the length and breadth of the Mediterranean. The artistic confidence and accomplishment of the Greeks was difficult to resist, and to begin with tended to overshadow Etruscan achievements. But by the 6th century BC, the Etruscans were freeing themselves from cultural subservience and reaching new heights of material prosperity and political power. They extended their influence down to Campania and north into the Po Valley to become masters of almost the entire Italian peninsula.

Around 600 BC, the Etruscan League of the Twelve Cities came into being – its inspiration partly religious, partly political. Once a year, the Lauchme (the princes or kings) of the member cities would convene at their most sacred shrine, the Fanum Voltumnae near Orvieto, for worship and discussions. Presumably, it was at such a gathering that the Lauchme agreed to a military alliance with the Phoenicians that would enable them to prevent Greek colonisation of Corsica in 540 BC. In 510 BC, however, the Romans toppled the Etruscan ruler of their city, and in 474 BC the Greeks, under Hieron of Syracuse, routed the Etruscan fleet off the coast of Campania. These twin blows were the end of Etruscan supremacy.

At the close of the 5th century BC, Etruscan culture enjoyed a final flowering, though with a melancholy note. The graves were just as elaborate, the gifts left with the dead just as splendid, but the mood of the frescoes was different. Where once bright and festive scenes of the joyous dead had illustrated a carefree existence in Paradise, now solemn and even disturbing themes predominated. Terrifying demons and monsters

---

EVERYDAY LIFE

A life of luxury

Greek writers tell of the extremely opulent lifestyle of the Etruscan upper classes, and these reports are borne out by the frescoes painted in the burial vaults of Etruria. Men and women alike were happy to flaunt their wealth, whether in the form of exquisite clothing or jewellery, or in the exotic furnishings of their homes. Rich Etruscans entertained their friends and trading partners with lavish banquets, at which slaves passed round wine in golden goblets, jugglers and acrobats performed, and musicians played dance music. In their leisure time, the Etruscans would meet for sporting contests.

conducted the dead into a dark and gloomy Underworld, whose god, Aita, waited in his wolfskin cowl.

The final downfall

The invasion of the Celts, who crossed the Alps and invaded the Po valley at the beginning of the 4th century BC, was a calamity for the Etruscans. Their last trading contacts and revenues were lost, and economic collapse quickly followed, causing enormous unrest throughout society. A rising power on the Tiber took full advantage. Until now, the Romans had modelled their political and civil systems on those of the Etruscans. They sent their children to the cities of Etruria to be educated; their alphabet and numbers were based on those of the Etruscans; they had even adopted key features of Etruscan

architecture – the Cloaca Maxima, for example, the main drainage system of Rome, had been built under Etruscan domination. Even the toga was the traditional garb of Etruscan men.

It is not unreasonable to say that many of the things we think of today as quintessentially 'Roman' would have been unimaginable without the Etruscans. Yet by the 4th century BC history was sweeping them aside. The Romans usurped their position of power in central Italy, annexing one city after another. By 250 BC, all of the Etruscan cities were under Roman control, though they retained their autonomy until 89 BC. In that year, Etruscans were granted Roman citizenship – nominally an honour – which absorbed them completely into the Roman state.

A merry dance
The Etruscans' *joie de vivre* is vividly shown in their frescoes. The artist scratched the outlines of the design onto the wall before applying the paint to the still wet plaster. A combination of constant temperature and the natural moistness of the tufa rock has helped to preserve many of their paintings, like this one at Tarquinia, through the centuries.

The rise of Rome

From a cluster of huts on a hillside above the River Tiber rose the greatest city the world had yet seen. Its people would create the mightiest empire of the ancient world, encompassing the entire Mediterranean – and far beyond.

The pride of Rome
Legionaries like this one took the burgeoning city of Rome to imperial greatness. This realistic, life-size bronze statue dates from the 2nd century BC.

Rome is not short of ancient monuments: some of the world's most majestic sights are to be seen here, from the Colosseum to Trajan's Forum and the Arch of Titus. It may seem surprising, then, that archaeologists should have lavished so much care and labour on unearthing some simple stone huts discovered on the side of the Palatine Hill. There may have been grander excavations, but few have been more charged with romance: for this iron-age settlement may have been the original site of Rome.

The chronologies of archaeology and legend come intriguingly close together with the agreement that people were settled here from the middle of the 8th century BC. Modern research has uncovered some signs of settlement in the vicinity from an earlier date, but this does not negate the tradition that the city of Rome itself was founded in 753 BC.

Mythical beginnings
One version of the legend tells that King Numitor of Alba Longa, a nearby city-state, was murdered by his brother Amulius who usurped the throne. Learning from an oracle that his line stood in danger from the future children of Rhea Silvia, his brother's daughter, Amulius presented her to the temple of Vesta, goddess of the hearth, to be one of her virgins.

But the war god Mars came down and slept with Rhea Silvia one night, and their union produced twin boys, Romulus and Remus. Their conception was considered unclean as it had taken place in violation of Rhea's position as a vestal virgin, so mother and sons were thrown into the River Tiber. The two boys survived and were found by a she-wolf, who suckled and raised them.

When the boys grew to manhood they killed Amulius in revenge and decided to build a city at the place where they had been found – at the foot of the Palatine Hill. They quarrelled, however, and Romulus killed Remus, becoming sole ruler of the new city, which he named Rome. Something of an outlaw himself now, Romulus took in vagabonds, criminals and runaway slaves to populate his city. But the community needed women, so he invited the neighbouring Sabine people to meet with the Romans at a festival. Amidst the merrymaking, Romulus and his men abducted the Sabine women and took them back to Rome. A bitter war ensued, but peace was eventually brokered by the Sabine women themselves, and the kingdoms came together under Romulus's rule.

Birth of the Republic
According to legend six further kings followed Romulus, each apparently more tyrannical than the last, until Tarquinius was expelled in 509 BC. From this time forward, Rome's leading citizens were determined to be rulers of their own city

Lucius Junius Brutus – reputed to be the first consul of the Roman Republic.

Symbolic stone
Important Romans had tombstones personalised to proclaim their lifetime honours and achievements. The folding stool and bundles of reeds were signs representing a consul.

and not submit to the authority of any king. Two consuls were elected annually to run Rome, and their decisions were scrutinised by an assembly of nobles known as the Senate. It was an effective and accountable system so far as it went, but it did not compare with the 'democracy' that Cleisthenes was introducing in Athens around the same time: only the nobility, the *patres* or protective 'fathers', had a voice in Roman politics.

The common people – the plebeians, or 'plebs', who included wealthy farmers and merchants – had no representation on the Senate and were not eligible for public office. Social mobility was actively discouraged and marriages across class-boundaries were forbidden. The only way that plebians could secure some of the privileges of the nobility was by becoming clients of a patrician, then serving and supporting him in return for his help and patronage.

The class-struggle between plebians and patricians intensified as a wealthy middle class of successful merchants came to the fore. The formation of a popular assembly in 494 BC, and the appointment of 'tribunes of the people', were seen as the sop they were and the conflict continued. The publication in 450 BC of the 'Twelve Tables', the first codified Roman laws, at least offered some protection to the plebeians against arbitrary behaviour by patricians, but it was not until 367 BC that the Senate was opened to plebeians – and then, only to the wealthiest. From 342 it was required by law that one of the consuls should always be a plebeian: some measure of popular representation had finally been attained.

Fighting for survival
By that time, however, the city was under threat from external enemies – not that the preceding century and a half had

passed peacefully. As leader of the Latin League – an alliance of states against the Etruscans – Rome had learned early that attack was the best form of defence. Since the League's inception in 493 BC, Rome had pursued diplomatic and military measures in turn – and sometimes simultaneously. The defeat and destruction of the Etruscan city of Veii in 396 BC was a major breakthrough. By 351 BC two more cities, Tarquinii and Falerii, had been neutralised as threats. Three years later, in 348 BC, came a revolt by Rome's Latin League allies. Perhaps they had recognised, belatedly, that their position in the 'alliance' was subservient: if not, Rome's crushing victory must have brought the point home.

The Romans were going from strength to strength: the next 50 years saw them become masters of central Italy. As their control spread, however, they came into conflict with Greek colonists around the coasts. In 280 BC King Pyrrhus of Epirus, a Greek kingdom in the Balkans, crossed the Adriatic to take on the Romans. His stated aim was to come to the aid of the Greek colonists at Tarentum, but he may have been trying to win for himself control of all the Greek outposts in Italy. He won the original 'Pyrrhic victory', defeating wave after wave of Roman legionaries, but sustained such heavy losses in the process that he was compelled to withdraw. 'One more such victory and I am lost', he is said to have cried.

The Romans would have claimed, justifiably, that these wars had all either been defensive in intent – fought against enemies who would have otherwise destroyed them – or to uphold alliances. But Rome was now the dominant power in the land, and was tightening its hold.

In 312 BC work began on the Via Appia, a road stretching south from Rome all the way to the 'toe' of Italy. This was

The Roman Forum
A focal point for the city of Rome from its earliest times, in the 2nd century BC the Forum was transformed beyond recognition into the social, political, religious and commercial heart of a mighty capital.

The capitol with the Temple of Juno, one of the most ancient shrines in Rome.

The construction, around 570 BC, of the famous drain known as the *cloaca maxima* opened up the marshy valley to development. Now the antique forum became a bustling commercial and civic centre, with a marketplace, city hall and assembly buildings.

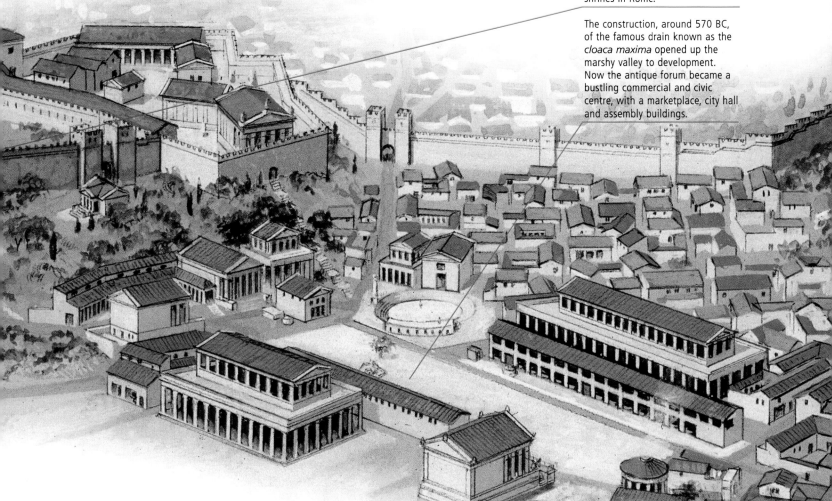

The rule of law

The first codes of Roman law were drawn up in 450 BC. These applied only to Roman citizens, but in the 3rd century BC another branch of law evolved to cover relations between Romans and foreigners. By the 2nd century BC, jurisprudence was acknowledged as an intellectual discipline in Rome.

The rule of law was fundamental to Roman ideas of the fitness of things. The ability to plead a case was an essential part of a young man's equipment for life, and an understanding of the law was central to citizenship.

Rome's expansion of power led to widespread application of Roman law. It remains in force in many countries to this day, in the sense that it formed the basis for many of the legal systems of modern Europe.

War at sea
The Romans fought their first naval battle against the Carthaginians in 264 BC, in ships copied from the Carthaginians' own vessels. Over time, Rome became a major maritime power.

the first of a network of roads, intended first-and-foremost for the rapid movement of troops and military equipment and dispatches, and only secondarily as arteries of trade. The engineering skills of the Romans have been much admired, but their roads were propaganda statements, too. They ran unswervingly over every type of terrain – carried as appropriate by magnificent bridges and viaducts over marshlands or tunnels through rocky outcrops – proclaiming the invincibility of Roman power.

The Punic Wars

One Roman enemy was determined to resist: the North African city of Carthage had much to lose by a Roman takeover of its possessions in Sicily and Sardinia. Originally a trading colony of the Phoenicians (hence the Carthaginians' Latin name, *Punici*), Carthage had become a great economic and naval power in its own right, surpassing the old Phoenician centres of Tyre and Sidon on what is now the Lebanese coast. A seafaring state, Carthage's empire did not extend to vast inland territories, but they ruled trading centres all around the Mediterranean.

When, in 264 BC, trouble flared between the Greek colonists of Sicily and the powerful Carthaginians, Rome could not resist the chance to get involved. Though their record of military conquest

ashore was impressive, they were unprepared to engage the Mediterranean's foremost maritime power. Yet Rome's engineers came through again. It says something about the Roman spirit and work ethic that when they found a stranded Carthaginian galley they set about copying it – and completed 100 seaworthy vessels in just 60 days. Going one further, they devised a simple contraption, the corvus or 'crow', which enabled them effectively to fight land-battles at sea. A hinged gangway with a hook at the end, the corvus could be swung round and dropped on to the side of an enemy ship. The legionaries could then swarm over and engage the enemy at close quarters. Ingenious as it was, the corvus could not redress the balance completely: though the Romans won the First Punic War, it took them 20 years.

The Romans had taken Sicily, but Carthaginian power was by no means broken. The Second Punic War began in 218 BC when the brilliant young general Hannibal came up from southern Spain, leading an army that famously included 37 elephants, to challenge Rome on its home territory. The epic journey took them over two great mountain ranges, the Pyrenees and the Alps, and across hundreds of miles of foreign territory – though the Celtic tribesmen flocked to the banner of a man who was out to

humble Rome. And Hannibal came very close to doing just that, with crushing victories at the Trebbia River, at Lake Trasimeno and at Cannae in 216 BC.

This last defeat in particular was almost the end of Rome: 45,000 legionaries are believed to have died that day, and seeing their opportunity the peoples of southern Italy rose in rebellion. But the dogged Romans returned to fight another day: they trained more troops, and by 212 BC had almost a quarter of a million in the field. Hannibal in his turn had won a Pyrrhic victory. Far from home, he was hopelessly outnumbered. As Rome mounted a counter-attack, landing an expedition in North Africa, he returned home to defend his native city. In 202 BC the Roman general Scipio – known thereafter as 'Scipio Africanus' – defeated Hannibal at Zama, outside Carthage.

An imperial dividend
In the peace settlement that was forced on the Carthaginians, their province of Iberia (Spain and Portugal) fell to Rome. Farther east, meanwhile, Rome had, since 211 BC, been at war with Macedon whose king, Philip V, had sided with Carthage. In 196 BC the Greek states of Rhodes and Athens pleaded for aid to counter Macedonian expansion. Rome obliged, defeating Philip, but the Greeks paid a high price, being taken into what was becoming an overseas Roman Empire.

In 190 BC the Romans invaded Asia Minor, whose Seleucid king, Antiochus III, had been another Carthaginian supporter. The Romans inflicted a damaging defeat in 189 BC, but made no attempt to annex Antiochus's dominions. They added Macedon in 148 BC, though, finally bringing to a conclusion a long series of difficult wars. Two years later they rounded once more on Carthage: this time, they razed the city to the ground and declared Africa a Roman province.

Rome's next acquisition was in Asia. Pergamum, in western Asia Minor, had long been an ally of Rome, sharing its interest in curbing the ambitions of the Seleucid Empire. When King Attalus III of Pergamum realised that he would die childless, he left his kingdom to Rome. He died in 133 BC and Rome had its first Asian province, a bridge-head for further conquests in the years to come.

Mediterranean metropolis
The Romans were now masters of the Mediterranean. As the tribute flowed in from their conquered provinces and trade flourished across the empire, the city at the centre of it all grew in wealth and power. Programmes of public building beautified Rome in the Greek style that the Romans had made their own. The Romans had fallen in love with the art and architecture of the Greeks early in the 3rd century BC when they encountered the Greek colonies of Italy's southern coasts. They acquired a sense of just how impressive a cityscape could be. Now the possibilities seemed limitless: colonnaded temples were going up every-where; the old Etruscan marketplace or forum was reconfigured as the civic and commercial heart of the capital and empire. Law courts and government buildings were built in the grandest, most imposing of styles, with Rome's supreme importance implicit in every stone.

The splendour of Rome was little more than skin-deep, however, as poverty and resentment seethed beneath the surface. Most Romans saw no benefit from world-domination. With their gaze fixed on imperial horizons, Rome's leaders failed to see the social and political problems building at home. They would not be able to ignore the tensions for long.

The mouth of truth
The *bocca della verita*, or 'mouth of truth', as it is known, can be seen in the Church of Santa Maria in Cosmedin, Rome. It is actually an ancient drainage cover.

The Scythians – nomadic warriors

From the 7th century BC they controlled the steppe region that is roughly today's Ukraine, but the Scythians were heirs to a rich culture and destined for a major place in history.

They drink from the skulls of their enemies, claimed Herodotus. 'They take scalps, and hang them from their bridle reins.' Such charges against the Scythians sound like the propaganda of an enemy, but modern archaeologists have discovered evidence that back up the Greek historian's claims: drinking cups quite clearly fashioned from human crania and marks of disfigurement on buried skulls consistent with scalping. In the Western tradition, the pastoral life has always been seen as essentially peaceful and quiet, but the reality of life among the pastoral nomads of the Asian steppes was very different.

Stretching from the Pacific in the east to the Hungarian plain or *Puszta* in the west, the steppes were a vast open arena of competition and conflict. The problem, unlikely as it sounds, was the question of living space: much of the area is mountainous or

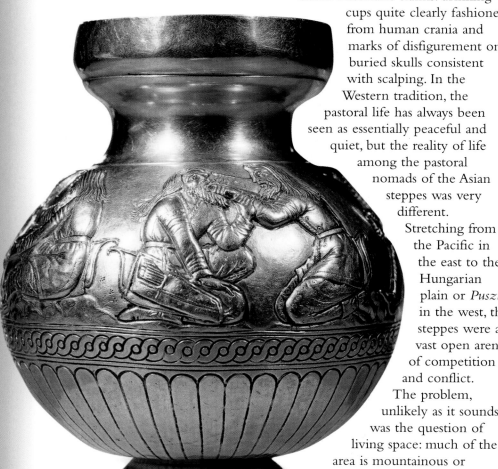

Steppe dentistry
A Scythian warrior receives dental treatment in the field. A painful moment, captured in precious gold.

marginal semi-desert – not the ocean of waving grass that is generally assumed. The pastoral way of life had to be nomadic to get the best out of variable grazing and water supplies, and that meant the need for enormous areas of territory to be protected. Add the temptation to make up losses in livestock – and women – by raiding other communities, and the unstable political environment of the steppe becomes apparent.

The steppe nomads not only fought each other, they terrorised settled peoples to the south and west of the steppe who had no real answer to the ferocity of these warriors. The nomadic lifestyle produced astonishing equestrian skills. Every rider could wheel and turn on an instant, and they could also fire arrows from their short bows with amazing precision while moving at a gallop.

All the great civilisations – those of the Far East, India, Persia, the Middle East, the Mediterranean, even Western Europe – have been profoundly affected by invasions of steppe nomads of one sort or another. They have included the Aryans and the Hsiung-nu or Huns, the Mongols and Turks of more recent times, and the Scythians of the 1st millennium BC.

A hazy history

Nomads travel light: they cannot carry archives with them – in fact they tend, like the Scythians, to be illiterate – and their connection with the land, though

In the saddle
Cutting a dash on his steppe horse, this image of a Siberian nomad from the days of the Scythians was miraculously preserved in the Pazyryk tomb in Siberia. Stirrups were still unknown at this time.

close, is not deep-rooted. There is no way of knowing today where or when the Scythians originated: they appear in recorded history only when they collide with established civilisations. That happened for the first time around the end of the 7th century BC, when raids were reported on outposts of the Assyrian empire – but no one supposes that this was really the start of the Scythian story. It seems likely that they belonged to the same Indo-European racial type as the Aryan invaders of India and Iran, without the more oriental features of the Huns or Mongols. They may have been descendants of Srubnaya tribes from the Volga–Ural region, who started drifting south from the middle of the 2nd millennium BC.

The animal style

Not surprisingly, animals take pride of place in the art and craftwork of the Scythians, especially the horse, the stag, the ibex (a kind of wild goat) and the boar. Predators are also popular, with beautiful panther and wolf designs, as well as bears and eagles. Sometimes fish are featured.

The 'animal style' may have originated in Central Asia around 1000 BC, and the Scythians never completely abandoned it. It is easy enough to see why: the figures display a restless grace that must have been familiar to their owners – all the energy and freedom of a gallop across the steppe.

The Scythians were not closed to other ideas, however. Their style was quite clearly influenced by the civilisations with whom they traded and fought, such as the Assyrians and Persians, and like many other peoples, they became voracious consumers of all things Greek.

Helleno-scythian art
In this artistic collaboration, the horseman is unmistakeably Scythian, the painted bowl unmistakeably Greek.

These tribes established themselves in an area to the north of the Black Sea, roughly corresponding with modern Ukraine. A related group appears to have taken up territories farther to the east, between the Caspian and Aral Seas, and ranging eastward as far as the frontiers of China. These were known as the Saka by the Persians, whose northern settlements they raided, but with whom they seem to have reached a workable compromise.

Several of the great empires found it easier to make deals with the Scythians than defeat them: Esarhaddon of Assyria may have married one of his daughters to a nomad leader called Partatua around 670 BC. A generation later, taking advantage of the power vacuum left by the Assyrian collapse, Partatua's son Madyes led his men against the Median kingdom of northwestern Iran. He pushed on westward into Asia Minor then turned south into Syria and Palestine – the Scythians are referred to briefly in a biblical narrative by the name of the Ashkenaz. Eventually, they reached the borders of the Egyptian empire, and though they could have gone farther, they allowed themselves to be bought off by Pharaoh Pstamtik I: as invaders they were more concerned with plunder than glory.

An elusive enemy

Scythian pragmatism was reflected in their response in 514 BC, when the Emperor Darius I of Persia decided that the nomads were an irritation he would bear no longer. He marched a huge army – said to have been more than 700,000 strong – across the Danube over pontoon bridges and out on to the steppe. Time and again, reports Herodotus, he challenged the Scythians to do battle. But they simply withdrew – and why not? They had no cities or infrastructure to defend, not even fields. With nothing to prove by engaging such an overwhelming force, they preferred to vanish into the steppe. Darius was chasing a chimera, while his army was harried in its flanks and rear. Having

melted away, the Scythians would reappear when least expected. Their incessant small-scale attacks drained the strength and moral of Darius's forces, leaving them demoralised and badly depleted – it was only by good fortune that the Persians escaped annihilation. The Scythians were a foe to be reckoned with.

A resting place in death

Some of the Scythian customs may have shocked more peaceable communities, but they were by no means mere savages. As nomads, they left behind no literature of their own, and neither did they leave splendid city-sites or ruined temples by way of monuments. There came a point in every Scythian's life, however, when he had no choice but to stop roaming and settle down. That point, of course, was the moment he died.

Herodotus described the elaborate ceremonies that accompanied the death of a Scythian chief. First, his body was carefully embalmed, then he was driven around in a wagon for 40 days. Only after this tour of his former kingdom could he be laid to rest. The body was placed in an underground chamber and a gigantic mound of earth was heaped over the top. Weeks of labour were involved. Finally, a statue of the man was placed on top, visible from far across the plain.

This reverence accorded to the dead goes hand in hand with the shamanistic traditions that many Central Asian peoples have followed since the earliest times. Sometimes aided by mushrooms or other hallucinogens, the shamans or priests went into a trance to communicate directly with the ancestors, who were the community's protective spirits. Herodotus also mentions a Scythian goddess of the hearth, Tabiti, and a sky god called Papaios. Not much else is known about the religious beliefs of the Scythians.

Many burial mounds, or *kurgans*, of the type that Herodotus describes have been excavated in modern times, and finds from sites like these have given archaeologists their best insights into this people. As with many other ancient civilisations, it was the Scythian tradition to equip the departed for the life beyond by including all manner of personal belongings in the burial. In some cases these possessions included other people: servants, wives or concubines – very likely, ritually murdered for interment with their lord. As would be expected of a people for whom livestock were both a means of

Nomads did not build or furnish splendid palaces. Their wealth had to be portable and carried either on horseback or in a wagon. Non-essential valuables had to be small, which explains their taste for jewellery and small ornaments. As might be expected, animals seem to have been a major theme of

Horn of plenty
This 5th-century-BC Scythian 'rhyton' or ceremonial drinking horn is beautifully ornamented in silver and gold. The wine was sipped through a hole in the bottom of the horn.

support and a measure of wealth, animals were buried in the *kurgans* too. The barrow at Kostromskaya, in the Kugan region northeast of the Black Sea contained the skeletal remains of 13 people, not counting the chief himself, as well as those of 22 horses.

Weapons were frequently buried with the dead, including the composite bow favoured by all steppe nomads. Wood, bone, antler and sinew were glued together in alternate layers to make bows that were short enough to be used from horseback yet still had enormous power. Arrowheads have also been found – generally made of bronze – and leather quivers. Iron was used for the tips of lances and also for shields, though the shield of the Kostromskaya chieftain was ornamented with a golden stag.

Mobile wealth

Domestic details were not forgotten: the Kostromskaya barrow contained a grind-stone for milling grain, and bronze cooking cauldrons have turned up in many mounds. So, too, have much larger items, notably the wooden wagons in which the women and children rode from place to place, along with tents, utensils, food and other essentials. Ornaments have also been found, some beautifully carved in antler bone and wood, but often exquisitely worked in bronze or gold.

Scythian art: horses, of course, but wild creatures such as stags as well, their forms often extended in a graceful leap.

Far to the east of the Scythian heart-lands, at Pazyryk in Siberia, a freak freeze preserved the more perishable contents of a barrow soon after burial. Silks from China were found here, as well as beautiful felt-work made by nomads themselves. Scythian tombs may well have contained comparable luxuries. Among the organic materials preserved at Pazyryk is the skin of the chief himself, richly tattooed with stylised horses and other ornamental forms. Scythian leaders are also said to have been tattooed, and this seems likely: it is another way in which wealth and status could be advertised without impeding mobility.

A prosperous partnership

The wealthier Scythians were rich indeed, a result partly of raiding, but also of the tribute they exacted in return for their 'protection'. Along the northern limits of their range, for example, in the more fertile fringes of the forest zone, farming communities made regular payments of grain just to be left alone. The Scythian communities on that part of the steppe kept some for themselves, to supplement a diet that was high in meat and dairy foods, then

Fighting it out
Full of strength and dynamism, a group of tiny warriors does battle along the top of this exquisite gold comb from about the 4th century BC.

Golden diadem
This golden headband, delicately trimmed with sphinxes, illustrates the breathtaking skill of Scythian metalworkers.

traded the surplus with other Scythian groups or with the Greek colonies along the Black Sea coast. It appears that the Greeks and Scythians got along together fairly well and their trading relationship must have been mutually advantageous. The Scythians are believed to have loved Greek wine as well as luxury arts and crafts. Greek vases, as well as vessels and jewellery made of gold, silver and bronze have been found in considerable quantities in Scythian barrows. Some items made by the Scythians have been found at sites in Greece, though for the most part they are thought to have traded raw materials like grain and hides.

Transcending trade

In time, the links between the Scythians and Greeks grew stronger. Along with the actual exchange of artefacts, there was a brisk and lively commerce in artistic styles. That the Scythians were open to the influence of Greek arts and crafts has been shown time and again in archaeological finds. There are also signs that Greek craftsmen produced luxuries specifically for the Scythian market – items designed to appeal to the Scythian taste for animal forms.

Some Scythian groups seem to have found their contact with the Greek colonies so rewarding that they settled down in the hinterland themselves. There are cases in which they apparently lived alongside the colonists – the two groups perhaps intermarrying, and certainly partaking of one another's culture. One example of this, dating from the early 5th century BC, has been found at Gute Maritzyn in the Ukraine. This is at the

mouth of the Dnieper, not far from the site of Olbia, which was the most important Greek settlement on the Black Sea's northern coast. Here a group of traditional Scythian barrows has been found, though the artefacts buried there were overwhelmingly Greek. Analysis of the skulls of the interred suggest that several of them were actually of Greek origin: Scythians and colonists laid side by side. In 330 BC, the Scythians came to the defence of Olbia, defeating the army of Zoporion which had set out to conquer the colony.

By the end of the 5th century BC, a settled Scythian kingdom existed in southern Ukraine. Its capital was at Kamenka, not far from Nikopol on the River Dnieper. A trading centre, and to some extent an industrial one, Kamenka had its own smelters for iron and smiths making weaponry and harnessing for horses. Its ruler, who had his own separate citadel walled off from the rest of the community, seems to have lived in great style. The kingdom would not last long, though: nor would the Scythian people as a whole, for in the 3rd century BC another group of nomads started invading their territory.

The Sarmatians originated in lands to the north and east of Scythian territory, but were themselves dislodged by commotions farther out on the steppe. As they were pushed westward, the Sarmatians encroached increasingly on the lands of the Scythians, pushing them farther westward in their turn. Finally running out of room to manoeuvre, the Scythians were made subject to the Sarmatians, who absorbed them into their own tribal groups. So the Scythians disappeared from history as abruptly as they had entered it – here and gone in the space of a few hundred years.

In the shadow of the Acropolis

In the 5th century BC, in the face of bitter wars with Persia, ancient Athens reached its zenith. Ultimately, however, it made too many enemies and would be humbled by Sparta.

In 493 BC, it is reported, the dramatist Phrynikos fell foul of the Athenian authorities and was fined. His offence appears to have been the staging of a play, *The Fall of Miletus*, which struck a very raw nerve. Miletus was a Greek city in Ionia, on the western coast of Asia Minor, which had been a colony since Minoan times, long before the main wave of Greek colonisation. Miletus had thrived ever since, taking the transition to Persian rule in the 6th century BC in its stride: the Persians, it turned out, were fairly easy-going overlords so long as basic loyalty was assured. Then in 499 BC, in the absence of the Persian ruler of Miletus, his deputy Aristagoras seized the opportunity to foment rebellion against Persian rule. Other Ionian cities followed his lead and Aristagoras called on the Greek cities for assistance. Athens responded by sending 20 ships – as half their total fleet, this was quite a commitment, but it was as nothing compared to the power of Persia. The outcome was tragic farce: a combined Athenian and Miletan force attacked the loyal Persian city of Sardes, but managed only to burn down a few houses in the outskirts before being driven off. The Athenian ships sailed

Periclean glory
Pericles (c.490-429 BC, background) presided over Athens in its days of greatest glory. The famous temples of the Acropolis were built at his instigation. The Parthenon was constructed between 447 and 432 BC. The Erechtheion (below) and the temple of Athena Nike were completed after Pericles' death.

home, the operation an ignominious failure – but they had succeeded in making an enemy of Darius I, the Persian emperor. It was an open secret that he would soon advance on Athens with an overwhelming force. Athenians had the desperate sense that they were living on borrowed time.

The defence of democracy

Athens had reason to be fearful: Darius I had decided that he could not tolerate continued interference from the Greek cities in the western provinces of his empire. Athens, the upstart democracy, was especially objectionable in the emperor's eyes: he made plans to reinstall Hippias, the now aged Peisistratid tyrant, on his former throne. In 490 BC Darius launched a direct assault across the Aegean: it was an attack on all Greeks, but the Athenians

The Earth-shaker
This bronze statue of the sea god Poseidon was created in Athens around 460–450 BC.

had most to lose. Apart from the city of Plataea, which sent a group of hoplites, the neighbouring city-states left Athens to fight alone. The Spartans sent the excuse that they had to attend a religious festival, which prevented their going to war. Some 15,000 Persians landed at Marathon, famously 26 miles northeast of Athens. The coastal plain here is broad, so Darius's forces had room to

manoeuvre. It was not the battlefield that Miltiades, the Athenian commander, would have chosen. Despite this, he led his phalanx of 10,000 Athenians and the 1000 Plataeans to an historic victory. It was vital that they withstood the impact of the Persians' first crashing cavalry charge, and as the Greek centre held firm their comrades on the wings circled inwards. Suddenly finding themselves almost surrounded, the Persians panicked, broke and fled for their ships.

A temporary Greek triumph

The Spartans arrived just in time to clear up after the battle: some 6400 Persians had fallen, compared to just 192 Greeks. By any standards, it had been an extraordinary victory. But if Persian pride was in tatters, its forces and fleet were still substantially intact: the Athenians had been unable to follow through their advantage and destroy the Persian ships. Some in Athens realised that the Persian problem was by no means solved. Over the following years one man, Themistocles, argued tirelessly for continued vigilance. Athens should be prepared for another war, he declared, and in particular they should build ships and become a naval power. The death of Darius I in 486 BC did not divert Themistocles from his cause; neither did opposition in Athens. His plans were boosted by the discovery of a new seam at the state-owned silver mines at Laureion. Themistocles succeeded in channelling the proceeds into the war effort.

The Persians return

By 480 BC, Athens had 200 triremes, most of them brand-new. They were not a moment too soon, as later that same year Darius's successor, Xerxes I, sent 700 ships and 100,000 men against the Greeks. This time, however, Athens and Sparta were united: the Spartans had 150 ships.
   The bulk of Xerxes' army came overland, crossing the Hellespont on a

An Athenian war-galley
The Greek triremes that triumphed over the Persians at Salamis were driven by sheer muscle-power. This detail from a Greek amphora depicts one in action.

pontoon bridge then marching down through Thrace and Thessaly. Their advance was briefly halted by a small Spartan force in a mountain ravine at Thermopylae. The action here of Leonidas, the Spartan king, and his 'brave three hundred' is the stuff of legend: they fought and died heroically, defying over-whelming odds, to keep the Persians at bay. They might well have succeeded had they not been betrayed by a Thessalian, Ephialtes, who literally 'sold the pass', showing Xerxes' troops a way over nearby crags which enabled them to come at the Spartans from the rear.

The Persians pressed on, burning and destroying as they went: soon they were in Attica, threatening the city of Athens. Themistocles's response was unexpected: he abandoned the city and withdrew the people to the port of Piraeaus. There they sat out the next few days, whilst the Persians rampaged through Athens, looting and pillaging, and destroying the ancient buildings of the Acropolis.

Meanwhile, the much-vaunted new navy seemed to have melted away without offering any resistance: the Persian fleet pursued them into the strait of Salamis. In fact Themistocles, who had taken personal command, had set a perfect trap. The Greek triremes now turned abruptly and engaged the enemy. Confined in the narrow waters of the strait, the Persian fleet was unable to manoeuvre and was severely mauled. With their navy destroyed, and no possibility of any real support so far from home, Xerxes' army found itself clutching an empty prize. There was no alternative but retreat.

The following year, in 479 BC, the Persians were back. This time, at the Battle of Plataea, the Greek hoplite armies fought side by side to complete the defeat of Xerxes and end the Persian threat.

- ▬ **Athens and its allies**
- ▬ **Persian Empire**
- ▬ **Neutral states**
- ➔ **Persian advance**

SEA OF MARMARA

MACEDONIA

Xerxes' Canal

Abydus

THESSALY

A E G E A N

S E A

PERSIAN

Thermopylae ✕✕

Marathon ✕

Sardes

EMPIRE

Salamis ✕ Athens

PELOPONNESE

Miletus

Sparta

Torch-bearers
Athletes carry torches in one of Greece's many sporting festivals. Athletes competed naked.

Woman cooking
Greek art is associated with ideal forms, but it also engaged with the everyday.

Athens in ashes

It was Athens' finest hour – or would have been had the city not been reduced to ruins, its historic heart destroyed by the Persian invaders. This was no cause for mourning, however, as the Athenian general Nicias told his troops: 'It is men who make the polis, not the stone and wood of its walls and buildings.' His remark perfectly expressed the new political sensibility that had seen Athens through this darkest of times. The mood of civic self-confidence and solidarity enabled the Athenians to see the destruction of their city as an opportunity, a chance to build a new future.

Appropriately enough, Themistocles, the man who had successfully led them through the war, was involved in the reconstruction. In peace, his priorities remained unchanged: he wanted Athens to re-fortify and re-arm, and he wanted it to do so as a seafaring power. Rather than rebuild the temples, he urged Athenians to construct a new fortification, a 'Long Wall', creating a continuous corridor between the city and the port of Piraeus. Its practical function was to protect seaborne supplies in the event of another war, but its symbolism was even more important. It turned what had been an inward-looking, agricultural polis into one which faced out to sea, a major merchant city and maritime power. Sadly for Themistocles, he fell from favour with the Athenians. He died in 460 BC, before the fortified wall was completed in 458 to 456 BC.

Pericles and the Acropolis renewed

Themistocles' plan for the Acropolis was to leave it as it was, its ruins a permanent reminder of the destructive power of the Persians. But such a cautionary vision was out of step with the times. A new figure brimming with optimism was coming to the fore. By 449 BC, Pericles was established as the leader of Athens. He would preside over his city's golden age.

His policies had as their centrepiece a massive programme of public building which would proclaim Athenian greatness to the world. Fine new temples, courts and council chambers would be built around the Agora to house the institutions of democracy in the splendour they deserved. The Acropolis had always had associations with the old, aristocratic order: it had been, after all, the ancient stronghold of the first warlords. But Pericles envisioned it as a stage, high above the city and visible from afar, on which he would mount a stupendous symbolic display of civic power.

Although Pericles (c.490–429) would not live to see his whole vision rise up in stone, he did see the completion of the Parthenon. This temple to Athena took pride of place, a perfectly poised master-piece in marble, the heartstopping symmetry of its colonnades and stunning beauty of its friezes unrivalled anywhere. Within stood an 11m (37ft) high, gold-covered statue of Athena, goddess of arts and crafts, industry and, of course, Athens itself. Outside, across the hilltop, the sacred precincts stretched away in grace and grandeur, with temple after temple and statue after statue. Some were the work of the city's leading sculptor, Pheidias; most had been designed by him – the entire complex was a coherent whole.

The agenda was unspoken but clear, the implications of Athenian destiny unmistakeable. The Erechtheion marked the spot at which Athena had founded the city and a sublime temple was built there, a new embodiment of what had been an ancient shrine; the southern portico was supported by pillars in the shape of maidens. The temple of Athena Nike, the spirit of victory, drove home the message of Athenian military supremacy, whilst awed visitors came and went through a magnificent gateway, the Propylaea.

The Athenian aesthetic

Shimmering through smog and heat-haze, high above the busy centre of modern Athens, the buildings of the Acropolis remain iconic as the ultimate expression of 'classicism' in Western art. Ever since the European Renaissance, the works of the artists, architects and sculptors of Periclean Athens have represented an aesthetic 'gold standard', hailed for their symmetry, regularity, order and restraint. This last accolade is actually unearned: the buildings and statues which seem so white

and pure today would in their own time have been painted in a gaudy spectrum of bright colours. The other qualities can hardly be disputed, however: Athenian architects and builders went to extraordinary lengths to achieve the appearance of perfect balance and virtual weightlessness.

Meanwhile, the Parthenon's decorative friezes (some of them controversially brought to Britain in the early 19th century as the 'Elgin Marbles') set new standards in capturing the strength and beauty of the human form. Though impressively grand, they also have a more haunting humanity, something that speaks of men and women as they really are.

The troubles of the human condition find no deeper expression than in the tragedies written by the great Athenian dramatists of this time. The works of Aeschylus and Euripides resonate as powerfully today as they did for the first audiences who watched them unfolding in the Athens of more than 2000 years ago. More informal entertainment was on

---

TIME WITNESS

The Greek art of education

The schools that started out in the stoas of the Athenian agora soon gave way to more permanent establishments in the suburbs, where there was peace and quiet, and space for the physical activities which the Greeks saw as inseparable from the development of the mind. Plato founded an academy northwest of the city in 387 BC – it would remain in business for almost 900 years, finally closing in the chaos that followed the collapse of Rome.

Plato's most famous student Aristotle set up a Lykeion (or Lyceum) on a site to the northeast. But it was Isocrates, an orator and rhetorician, who around 354 BC formulated the main values of Greek education in his book *Antidosis*. He believed the role of education was to teach skills of

analysis and expression, rather than a body of knowledge. The good citizen should be able to master any brief and plead any cause: it was essentially a course in rhetoric and persuasion.

An organised education
The decoration on this ceramic Greek bowl, found in Cerveteri, Italy, shows lessons in oratory and playing the lyre. Education played a major role in disseminating Greek culture in the 3rd century BC: wherever the Greeks settled, they set up schools.

Site of the oracle
The temple of Apollo at Delphi was home to the most famous oracle in the ancient world. The political repercussions of predictions made here were often felt the length and breadth of Greece.

offer in the colonnaded walkways or 'stoas' around the agora, in whose shade men liked to spend their leisure hours. There were taverns and barbershops, market stalls and pedlars, acrobats, musicians and hustlers of every kind. There was even philosophy for sale: various sages offered tuition to bright young students keen to make their mark as speakers in the Athenian assemblies. Socrates plied his teachings here. His most famous pupil, Plato, founded a more formal academy in 387 BC; the school's illustrious alumni included Aristotle. These three men are generally thought to have come up with all the main questions of Western philosophy – questions which have haunted thinkers to this very day.

Rebuilding the economy

The reconstruction of the Acropolis was a reconstruction of the Athenian economy.

Pericles seems to have conceived it as something of a 'new deal' for Athenian citizens. Inscriptions on stone slabs, found by archaeologists, indicate the amount of employment the work created. In one year (409 BC), relating to a single temple (the Erechtheion), the lists ran to 2650 lines. The categories of worker included stone-masons, carpenters, hoist-operators, scaffolders and gilders. Citizens and slaves worked together, though the latter's earnings went to their masters. Many thousands of people were involved, and the prosperity trickled down to other areas of the economy, benefiting everyone.

The Delian League

Athens had exploited more immediate – and highly controversial – ways of raising money to get its ambitious rebuilding project started. It drew heavily on the treasury of the Delian League, an alliance established by the main Greek islands and seafaring cities in 479, after the defeat of Xerxes, as a bulwark against future Persian aggression. It was called the Delian League after the island of Delos, its ceremonial centre and legendary birthplace of Apollo and Artemis. Athens' dominance of the League began as a privilege but turned into a liability as the alliance became, in effect, an unacknowledged Athenian empire. This was made clear in 470 BC when the island of Naxos tried to leave the 'alliance' – it was blockaded by the Athenian fleet and compelled to continue.

The Peloponnesian War

The manipulation of the Delian League gave rise to resentment among the other members – and they were Athens' friends. Non-League states found the ascendancy of Athens quite intolerable, but events seemed to conspire to cement its pre-eminence as first city, not just in Greece but in the world.
Sparta, its traditional

rival, was bogged down in its own problems: uprisings of its slaves, the helots, had been flaring on and off for years.

A further Athenian victory against the Persian navy at the Eurymedon River in 469 BC served only to increase the complacency of Athens, which knew no bounds when the Persians were expelled from Egypt in 460 BC. Egypt had been one of the great granaries of the Persian Empire – now all its produce belonged to Athens, first city in the world.

The tide was turning, however: in 454 BC the Persians won back Egypt, and that same year Sparta succeeded in suppressing the helots back into submission. Despite a peace treaty between Athens and Sparta, signed in 446 BC, the two major powers of Greece were on a collision course. Sparta headed its own alliance, the Peloponnesian League, and in 431 BC the two sides went to war. It was a bewildering and inconclusive conflict, involving many small armies from many small states fighting in countless scattered skirmishes. And it was draining, particularly for Athens, which was badly led and on the back foot from the start.

Pericles himself was largely to blame: an inspirational leader in peace and prosperity, he made basic errors in his handling of the war. Worse was to come: Athens was hit by an outbreak of plague that raged through a city overcrowded with all the citizens of Attica, who had retreated behind its walls for protection. By 429 BC a quarter of Athens' population had died – including Pericles himself. The war dragged on until an uneasy peace was agreed in 421 BC.

Disunity and decline

Whatever its reverses, Athens was still Greece's greatest city, but with hindsight the passing of Pericles seems symbolic – the

The oracle at Delphi

Delphi was believed to be the most important oracle in all Greece. The site was important as the reputed birthplace of Apollo, but its position at the centre of Greece (and therefore, it was assumed, the centre of the world) gave it special status as the navel of the world.

The idea seems to have been prompted by the hollow in the temple at Delphi; the responses of the oracle were said to come up through the cleft in the ground in the form of vapours. As the priestess, or Pythia, breathed in the fumes, she went into a trance and uttered the pronouncements of Apollo in the form of verses, invariably ambiguous in meaning.

The navel of the world
This stone marked the cleft, called the *omphalos*, through which the oracle was believed to speak.

Philosophical hero
The Greek philosopher Socrates (469–399 BC) lived through the Periclean age and the Peloponnesian War. Despite leaving no written works behind him, he is one of the most famous philosophers in history. The direction of his thought is known to us entirely through the writings of his loyal pupil, Plato.

Dinner is served
This detail from a 4th-century-BC vase shows slaves serving at a banquet. Food and drink are already laid out on small tables balanced on their heads.

golden age was gone. Internal strife did not help: debate in the Athens Assembly was degenerating into rancorous enmity between the conservative Creon and a more radical group led by Alcibiades. It was at Alcibiades' urging that, in 415 BC, Athens took the decidedly risky step of invading Sicily – an 'all or nothing' gambit intended to show that the city was still an imperial power. The adventure might even have succeeded had Alcibiades not been called home from the campaign by his enemies to face trumped-up charges of sacrilege: he was tried in his absence and sentenced to death. So Alcibiades went over to the Spartans and helped them to frustrate Athenian plans. Athens was defeated, once and for all, in 404 BC.

The magnanimous Spartan general, Lysander, allowed Athens to continue conducting its own affairs. An oligarchy displaced the democratic system which seemed to have been so comprehensively discredited. It took only a few months of bungling by 'The Thirty', however, to make democracy look appealing again: it was restored in 403 BC and remained in force another 80 years. During that time,

Spartan bullying became as irksome to the Greek cities as Athenian arrogance had been: Athens even regained minor prominence as a focus for opposition to Spartan dominance.

Philip of Macedon

In the end, the squabbles of the city-states would matter little: all would be swept away when Greece was conquered by Philip II, King of Macedon. He seized power in his own country in 359 BC, his ascent attracting little attention in the world at large: Macedon was only a small impoverished land in the mountainous north of mainland Greece. But Philip's talents as a general and diplomat were going to win for it a significant empire. He started by turning its army into a professional, full-time fighting force, drilled in discipline and *esprit de corps*. He used the standard Greek-style phalanx, but equipped his hoplites with the *sarissa*, the 5m (16ft) long, wickedly bladed Macedonian pike. Enemy hoplites could not get close enough to the advancing Macedonian phalanx, which moved forward in a wedge, opening up a gap for its cavalry to make a shattering charge.

The Greek cities had seen the danger but seemed helpless before the threat. Arguments raged – Philip doing his best to stir up dissenting factions. In 344 BC he started his inexorable push through northern Greece. Athens and Thebes finally set about organising the Greek cities in a united resistance, but it was too late. The Greek forces met the Macedonians at Chaeronia in 338 BC, and were decisively defeated. Philip enjoyed power for just two years before he was assassinated, in 336 BC, but he had killed off the power of the Greek polis for ever.

The unknown Celts

The great migrations of Celtic tribes began around 500 BC, spreading the Celts as far as Ireland and Asia Minor. For centuries the dominant force in Europe, their popular image is one of war-like strength combined with mystic glamour.

A few miles northeast of Rome, on a dark day in 390 BC, the consul Marcus Popilius Laenas addressed his forces. They were a well-drilled and disciplined army, many of them seasoned veterans of the wars against the Etruscans by which Republican Rome had won for itself the leading role among the Latin states. This time, however, the danger they faced was of a different kind and altogether more ominous. In an account written by the Roman historian Livy some four centuries later, these are the words with which Laenas urged on his troops: 'You are not facing a Latin or a Sabine foe who will become your ally when you have beaten him. We have drawn our swords against wild beasts whose blood we must shed or spill our own.'

The Roman army was outnumbered by an estimated three to one, so it is perhaps not surprising that it was overwhelmed. Nothing could then stop the Celts entering Rome, where they indulged in a spree of pillage and destruction. The last of Rome's soldiers retreated to the citadel on top of the Capitoline Hill, where they held out against attempts to dislodge them. The Celts settled down to a siege: they were in the city some six months, before an outbreak of plague and a payment of 1000 lbs of Roman gold persuaded them to leave.

The Romans would neither forget nor forgive this humiliation at the hands of the Celts. Perhaps more than any other event, the sack of Rome set the tone for how Celts have been defined in the historical record – an image that has lasted

The Gundestrup cauldron
Found in a peat bog in Denmark and dating from the 2nd or 1st century BC, this silver cauldron is one of the masterpieces of Celtic art. Made of a circular base and 12 detachable plates, the cauldron is 69cm in diameter and 42cm deep (27 x 16½in). The images are thought to represent Celtic gods and ritual practices.

Human offering
This detail from the Gundestrup cauldron depicts a human sacrifice, thought to be to the Celtic god Teutates.

right up to modern times. We might know the Celts better today if they had left chronicles of their own, but they were not a literate people – their religion actually seems to have prohibited the use of written script. The Druids, the keepers of Celtic knowledge, depended on memory. So our accounts of the Celts have come from writers of the classical world. For some, they were vicious, uncultured, even subhuman; to others they were 'untamed', with a freedom of spirit that more 'civilised' societies had lost. Neither view made any real attempt to understand the Celts as they really were or as they saw themselves. History, as we know, is written by the victor, and Roman power would sweep aside Celtic culture across Europe.

The reputation of these people, therefore, obstructs our view of their reality, but the archaeological record furnishes a certain amount of information that enables modern historians to use the classical writings as Celtic sources. Much is still unexplained, but an outline history of these people, once Europe's dominant cultural and military force, can be pieced together.

Alpine beginnings

In a bleak ravine, high above the village of Hallstatt in the Austrian Alps, is a salt mine which has been worked throughout recorded history. Right up to the modern-day, miners have been turning up

prehistoric finds in the winding tunnels. Literally salted away here, preserved by the mineral deposits, lay the equipment and possessions of men who worked these tunnels almost 3000 years ago. Tasselled leather hats gave limited protection to their heads while they hacked at the salt seams with picks and mallets, scooped up the salt in wooden shovels and loaded it into hide haversacks. They lit their way with torches, bundled twigs of spruce and pine, and used bone whistles to signal to one another in the gloom. Arriving at the bottom of the shaft, they poured the salt into big wooden buckets that were hauled to the surface on ropes of twisted bark.

It has been estimated that it would have taken 2 to 3 years of digging through rock just to reach the seams of salt. Whoever started this mine was clearly thinking in the long term, and it was a large-scale operation. Archaeologists have identified 4km (2½ miles) of prehistoric galleries extending up to 1.6km (1 mile) into the hillside and reaching a depth of about 300m (1000ft). Yet the entrepreneurs who established the mine and the industrial community that arose around it are one of the first Celtic communities that we know of. Archaeologists speak of an early-Celtic 'Hallstatt' culture.

Iron-age innovations

It was the Celts' acquisition of ironworking skills that gave central Europe an industrial revolution in the early 1st millennium BC. With the help of iron blades, forests could be more easily cleared for fields, the earth cultivated and crops harvested more efficiently. They made drills and chisels for working wood, hammers and nails for construction, iron knives and pots for cooking. The basic tools

BACKGROUND

The Druids
The Celts inhabited a landscape steeped in religious significance, and beset by duties and taboos. They had scores, possibly hundreds, of deities: every stream, wood and valley may have had its own god or goddess. All masculine deities descended from the same father-figure, the Dagda or 'good god' of Irish myth; all goddesses were of the same earth-mother or Great Queen.

The Druids were the keepers of this complex religion, as well as other important knowledge. They knew which gods to placate in different circumstances and with what sacrifices. They decided when the time was right to plant, harvest and hunt, and they served as doctors, advisors and judges in disputes. The Romans distrusted them implacably.

invented by the Celts at this time were so effective that they have changed very little since: most are easily recognisable from the tools we use today.

Celtic smiths greatly improved mobility when they learned to make iron 'tyres', fashioning them just that bit smaller than the wheels for which they were destined. The iron ring was heated till it expanded, then slipped over the wooden wheel; as the iron cooled it shrank to clutch tightly round the wooden rim in a perfect fit. There is also some evidence that the Celts were responsible for roadbuilding in many lands subsequently conquered by the Romans: serviceable roadways, surfaced with tree-trunks, have been found. In places, Roman engineers may simply have paved such highways with stone. Other Celtic innovations include glassmaking, which they brought to central Europe, and they were also the first people north of the Alps to use the potter's wheel.

A warrior elite

This picture of industrious and innovative Celts could hardly be further from the romantic stereotype, but the popular image is not altogether wrong. The Celtic smiths were also skilled in weaponry. They made long iron swords and lances, which were enhanced by the advent of steel – the higher carbon content of the metal made it far superior in strength and durability. The Celts were also the first Europeans to make chainmail from inter-locking iron rings, although only wealthy warriors could afford it. Technological and economic advances like these may well

have contributed to the emergence of the warrior culture. Classical writings from after the Celtic expansion are particularly helpful in describing this culture.

'The Celts are tall of body, with rippling muscles, and white of skin,' noted Greek historian Diodorus Siculus in the 1st century BC. 'Their hair is blond, and not only naturally so, but they also make it their practice by artificial means to increase the distinguishing colour which nature has given it. For they are always washing their hair in limewater, and they pull it back from the forehead to the top of the head and back to the nape of the neck. ... Some of them shave the beard but others let it grow a little; and the nobles shave their cheeks, but they let the

Skull trophies
The Celts considered the skull to be the seat of the soul. They decapitated important enemies killed in battle and collected the heads as trophies, believing that this transferred to them the strength and power of the enemy. The skulls set into the gateway below, at the Gaulish cult site of Roquepertuse in southern France, may have been the result of human sacrifice.

Celtic weaponry
This dagger dates from the Hallstatt period in the middle of the 1st millennium BC. The bronze helmet dates from around 50 BC; it was found in the River Thames, where it may have been cast as a votive offering.

moustache grow until it covers the mouth.'

Julius Caesar kept detailed records of his encounters with the Celts in Gaul and in Britain, which he invaded in 55 BC. He had this to say of their fighting style:

'In chariot fighting the Britons begin by driving all over the field hurling javelins, and generally the terror inspired by the horses and the noise of the wheels is sufficient to throw their opponents' ranks into disorder.... By daily training and practice they become so skilled that even on a steep slope they can control their horses at full gallop and check and turn them in a moment. They can run along the chariot pole, stand on the yoke, and get back into the chariot as quick as lightning.'

Diodorus Siculus commented on Celtic helmets and the 'individual fashion' in which the 'man-sized shields' the Celts carried were decorated: '... some of them have projecting bronze animals of fine workmanship.... On their heads they wear bronze helmets which possess large projecting figures lending the appearance of enormous stature to the wearer. In some cases horns form part of the helmet, while in other cases it is relief figures of the fore parts of birds or quadrupeds.'

Classical accounts hint not only at the widely admired skill of Celtic craftsmen but also at the way in which the Celts saw themselves – not as a regimented people, but as individual warriors and heroes. The writings imply that in battle the Celts were a brave but ultimately undisciplined force with a highly individualistic warrior culture. In this respect, the Celts had more in common with Homeric heroes rather than the disciplined hoplites of Greece or legionaries of Rome.

Conspicuous consumption

Status was important to the Celts. Poseidonius, another Greek writer, remarks:

'When a large number feast together they sit around in a circle with the most influential chieftain at the centre, like the leader of a chorus. His position is accorded on whether he surpasses the others in war-like skills, or nobility of his family, or his wealth.'

Celtic sites – ritual enclosures

Dun Aonghus
Perched dramatically above the Atlantic on top of a 90m (300ft) cliff, the ancient site of Dun Aonghus dominates the isle of Inishmore off the western coast of Ireland. It is believed to have been built not for defence but for ritual purposes.

Across central Europe and France, and also in Ireland, extensive enclosures have been found, ringed with walls and ditches that appear to have been for defence. It was long taken for granted that they were hillforts – or in some cases small fortified towns. What else could they possibly be?

As time went on, however, and excavations continued, archaeologists began to ask themselves why they were not finding any signs of habitation. It appeared that these impressive ramparts had been constructed around empty space. In some cases deep shafts were found, with human remains at the bottom, but these did not seem to represent burials of the usual kind.

Today, scholars have come to the conclusion that these must have been sacred sites, set apart by their walled enclosures for special religious rituals – and perhaps also as a meeting place and seat for trials.

The Celts were notoriously fond of wine and feasting, but there was more to their consumption than mere gluttony. Banqueting is one of the best ways of advertising power and wealth. Another is personal adornment, which was another Celtic passion described by Diodorus:

'They amass a great amount of gold which is used for ornament not only by the women but by the men. For around their wrists and arms they wear bracelets, around their necks heavy necklaces of solid gold, and huge rings they wear as well, and even corselets of gold.… The clothing they wear is striking – shirts which have been dyed and embroidered in various colours, and breeches which they call in their tongue *braccae*; and they wear striped cloaks, fastened by a brooch on the shoulder, heavy for winter wear and light in summer, in which are set checks, close together and of varied hues.'

The Celtic taste for luxury has been confirmed by spectacular finds at burial sites. Important individuals were interred with vast quantities of gold. Excavation of the great barrow at Hochdorf in Germany yielded exquisite jewellery and daggers dripping with gold, as well as larger items: a full-sized wagon, a bronze couch and an enormous cauldron.

Around 500 BC, Celtic craftsmen developed an ornate artistic style known as 'La Tène', after the lakeside site in Switzerland where it was first uncovered. Swords, spearheads and other weaponry were recovered from the shallow waters – thrown in deliberately, perhaps after their owners' deaths. Many of the pieces have ornamentation that is unmistakeably Celtic – swirling, spiralling leaves, and looping animal forms.

The presumed 'princess' of Vix in eastern France was buried with a torque (a solid necklet) of gold weighing over 450g (1lb), as well as detailed animal and other pendants of staggering delicacy. Also buried with her was an enormous bronze wine-mixing cauldron designed to hold some 1250 litres (275 gallons). It too is richly decorated, but not in the La Tène style. Around the neck of the cauldron is a frieze of warriors, chariots and other designs in the Spartan style. It is clear that contact began early between the Celts of central Europe and Greek merchants who traded up the River Rhône from their colony at Massilia (Marseilles).

Celtic expansion

From the 6th century BC, the Celtic tribes spread outwards from their heartlands in the eastern Alps, southern Germany and eastern France. The reasons for this expansion are not clear: possibly the population had outgrown the land available; or perhaps elite Celts needed to expand to maintain their status. Alongside the Druids at the top of Celtic society was the nobility, a wealthy elite who controlled the wealth and resources, leading lives of leisure and luxury punctuated by bouts of heroic warfare. As time passed and the population grew, the elite had to travel to secure these things. A Celtic chieftain had to maintain a certain lifestyle to preserve his status, and he had to buy loyalty from his retainers with gifts of cattle, land and luxury goods, so he needed to conquer, plunder and ultimately settle new territories.

Whatever the reasons, expansion would take the various Celtic groups and tribes westward across France and over the sea to Britain. They went southward into Spain, where at first they fought but eventually mingled with the native Iberians to create a new and distinctive 'Celtiberian' culture. Other groups went over the Alps into

Man with mustache
Uncovered at a sacred Celtic site in the Czech Republic, this carved head from the 2nd–1st century BC is believed to represent a Celtic god. It is the closest image that has yet been found to a realistic portrait of a Celtic face.

The Battersea shield
This beautifully fashioned Celtic shield, found in the River Thames beneath Battersea Bridge, was probably made for ritualistic purposes. The Celts went into battle carrying long, oval wooden shields.

northern Italy – including the tribe who eventually sacked Rome. The Celts would remain a presence in the Italian peninsula for well over a century, and a sizeable population settled in the Po valley. From here, they seem to have developed a cycle of winter restovers and summer raiding – 'commuting' south in spring and returning in autumn laden with booty.

During the 4th century BC, other groups moved southward down the Danube, settling in what are now Serbia, Hungary and Romania. The collapse of Alexander's empire after the conqueror's death in 323 BC must have seemed a heaven-sent opportunity for the Celts. Instead of a strong empire, they now faced a ramshackle leaderless state, powerless to resist an attack like theirs. At the same time, however, the Celts in northern Italy were coming under pressure: by now, Rome was no longer a young statelet but a mighty military power. This, rather than the vacuum in the Balkans, may have been what dislodged the Celts from the land the Romans called 'Cisalpine Gaul' – literally, Gaul (the land of the Gaels or Celts) on this side of the Alps – and sent them spilling southeast over Slovenia into the lower Danube. Whatever the explanation, in 279 BC a huge force of Celts swept down through Thrace and into northern Greece.

The sacking of Delphi by the Celtic force at this time, and the killing of the priestess there, was as shocking as the destruction of Rome. Greece still stood for civilisation, and the Delphic Oracle was famous far and wide. Raids like this did not show the Celts at their more civilised. The Greeks were able to resist the Celtic advance, but some pushed on across the Dardanelles into Asia Minor. They arrived there as raiders, but stayed as mercenaries for local kings. Some settled in what became known as Galatia in present-day Anatolia.

Pushed to the margins

The Celts are now associated with the farthest Atlantic fringes of Europe: Galicia in Spain, Brittany in France, Scotland, Wales and Ireland. They were driven back into these areas by Roman power, but by then they had created the first city civilisation north and west of the Alps. In his account of the Gallic Wars, Julius Caesar describes their *oppida*, or towns. The Celts' fortified settlements were indeed the size of towns and some formed the core of cities inhabited to this day. Paris goes back to the *oppidum* of the Parisii tribe, while Avaricum (now Bourges) sheltered some 40,000 during the Roman siege. In times of peace they were home to the nobility, craftsmen and traders, and were market centres for the rural communities around. Caesar was particularly interested in the construction of the *murus gallicus*, or 'gallic wall', built around these settlements as defence. Wooden frameworks were filled with earth and rubble, and this resilient core was then clad in a layer of stone.

But Celtic earthworks and heroic warriors, even the fierce resistance of Vercingetorix, could not hold out against the Roman war machine. Leader of the Arverni tribe in the Rhône Valley, Vercingetorix briefly united the Gallic tribes against the Romans, but Caesar's disciplined soldiers, tactical brilliance and good luck saw him through to a crushing victory at Alesia in 52 BC. The Celts never recovered. In 15 BC, a Roman army crossed the Alps into Celtic lands in southern Germany virtually unopposed.

The Romans first raided Celtic Britain under Julius Caesar in 55 BC. They returned in AD 43, in the reign of Emperor Claudius, and established their hold over all but the far north and west. The uprisings of Caratacus (AD 47) and Queen Boudicca (AD 60) were more dramatic than militarily realistic. The last stand of the Celtic Picts came at the battle of Mons Graupius in Scotland, around AD 80, when the Roman general Julius Agricola won a resounding victory.

The Roman Republic in crisis

At what might have been its moment of utmost triumph, the Roman Republic began to spiral into civil war and dictatorship.

Emperor in all but name
More successful as a general than a politician, Gaius Julius Caesar (c.100–44 BC) did not enjoy ultimate power in Rome for long. He paved the way for his nephew and heir Octavian to assume imperial powers as Augustus Caesar.

The successful conclusion of the Punic Wars, with the destruction of Carthage in 146 BC, left Rome the undisputed superpower of the Mediterranean. As the celebrations subsided, however, many began to count the cost: decades of war had disrupted both Rome's economy and its institutions. The strain was starting to show, and grievances, unnoticed in the heat of war, were being expressed in a rising clamour.

Even the countryside was in crisis. The peasant farmers provided the backbone of the Roman army, but the demands made on them in recent times had been extraordinary. They returned to their smallholdings to find them neglected and badly affected by unfair competition. Roman patricians, enriched by war, had established huge estates or *latifundia*: worked by slaves, these enjoyed huge economies of scale. Traditional farming became increasingly unprofitable, and many thousands were forced off the land only to end up as an idle and disaffected element in the towns.

In 133 BC the People's Tribune, Tiberius Sempronius Gracchus, attempted to tackle the problem by distributing state-owned lands among the dispossessed. When the patricians of the Senate resisted, Gracchus went directly to the People's Assembly with his

Battling with the barbarians
From the end of the 2nd century BC, Rome made continuous conquests in Gaul and in western Germany.

Rome's hard-won image as a military juggernaut. The uprising of King Jugurtha of Numidia in North Africa was put down, but it took an embarrassingly long time. Accusations of incompetence and corruption among the Roman ruling elite were rife. Then in 105 BC the Cimbri and Teutones – two Germanic tribes which had migrated into Gaul – defeated a Roman army outside Arausio (modern Orange). They were subsequently crushed, but the damage had been done. Rome's people were thoroughly disenchanted with a leadership that only a generation earlier had been riding high.

The Social War

Next it was the turn of Rome's Italian allies to register their discontent. They, too, had fought in the Punic Wars and now they felt their sacrifices had been for very little return. Where were their rewards of victory?

Rome recognised the 'freedom' of its allies or *socii*, but was reluctant to concede the citizenship that many demanded. Resistance came from both the patricians and from the poor. For the latter, citizenship was perhaps the only privilege they felt they had, and they were readily moved by the xenophobic speeches of politicians like consul Gaius Fannius. 'If you give citizenship to the Latins,' he exclaimed in 122 BC, 'do you think that there will be room for you at rallies as there is now, or that you will be able to attend games and festivals? Don't you think that they will take up all the room?'

The more moderate tribune Marcus Livius Drusus argued for the extension of citizenship to the allies, but he too was assassinated in 91 BC. With all avenues of peaceful reform apparently closed by this act of violence, the resentment of the *socii* flared into the Social War. Rome brought the conflict to a conclusion in 88 BC, but at a price. From then on, every Italian male who originated south of the River Po had the right to claim *Cives Romanus sum* – 'I am a Roman Citizen'.

proposals. Why, he demanded, should those who had fought and died to make Rome great have enriched only others, deriving no benefits for themselves and their own families? Not surprisingly, his words struck a chord, but enthusiasm turned to outrage when Tiberius was assassinated later that year. The suspicion was that he had been the victim of a patrician conspiracy.

Ten years later, Tiberius's brother Gaius took up the cause, but he too was assassinated. This time public anger was brought to boiling point. The mood was not improved by a series of military defeats in the final years of the 2nd century BC, which took the gloss off

Sulla the strongman

Despite supposed victory in the Social War, in Rome itself it was seen as another humiliation and Rome's leadership was now dangerously lacking in authority. When the tribune Publius Sulpicius Rufus took the command of a campaign in Asia Minor away from Lucius Cornelius Sulla to give it to a favoured friend, the general made his contempt clear. He returned with his army and marched on Rome, seized the city, executed Tribune Rufus and established his own associates in power. He then headed back to Asia.

Though Sulla's supporters were driven out of Rome in 87 BC, he was building a formidable power base for himself in Roman Asia. He kept the loyalty of his officers by allowing them to extort money from the Asian cities, and in 85 BC he returned to Italy as an invader. After two years of horrific civil war, Sulla emerged as the victor. In 81 BC he had himself named as dictator in Rome.

Sulla restored senatorial government before his death in 78 BC, but he had set a sinister precedent for Roman politics. With an extensive and often unruly empire to be run, generals in the field had to be given considerable resources and a great deal of autonomy. The potential for them to make themselves mini-monarchs in their distant provinces was bad enough without the threat of them coming back to interfere forcefully in the rule of Rome. To make matters worse, a populace now thoroughly dissatisfied with its established rulers was starting to succumb to the allure of strong men like Sulla.

Pompey the Great

This was clear from the adulation given to the young general Gaius Pompeius, a protégé of Sulla's (he had supported Sulla in the civil war) and an early emulator of his mentor's methods. In 77 BC, 'Pompey' used his troops to intimidate the senate into giving him what he wanted – the command of a campaign in Spain. Seven years later he was given a consulship, despite his ineligibility in both age and experience. A series of overseas assignments removed him from Rome, but these bolstered his growing reputation as a man who could get things done. In 67 BC, asked to tackle the problem of piracy in the Mediterranean, he fought a whirlwind naval campaign which succeeded in just 40 days. He then went to Asia Minor to put down the longstanding unrest there, then moved south to Syria where he annexed the Seleucid Kingdom to the empire.

By the time Pompey returned to Rome in 62 BC, tensions in the city were at fever pitch. The year before, Lucius Sergius Catilina ('Catiline') had attempted a coup. Catilina failed to seize power only because of the actions of consul Marcus Tullius Cicero, whose eloquent and impassioned speeches in defence of Roman liberty are still considered literary classics.

Defender of freedom
Marcus Tullius Cicero, the great writer and orator of the Roman Republic, was implacably opposed to the First Triumvirate. He was assassinated on Mark Antony's orders in 43 BC.

The First Triumvirate

The respite Cicero won for the principle of freedom was only temporary. Rival generals were now circling the senate like sharks. It was not very long before the most important among them came to a compromise. In 60 BC Pompey and Marcus Licinius Crassus – both Consuls since 70 BC – joined with Gaius Julius Caesar in the First Triumvirate. The alliance between the *tres viri* (three men) was unofficial, but for the next few years they were the power in Rome.

There followed an uneasy truce between Rome's three new rulers – and a period of apparent success for the empire, which over the next decade was enlarged by Caesar's conquests in Gaul. These extended beyond the borders of modern

Colonial style
An expanding empire offered plenty of opportunities for leading the good life: this villa is at Stobi in Macedonia.

France to include Belgium, parts of the Netherlands and all Germany west of the Rhine. Pompey and Crassus looked on with envy, but Crassus' attempts to emulate Caesar's success ended in disaster. In 53 BC he suffered a catastrophic defeat at the hands of the Parthians at Carrhae in Asia Minor; his army was destroyed and Crassus was killed. With Crassus' death, the Triumvirate alliance collapsed and Pompey was elected Rome's sole Consul.

Crossing the Rubicon

Caesar was enraged. Defying direct orders from the Senate to disband his army, he marched back to Rome in 49 BC. By crossing the River Rubicon near Ravenna, the border between Gaul and Italy, he triggered civil war. Pompey had the political support, but Caesar's generalship was unstoppable. In three months Caesar had made himself master of Italy, and the following year he defeated Pompey's forces in Thessaly. Pompey fled to Egypt, where he was assassinated.

Hopes that Caesar would restore the Republic were soon dashed, however.

In 45 BC, he had himself made 'dictator for life'; worse still, he seemed to be adopting the regal trappings of the eastern kings. This was not the man for whom many of his supporters had thought they were fighting, and on the ides of March (the 15th) in 44 BC he was assassinated outside the Senate on the steps of the Capitol. No fewer than 60 senators took part, led by Marcus Junius Brutus and Gaius Cassius. Honourable as their intentions may have been, the message that their action sent out was not that the Republic should be restored, as they had hoped, but that Rome's destiny was to be decided by violence.

'Friends, Romans, countrymen...'

The events surrounding the assassination of Caesar are familiar through the famous drama of William Shakespeare, as good a guide as any to this turbulent time. Caesar's friend Marcus Antonius (Shakespeare's Mark Antony) did attempt to whip up support for his own ambitions among Caesar's following, despite assuring the conspirators of his sympathies. But

Antony found himself losing his position at centre-stage on the Roman scene to Caesar's nephew and adopted son and heir, the young Giaus Octavius (Octavian).

Only 19 when Julius died, Octavian quickly showed his fitness to follow in the dictator's footsteps. He attempted to gain support for a coup among Caesar's loyal veterans, but when this failed he formed an alliance with Antony and Marcus Aemilius Lepidus, another of Julius Caesar's supporters. These three took power as Rome's Second Triumvirate. One of Antony's first acts was to order the assassination of Cicero, who had been an outspoken critic of his drive for power.

Return to civil war

Meanwhile, Brutus and Cassius had taken hold of the Eastern Empire, and the scene was set for a showdown. At Philippi in Greece, their armies were defeated by those of Antony and Octavian. The Triumvirate were left rulers of the Roman world, but three was felt to be a crowd so Lepidus was promptly sent off to take charge in Africa. Then in no time at all Octavian compelled him to retire; he was 'promoted' into what had become the fairly meaningless position of *pontifex maximus*, the 'high priest' of Rome.

At first, Antony fared better: he was given the east to rule on Rome's behalf. His notorious love affair with Cleopatra

of Egypt was a slight to Octavian's sister, to whom Antony was married, but Octavian was more concerned that Antony was growing increasingly wayward. Octavian demanded that all cities in the empire assure him of their loyalty personally. Antony defied the order, as Octavian had assumed he would, and in 32 BC their armies met in battle and Antony was defeated. With the help of Cleopatra's Egyptian fleet he tried to reverse the result at sea, but their force was smashed at the Battle of Actium in 31 BC.

Antony and Cleopatra both committed suicide, and Egypt became a province of Rome. Octavian's pre-eminence was now undisputed. In 27 BC the Senate awarded him the title Augustus – literally, august or glorious – along with unlimited authority. Quietly, without undue fuss, he took on the *potestas tribunicia*, the power of the tribunes, assuming responsibility for the representation of the common people. At the same time he became commander in chief and organised the creation of a personal praetorian guard for his own protection. Thus the institutions of the Republic were concentrated in one man: the empire had acquired an emperor.

In memory
With Brutus' head on one side, daggers and the ides of March 'Eid Mar' on the other, this coin was minted in commemoration of Caesar's assassination.

EVERYDAY LIFE

A slave's life

Slavery was taken for granted in Rome, as elsewhere in the ancient world. Many became slaves through 'debt-bondage', forfeiting their freedom on being unable to discharge a significant debt. Most slaves, however, were won by conquest. Rome's expansion brought an enormous influx of slaves: 65,000 Sardinians, for example, were sold in Rome after the island was conquered in 177 BC. By the 1st century BC, there were up to 3 million slaves in Italy – a third of the population.

The work that slaves had to do, and the conditions in which they lived, varied enormously. Those forced to labour in mines led dreadful lives; the big farms were rather like the plantations of the American South in the 19th century; gladiators were trained for public slaughter. The desperation of slaves led to revolts, in Sicily in 136–132 BC and, most famously, the uprising led by Spartacus in 73–71 BC.

Others were more fortunate, however, working in a wide range of domestic roles, or as craftsmen. Some were respected artists, architects and even philosophers, enjoying every privilege except their freedom.

Slave in chains
An African slave crouches in fetters, awaiting sale.

Threat from the north: the Germanic tribes

To the north and east of the Roman Empire lived Germanic tribes: were they as wild as the lands in which they lived?

The wild ones
This Roman relief shows Germanic tribesmen charging into battle half-naked and armed with primitive clubs. But how much of this image is Roman propaganda rather than realistic depiction?

In AD 9, the Roman governor of Germania, Publius Quinctilius Varus, led an expedition deep into the Teutoburg forest. The tribes of the region had undertaken one raid too many: the time had come for the Romans to teach them a lesson in civilised manners. Varus was equipped to do just that. He had with him three legions, the XVII, XVIII and XIX, along with extra cohorts and cavalry squadrons – in total, around 25,000 well-armed, well-trained and well-disciplined men. At first, as they made their way through the woods, there was no sign of opposition: common sense seemed to have prevailed among the peoples of the Weser valley. Progress slowed, however, as the forest grew denser and the undergrowth thicker. Soon, every semblance of military order was lost as the men were forced to make their way through increasingly boggy conditions. To make things worse, heavy rain was lashed by a gusting wind.

Then, quite abruptly, it became a massacre. Through the squalls of rain came a hail of spears. Before the Romans could react, Germanic fighters appeared from nowhere, material-ising as if by magic between the trees. They closed quickly, slashing with swords and thrusting with daggers. A surprising number wore basic armour of the Roman kind; others wore woollen rags that did not impede their agility – they ran, ducked, dodged, stabbed and then were gone. The attackers were never in sight long enough to engage with, and it was impossible to form ranks or wield heavy weapons in the trees. Varus had led his legions into a lethal trap. For three days the German attack continued relentlessly, and the Romans were slaughtered. A man defeated, Varus fell on his sword; only a few thousand of his soldiers made it home.

'Quinctilius Varus, give me back my legions!' the emperor Augustus is said to have cried at the news. Roman rule in Germany beyond the Rhine was at an end: the notion of an eastern border at the River Elbe was abandoned.

To add insult to injury, Arminius, the leader of the German revolt, turned out to have served as a Roman auxiliary. That explained the armour and equipment some of his men had been seen with. The detail merely confirmed what all Romans had already concluded: the Germani were a race beyond redemption.

A rural culture

The Germanic peoples left no great cities, palaces or temples as monuments. Their settlements did not rival the prosperous *oppida* of the Celts; nor, apparently, could they compete as craftsmen with the creators of La Tène work. The culture they created was appropriate to the environment in which they lived, which covered some of the most inhospitable lands of northern Europe. Theirs was a small-scale, low-tech lifestyle that coaxed a livelihood out of what were often inadequate soils in an unsympathetic climate. In short, the Germani could cope with conditions which utterly demoralised other people.

Archaeological evidence from around 1000 BC points to the emergence of a distinct culture centred on northern Germany, Jutland, Denmark and southern Scandinavia.

Goddess of the home
This carved wooden head from a site in southern Germany is thought to represent a goddess who protected the home. The iron-age people who revered her lived in scattered farmstead communities like the one in this artist's reconstruction (background, below).

The impression that these were a 'bog people' is partly accidental – the peat bogs of northern Germany and Denmark preserved organic items which would otherwise have decayed – but everything points to their having favoured sites close to coasts or in marshy valley bottoms. Houses of wooden construction were built, raised up on mounds of earth, clay, reeds and other debris to prevent flooding. Remnants of wooden tools and boats have also been recovered, as have remains of sacrificed bodies. Over time, this culture seems to have spread southward,

Ornamental stone
This beautifully decorated stone was found on the island of Gotland, southern Sweden.

up the River Oder into eastern Germany and west along the Weser valley. From around the 5th century BC, the Germanic people had ironworking skills, but these were hampered in the north by a shortage of high-quality ores. Important orefields would eventually be opened up in the Schleswig-Holstein region, in the valleys of the rivers Elde and Oder, and along the Vistula in Poland's Lysa Góra region.

Some groups grew comparatively wealthy on the proceeds of the ironworking trade. At Hjortspring in Denmark a warship has been found buried in a peat bog, along with a large quantity of weaponry including 150 wooden shields, 138 iron spearheads and 20 chain-mail tunics. This treasure from the 3rd century BC may have been an offering to a god in gratitude for victory: it implies there was a wealthy warrior elite along Celtic lines. Even so, the Germanic culture was recognisably different from that of the Celts, which was then developing in Alpine central Europe and being exported into western areas of Germany.

The struggle to survive

For most of the Germanic peoples there was no warrior lifestyle, just a daily battle for survival. Writing in the 1st century AD, the Roman writer Pliny the Elder described one settlement he visited along Germany's North Sea coast, where the elements made it questionable 'whether it belongs to the land or is part of the sea'. Of the people's lifestyle, Pliny records:

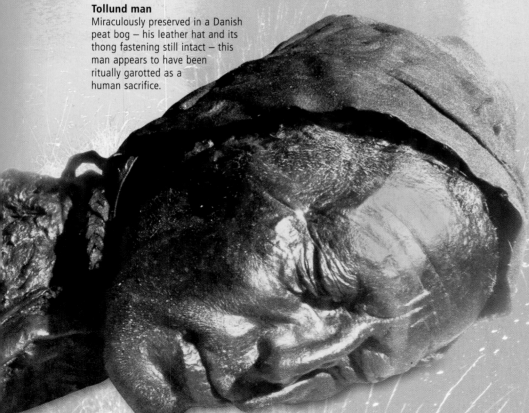

Tollund man
Miraculously preserved in a Danish peat bog – his leather hat and its thong fastening still intact – this man appears to have been ritually garotted as a human sacrifice.

'Here lives a poor people on high hills or trestles erected by human hands, raised to the height of the highest floods. Here they also build their houses, and are like seafarers when the water covers their surroundings, as if shipwrecked, when the water retreats. Near their huts they catch fish on the descending tide, and they cannot keep livestock or nourish themselves from milk like their neighbours. They cannot even hunt the wild creatures, for far and wide there is neither bush nor shrub. They make their fishing nets from lines woven out of sea grass or rushes. With their hands they gather peat, dry it more in the wind than in the sun and use it to cook their food and warm their limbs, numbed stiff from the ever-blowing North wind. To drink they have but rainwater, which they gather in holes before their huts.'

Yet poor as they are, he concludes, these people love their freedom. Pliny's account rings true, even if most would not have lived quite as uncomfortably as this – like the 'neighbours' Pliny refers to, most would have had livestock. The Germanic family's cattle, sheep and pigs were its wealth, and were well cared for, in many cases sharing the family home. The typical 'longhouse' of the period was divided into sections, with space for men, women and children at one end and stalls for livestock at the other. In larger, more well-appointed houses, the two might be separated by a central workshop area.

A settlement of longhouses like these was found at Feddersen Wierde, at the mouth of the River Weser. Raised up on banks of clay the houses had timber frames, roofs of reeds and walls of wattle – reeds woven in basket-style. Some were big, with space in the built-in byre section for up to 20 cattle. Near each house stood a separate structure, raised up on piles, believed to have been granaries; the stilts would have given some protection against floodwater and vermin. The village seems to have been established in the 1st century BC. It was atypical only in the extent that it grew, over time – Germanic farmers generally lived in isolated farmsteads or small hamlets. Feddersen Wierde, by contrast, eventually comprised 50 houses, with separate workshop buildings and even a banqueting hall.

On the move

This substantial settlement was abruptly abandoned in the 5th century AD after a series of storm tides made the low-lying lands near the coast too salty for successful cultivation. Perhaps it was the sense that, however hard they tried, they were always battling against the odds which prompted the general tendency of the Germanic peoples to drift southwards. The first groups to do this were the Cimbri and the Teutones of Jutland, who in 105 BC cut down a Roman army outside Arausio in Gaul. The Romans had their revenge, however. An army led by Consul Gaius Marius met the Cimbri and Teutones in 101 BC; this time they won the battle and wiped the barbarians out.

TIME WITNESS

An example of loyalty and respect

The fullest account we have of the lives and customs of the Germanic tribes is in a volume called *Germania*, written in the 1st century AD by the Roman writer Tacitus. However, it is not clear how much it can be relied upon. Tacitus never visited what he was convinced was a deeply unappealing country, all impenetrable forests and pathless swamps. This must have been an oversimplification – even if it was true that the *Germani* had a genius for creating a subsistence living in inhospitable territories.

Yet Tacitus found much to praise in these peoples: their friendliness in peace and their courage in war. He admired the loyalty they invariably showed to their leaders and respected the tribal councils or 'Things' at which matters of moment were discussed and decisions taken.

No doubt he felt such institutions embodied some of that spirit of solidarity which had been present in the earliest senates of Republican Rome. It is certainly the case that he contrasted the noble simplicity of Germanic lives with the decadence and corruption of his fellow-citizens.

Germanic strength
For the Romans, the Germans seemed uncivilised, but full of raw physical strength, as captured in this decorative marble statue.

Successful integration
Seen on the right in this ivory diptych, with his wife Serena and their son Eucharius, Stilicho was one of many German warriors who rose high in the Roman army.

Breaching the limit

But the threat from the north was not to be dealt with quite so easily. Other Germanic peoples pushed south in the centuries that followed. The Roman conquests of northeastern Gaul and parts of Germany were justified on the grounds that they would create a buffer against future incursions, but towards the end of the 1st century it was decided to build a physical barrier. This *limes* or 'limit' began on the Rhine in the Neuwied Basin and ran 550 km (340 miles) eastward, almost to Regensburg on the Danube. It was a European version of Britain's Hadrian's Wall, which dated from around the same time, but was less effective in keeping out unwanted tribes. In the 2nd century AD, Lombards from the Elbe and Marcomanni

from Bohemia pushed southward into the empire. They were followed a century later by the Vandals, Burgundians, Goths and Alamanni. As yet, this was not a mass invasion; the newcomers were absorbed into the empire, the menfolk welcome recruits as auxiliary soldiers for an overstretched army. The sheer size of the empire, the length of its frontiers, meant that it could no longer be protected purely by citizens from the Italian heartland. The problem the Germani posed was not as an attacking enemy, but as a destabilising presence in the Roman army. They were aliens, and however well-disposed could not share in the required civic spirit or patriotic fervour. At first this did not matter, but in the 4th century, as Rome's political crises deepened, the army's loyalty began to matter a great deal.

Then, in the early 5th century AD, invaders originating out on the Central Asian steppe, the Huns, began putting pressure on Germanic tribes encouraged to settle in southeastern Europe. Tensions mounted between the Visigoths and succeeding Roman emperors. In AD 410, under King Alaric, the Goths poured into Italy and sacked Rome.

Far to the west in Spain, meanwhile, Germanic Vandals had settled. They now struck south across the Strait of Gibraltar to establish a kingdom in North Africa. The Franks and Burgundians carved out realms in what had been Celtic France, while the Lombards set up home in the northern provinces of Italy. With Roman rule collapsing, Germanic chieftains were among those quickest to take advantage.

The Roman Empire

Under the rule of its emperors, Rome became the dominant power in the western world, the yardstick by which all great empires would subsequently be judged.

Augustus Caesar
Rome's first emperor was born in 63 BC, the nephew of Julius Caesar. He reigned for 41 years. Behind him here is the triumphal arch of the Forum Romanum, which he had reconstructed.

Anno Domini, 'In the year of the Lord': history began again here – albeit only in the west, and only in hindsight. Even in Palestine, the year of Christ's nativity passed largely unnoticed. For there was only one 'Lord' in the Mediterranean world at that time, and he had been born 63 years earlier.

Augustus, the first Roman emperor, had begun his reign in 27 BC when, having seen off the threat of his rival Marcus Antonius, he was able to create his own monarchy. He assembled it from bits and pieces of the Roman Republic – the powers of the people's tribunes here, the authority of the senate there. Augustus never quite got round to abolishing these functions: he simply took them over. His main innovation was the idea of the *princeps* or 'first man'. He kept things in the family by putting his stepsons Drusus and Tiberius in charge of military campaigns which suppressed unrest in the Balkans and added Pannonia (Hungary) and Dalmatia to the empire, pushing its boundaries back to the Danube. On the death of Lepidus, once his fellow triumvir, in 12 BC, Augustus added the title of *pontifex maximus* to his other honours; his own lares and penate – household gods – were singled out for wider worship by Rome at large. As high priest in his own cult, the emperor was arguably coming close to self-deification, though that final step would be left to his successors.

The Augustan age

Augustus' handling of the office of *pontifex maximus* shows him cautiously treading a tightrope between open self-advancement and apparent self-effacement. He showed a similar adeptness in the programme of public building and beautification that he embarked on in the empire's capital – not, he insisted, for his own glory but for that of Rome. Civic not personal pride inspired his building projects. His reign saw a surge of energy in all the arts, buoyed up by self-confidence – and by public commissions. The new buildings needed paintings, statuary and mosaics to adorn them. But Augustus was careful. In his restoration of the Forum, and of several of the capital's most famous temples, he stressed the continuity of his

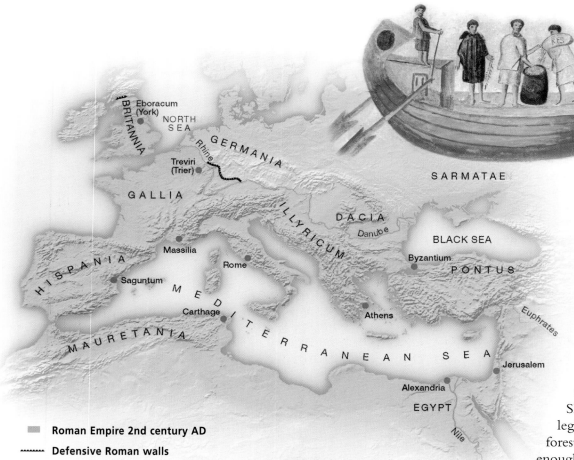

Roman Empire 2nd century AD

------- **Defensive Roman walls**

added to the lustre of this remarkable artistic empire, from the history of Livy to the verses of Ovid and Horace.

Trouble at the top

The age of Augustus was a time of prosperity and, for the most part, peace. Shocked by the loss of his legions in the Teutoburg forest, Augustus was happy enough to retrench. After his death in AD 14, however, Rome struggled to fine his equal. Augustus was succeeded by his stepson Tiberius, who seems to have been a reluctant ruler. In AD 23 he withdrew to Capri, leaving the empire in the hands of Sejanus, the Prefect of the Praetorian Guard. Sejanus was accused of plotting over the succession and executed in AD 31.

Worse was to follow in the reign of Caligula, Tiberius' successor, who was assassinated by his own bodyguard in AD 41. After Caligula came Claudius, whose death in AD 54 was widely rumoured to have been by poisoning. Claudius' adoptive son Nero won a gory reputation even by imperial standards: he had his own mother murdered and his wife executed in AD 59. He survived an assassination attempt in AD 65, but three years later, as his armies massed outside Rome to overthrow him, he took his own life.

Such cloak-and-dagger dealings of the imperial family barely touched the empire beyond. Claudius's conquest of Britain in AD 43 was the only event of any great

reign with the republican age that had gone before. Like the builders of republican Rome, Augustus found inspiration in the art and architecture of classical Greece, with its understated grace and quiet order. Augustus promoted a return to this purity, implying that he was a man who had reintroduced the 'Golden Age', but that he himself was modest in his tastes. He had no need to praise himself, when there were so many poets to do it for him. Extraordinary achievements in writing included Virgil's great epic poem, the *Aenead*, which urged on Romans their divinely ordained destiny to 'rule the nations'. Its exiled Trojan hero, Rome's legendary founder Aeneas, was an idealised Augustus: brave, honourable, generous, yet unassuming. Other works of literature, less obviously ideological, also

Trapped in time
The eruption of Mount Vesuvius in AD 79 destroyed the cities of Pompeii and Herculaneum. Thousands of men, women and children – and their animals, like this dog – were encased in falling ash.

significance; the outbreak of rebellion in Judaea in AD 66 left Rome unperturbed. But then there was the bloody farce of the 'Year of Four Emperors' in AD 68–69: Galba, Otho and Vitellius all took power and were murdered in the space of a year. The army restored order, ending the faction-fighting by imposing the next emperor, Vespasian, in AD 69.

Despite having violent beginnings, Vespasian's reign was largely peaceful at home, with more conquests in Britain and Germany. The construction of the Colosseum was begun, but did not finish until AD 80, a year after his death (of natural causes). By then, his son Titus was in the middle of his short reign. Before he died, in AD 81, Titus sacked Jerusalem, burning its Temple and breaking the force of the Jewish insurrection in Palestine.

There had been conflagrations closer to home, too. First, the eruption of Vesuvius in AD 79 had destroyed the cities of Pompeii and Herculaneum on the Bay of Naples. Then a huge fire destroyed large tracts of the city of Rome: Titus was praised for his rebuilding work.

He was succeeded by his younger brother Domitian, who reintroduced the tradition of violence at court with a vengeance: anyone whose ambitions he feared was executed. Domitian was assassinated in AD 96 by officials alarmed at the thought that they might be the next objects of his rampant paranoia.

The 'adoptive emperors'

Neither Domitian nor his successor Nerva had sons, so there followed a series of three 'adoptive' emperors. Trajan (ruled

On parade
From the first, the legions were the backbone of the Roman Empire. Increasingly, however, they did not just carry out their emperor's commands: it was they who decided who should rule.

The Villa Hadriana
In the grounds of Emperor Hadrian's personal pleasure-palace at Tivoli, Italy (above and background). He had copies made of sights which had impressed him on his travels

AD 98–117) was the first emperor to have been born outside Rome – in southern Spain – though he came from a distinguished Roman family. The famous column in the Forum commemorates his campaigns against the Dacians (101–105) and his conquest of their territory beyond the Danube (modern Romania). Trajan added Arabia to the empire and, after defeating the Parthians, also Armenia, Assyria and Mesopotamia. Culturally, his reign is a culmination, with important building projects undertaken (including a new forum) in Rome and new roads, bridges, aqueducts, amphitheatres and baths to further Romanise the provinces.

Trajan's ward, Hadrian, would also be celebrated for his ambitious construction projects, but as emperor he built for security as well as status. Two projects in particular sum up Hadrian's aims. With its Greek porticoes and Egyptian temples – even a long pool designed to suggest the River Nile – the Villa Hadriana at Tivoli was a fitting playground for a man who loved to travel throughout his empire. Far away in Britain, the great wall which bears his name reflected Hadrian's aim to consolidate Rome's hold on the empire with a fixed frontier. In keeping with this policy of retrenchment, he gave up his predecessor's Parthian conquests.

Hadrian's adoptive son Antoninus Pius (reigned 138–161) extended the empire, building his own (provisional) 'Antonine Wall' across Britain between the Forth and Clyde, and extending the *limes* (defensive walls) in Germany eastward. Notably, he kept the idea of the fixed frontier – the idea of the empire as an open-ended, ever-expandable dominion appeared to have been abandoned. There was a feeling that it had reached its largest viable extent.

This was confirmed in the reign of Antoninus's adoptive sons, Marcus Aurelius and Lucius Verus, who ruled jointly until the latter's death in 169. Attacks by German tribes were a reminder that the empire was surrounded by a hostile world. Marcus Aurelius was a great and thoughtful ruler: his philosophical *Meditations* are still an inspiration. But this did not rule out ruthlessness, as Christians discovered when, in 177, he confirmed their punishment as death.

All change

On Marcus Aurelius's death in 180 the succession passed smoothly to his son Commodus – the age of adoptive emperors was at an end. This did not mean stable rule, however, for Commodus was a tyrant. In 192 he forced the Senate to proclaim his divinity, then was assassinated in the same year. His two successors, Pertinax then Didius Julianus, were both put in place by the Praetorian guard, but neither lasted more than a few weeks. The slide into anarchy was checked by Septimius Severus, who was proclaimed emperor by his legions in 193, though it would be another four years before he really had authority over his whole empire. In 197, with a series of victories over his Roman rivals behind him, Septimius was finally able to go out and attack a foreign foe. His campaign against the Parthians was a resounding success, and Mesopotamia once more became a Roman province.

Silver goblet
Skeletons hold up masks in the macabre decoration on this Roman goblet, found in an excavation at Boscoreale, near Pompeii.

Septimius Severus was a career soldier, which perhaps explains how he restored a mood of expansionism in Rome. He died in 208 on his way to conquer Scotland. That project fell by the wayside under the joint rule of his sons, Caracalla and Geta, who were too busy fighting one another. In 211, Caracalla had Geta murdered and took sole charge. He extended Roman citizenship to all freeborn inhabitants of the empire, which increased tax revenues and perhaps also helped provincials to feel more part of a common project. However, critics complained that it diluted the concept of citizenship and corroded the integrity of the Roman Empire.

Caracalla was killed in the wars in 217. Macrinus, Caracalla's chief assassin, was proclaimed emperor by his soldiers, but then a rival candidate emerged: a 14-year-old Syrian boy named Elagabalus, said to have been Caracalla's natural son. A brief civil war ended with Macrinus's death and Elagabalus being elected emperor. He proved so despotic, however, that the Praetorian Guard assassinated him in 222.

Severus Alexander then took charge, his reign being marked by two ominous events: the emergence of the Persian Sassanid dynasty in the east, and attacks by Germanic Alamanni in northeastern Gaul. Severus Alexander's readiness to buy off the tribesmen with tribute outraged his military chiefs: he was murdered by soldiers in Mainz in 235.

Meltdown

With this death, what had been a tense situation descended into total chaos. No coherent account of the ensuing period of Roman history can really be offered. It was a murderous merry-go-round that saw 50 emperors in as many years; no fewer than 17 of their reigns ended in assassination.

While the coups and countercoups that followed the death of Augustus may not have affected the empire at large, now the imperial candidates were leading army officers, proposed and fought over by

---

EVERYDAY LIFE

Bread and circuses

The urban poor had been a problem for Rome's rulers since comparatively early in Republican times, when crowds of landless peasants began arriving in the city. Ever since, their discontent had been appeased with doles of grain when times were hard, and lavish entertainments staged on the ever-increasing number of festivals.

By the 1st century AD, in Rome quite literally every other day was a holiday – though this may not have interfered as much as it sounds in a work-regime where days began early and finished in the early afternoon. Emperors bought the support of the public with (often gory) spectacles offering everything from horse and chariot races to gladiatorial shows. The Colosseum could seat 40,000 for shows which, in some cases, went on for days. Lions, leopards and other exotic animals were imported from afar to be slaughtered in the ring. There were even special stadia which were flooded for staging mock sea-battles or *naumachiae*.

Victory parade
The winning charioteers in the Circus Maximus.

A ritual reading
In a fresco from the 'Villa of Mysteries' excavated at Pompeii, a young boy reads aloud the words of a ritual, while a young woman carries a plate of offerings.

military factions. The fighting enveloped the empire, and went right to its institutional heart. It is probably more a sign of the difficult political times and the need for a scapegoat that the persecution of Christians increased through this period.

The Germanic tribes were not slow to sense the power-vacuum: the emperor Decius was killed in action against the Goths in 251, while the Sassanids were pushing hard on the eastern frontier. In 259 the emperor Valerius was captured by the Sassanids during a campaign. He was paraded as a prisoner, then executed. Death in war was more of a risk for this new breed of emperors than it had been for their predecessors, whose authority came from the support of their men.

Breakaway provinces

For the first time, a mood of crisis could be sensed in the empire, deepened by the creation of an 'alternative empire' in Gaul the following year. The general Posthumus had placed himself in charge of an independent realm that included Gaul, Britain, Spain and parts of western Germany. It survived for almost 14 years, constantly buffeted by war as Rome tried to reclaim it. The legitimate empire, meanwhile, was equally harassed by enemies. Germanic

pirates based in the Black Sea plundered and sacked the city of Athens. Across the Aegean in Asia, things were no better: in 267 Queen Zenobia proclaimed an independent kingdom in Palmyra, Syria. Her late husband, King Odenathus, had been a willing client of Rome, but his widow was made of sterner stuff. Her revolt threatened to do for the empire's eastern provinces what Posthumus' had done for the west, destroying what was already a decidedly fragile peace.

In 273, however, Emperor Aurelian brought both Gaul and Palmyra into line: the empire's integrity was restored. It was significant, though, that Aurelian had felt the need to abandon Dacia as an unnecessary distraction. He also commemorated his victories with defensive constructions in Rome. Completed by Aurelian's successor Probus in 282, the Aurelianic Wall (much of which still remains) was by any standards impressive. It was 19km (12 miles) in overall length, with no fewer than 383 towers and 18 major fortified gateways (plus many smaller ones), enclosing an area of over 13km² (5 square miles). A splendid sight, and one to send a shudder down the spine of any enemy of Rome – though it would not have escaped their notice that it was defensive. Why did the world's greatest city, the ruler of the nations, feel the need for such protection? The message was clear: Rome no longer regarded itself as invulnerable.

Diocletian's dilemma

The accession of Diocletian in 284 brought a much-needed respite from all the fighting both in and beyond Rome. He was destined to reign securely for just over 20 years. Yet the empire he had inherited was creaking, the stresses and strains at provincial level making it all but impossible to govern it as a seamless whole. How, then, to reinforce the overall coherence of the empire while accommodating its local aspirations and concerns? An administrator of genius, Diocletian hit on the solution of dividing the empire into a number of semi-autonomous zones. First, in 286, he raised his friend Maximian to his own rank, naming him Augustus, a co-emperor, with powers equivalent to Diocletian's own in the western Empire. Then, in 293, the duarchy became a tetrarchy with the appointment of two subordinate caesars, or deputy emperors: Galerius for the east and Constantius for the west.

All of these rulers took up residence wherever they thought their presence was most needed. Diocletian settled in Nicomedia, Asia Minor, while Maximian made Mediolanum (present-day Milan) the centre of his rule. Diocletian's deputy, Galerius, divided his time between Thessalonica, Macedonia and Sirmium, Dalmatia. Constantius commuted between the cities of Augusta Treverorum (Trier), in western Germany, and Eburacum (modern York).

The politics of persecution

Left to his own devices, Diocletian would probably have been a tolerant ruler, but under pressure he was not above availing himself of any scapegoats that were to hand. The Roman Empire of the time had several religious groups – not just steadily increasing numbers of Christians but also followers of various mystic cults from Egypt and the east. Among the military, Mithras, the Persian god of light and truth, had enjoyed a wide unofficial following since the 1st century AD. Mithraism was a male-only cult, with tough initiation rites, so naturally appealed to battle-hardened men. Manichaeism, a more rarefied Iranian religion which saw life as an irresolvable battle between light and darkness, seemed to represent more of a threat. Both Manichaeists and Christians were persecuted in Diocletian's later years: 10,000 Christians are said to have been slaughtered in a single day in Nicomedia in 303.

Diocletian's legacy

Diocletian and Maximian both abdicated in 305, handing over to their deputies. Diocletian's bequest to the empire is debatable. He had very likely saved it, but his radical policy of division had probably made its eventual disintegration inevitable. He had also introduced the previously unthinkable idea that the Roman Empire might not be ruled from Rome.

Diocletian and the tetrarch
Shown in a sculpture of the time, near the end of the 3rd century AD, Emperor Diocletian stands with his three co-regents. The Colosseum (background) was built much earlier, in the 1st century AD, but was still very much in use for gladiatorial games.

The rise of Christianity

At first it was no more than a local sect, one of many to find followers among the cosmopolitan masses of the Roman world. But Christianity went from strength to strength, and by AD 380 it was the official religion of the Roman Empire.

Paul, the Apostle
Through his writings and constant preaching, St Paul was hugely influential in turning Christianity into a world religion.

The title 'Christ' comes from *Christos*, a Greek word for the Jewish concept of 'Messiah': a leader sent by heaven to redeem a sinful world. The linguistic mix is appropriate, for Christianity would have been equally unthinkable without either its gentile elements or its Jewish roots. Jesus of Nazareth was a Jew, most probably born some time around what we now call 7–6 BC: the dating of Anno Domini, 'the year of the Lord', is medieval in origin and has since been disproved.

According to the scriptures, Jesus grew up in Galilee, in the north of what is now Israel. After a short ministry, during which he gathered many followers, he went to Jerusalem where he was crucified by the Romans, at the behest of the local Jews, in AD 30.

The Romans saw Jesus as a rebel, even though his radicalism had never been political: it was the lives of his fellow Jews that he wanted to transform. History abounds in examples of mass-movements believed to have been shut down by the killing of their leaders, only to gain momentum from their martyrdom. Christianity went one better: reports that Jesus had risen from the dead set a tiny sect on the long road to becoming a world religion.

The apostle of the gentiles

An incident on another road was almost as important in giving impetus to the rise of Christianity: the vision of Saul on his was to Damascus. Though a Jew, Saul was born in Tarsus (in Cilicia, modern Turkey), spoke Greek and was a Roman citizen. That he inhabited this far more cosmopolitan world than the mainly poor and uneducated followers of Jesus would ultimately have profound and positive implications for the development of Christianity.

To begin with, however, Saul's orthodox sensibilities were outraged by this upstart sect that dismissed tradition. He was an implacable persecutor of the infant faith. Then one day around AD 35, as he was on his way to Damascus to attack the Christian community there, he was transfixed by a blinding light and a voice from heaven asked him why he insisted on persecuting Christ. Temporarily blinded and struck dumb with awe, Saul became a convert on the spot. From that time on 'Paul' (as he became) poured his considerable mental and physical energies into preaching the message of his old enemy, suffering terrible persecutions himself in the process. He started out preaching the 'good news' in Syria, Cyprus and southern Asia Minor, including his native Cilicia.

Soon, however, he was in conflict with the main Christian leadership. Led by the Apostle Peter, Christianity showed little sign of expansion: it was restricted from the start by the insular attitudes of many of its members. Another leading apostle,

Being thrown to the lions was a fate suffered by some early Christians, as this mosaic illustrates, but persecution was not so rife as many accounts would have us believe.

The catacombs of Callistus
In times of persecution Christians literally 'went underground' in Rome, tunnelling out the rock beneath the city. In those early days, the recognisable symbol of Christianity was not the cross, as today, but the fish (background).

James, who had charge of the Christian community in Jerusalem, had taken Peter to task for sharing his meals – and his message – with non-Jews. The issues involved were important to Judaic tradition: the gentiles were uncircumcised, and many of the foods they ate were forbidden by Jewish law. At one time, Paul would have been equally offended at the idea of eating in such company, but now he saw such taboos as exactly the sort of legalistic trivia that Jesus' divine teachings had swept away. It was not that Paul objected to Jews who had become Christians following their own ancient traditions, but that he saw no need for gentile Christians to keep these laws. Still less did he feel there was any justification whatsoever for denying Christ's saving message to non-Jews. For Paul, Christianity was a faith for all, and he felt the manner of his own conversion marked him out as God's 'chosen instrument' for the conversion of the gentile nations.

The first missionary

A meeting of leading Christians was held in Jerusalem in AD 48. Despite opposition, Paul's interpretation of Christ's message carried the day. With the backing of his church behind him, he embarked on his second great missionary journey, which took him to Cilicia, Macedonia, Athens and Corinth, where he stayed for over a year. In AD 56 Paul revisited Christian communities in Asia Minor, Macedonia and Greece.

Back in Judaea again, he fell foul of leading Jewish teachers: their antagonism was soon provoking widespread public disorder, and the Roman authorities responded by arresting the troublemakers. Paul was imprisoned for two years, and then taken to Rome where he invoked his Roman citizenship and regained his freedom. In the early AD 60s he was on the road again, preaching in Malta, Sicily and southern Italy. Around this time, Peter is believed to have come to Rome.

Persecution and perseverance

The growing geographical range of the Christian community is illustrated by the extent of Paul's travels, and all the different recipients of his pastoral letters or 'epistles'. Far-flung as its members may have been, however, they remained small in number. Tiny groups gathered in one another's houses to hold services.

To Nero, the emperor who set in motion the first major persecution in AD 64, they were more a convenient scapegoat than a credible threat to Roman rule. Whatever the motivation, this early crackdown seems to have cost Christianity its two leading proselytisers in the same year: both Peter and Paul are believed to have been among its victims.

But Christianity kept on growing, and if the first generation of Christians was dying, there was no question of Christ's message dying with them. New converts could read about Christ's life and teachings from the Gospels. Mark's Gospel seems to have been written in about AD 65, Matthew's approximately a decade later, with Luke's around 80. The more mystic John's Gospel followed in about 90. All around the eastern Mediterranean, communities drew inspiration from what they regarded as the 'Word of the Lord'.

The Church of Rome

Apart from sporadic outbreaks of persecution, the Christians were largely tolerated by the Roman authorities. The concept of throwing Christians to the lions is not entirely mythical, but it actually happened to very few. During the 2nd century, the site of Peter's supposed tomb became an important place of pilgrimage for Christians; and it made administrative sense for the world metropolis to be Christianity's capital, too.

The idea that the Bishop of Rome and his hierarchy were divinely sanctioned as inheritors of the original Apostles' ministry – the concept of apostolic succession – was already beginning to take hold. Around 200, Tertullian became the first author to write theological texts in Latin, further cementing the idea that this was a 'Roman' church. Some emperors did not agree: there were renewed persecutions under Decius (249) and Valerian (257), then worst of all, under Diocletian at the beginning of the 4th century. Written as propaganda, the early Christian accounts of these persecutions are unreliable, yet it seems certain that many thousands died. Such periods of persecution were the exception rather than the rule, however: by 311 normal tolerance had been resumed and Christians were allowed to rebuild their churches.

The sign of the cross

The new faith found a powerful backer the following year, when Emperor Constantine the Great had a vision the night before an important battle. He saw a cross overlaying the sun (the object of his own worship up till then) with the words: *in hoc signo vinces*: 'in this sign, prevail'. In a spirit more of superstition than spiritual enthusiasm, Constantine adorned his army with Christian symbols – and his forces conquered.

In the years that followed, Constantine gave Christianity his own personal favour, building up its institutions and organising the first great council of the Church at Nicaea in 325. Despite his energetic patronage, the emperor himself seems only gradually to have taken on real Christian convictions: he converted and was baptised just before he died in 337. Under the rule of his sons Constantine II, Constans I and Constans II, the church continued to thrive: Emperor Julian's attempt to put the clock back in 361–363 was doomed to failure. For now, the future was Christian throughout the empire,

EVERYDAY LIFE

The persecution of the Christians

Savage in its repression of civic unrest, Rome was generally tolerant toward what it saw as the religious peculiarities of its subject peoples – so long as they did not seem to threaten the stability of the empire. This attitude of indulgence applied to Christianity, just as it did towards other sects, and stories of Christians being persecuted constantly and on a massive scale are much exaggerated.

But empires have their ups and downs, and scapegoats are useful for rulers when things are not going well. From time to time, and especially under the rule of Nero and of Diocletian, Christians faced persecution and repression, many of them dying for their beliefs.

Christian martyrs
During periods of persecution, all manner of cruel methods were employed for torturing and killing early Christians.

The Chi-Ro
In Greek lettering, the cross makes an X or 'Chi', the 'P' a 'Rho' or R, spelling out the start of the name 'Christ' – the 'Messiah' (above). Painted glassware (background) with inscribed figures was often buried with Christian dead.

although Constantine's transposition of the capital to Byzantium (or 'Constantinople') was symbolically crucial. In time, a rift would grow between the eastern (Byzantine) and Roman churches; but for now, what mattered was the leaving behind of the pagan past.

In 380, Emperor Theodosius the Great, from his seat in Constantinople, ordained that Christianity was the official religion of the Roman Empire. Rome, the 'old' centre of the empire, was the last stronghold of paganism: conservative patricians still made offerings at the altar of the goddess of Victory in the Senate. In 382, however, that altar was removed on the orders of Ambrosius (St Ambrose), Bishop of Milan.

The Church and its teachers

That intervention speaks volumes about the shifts in power-relations within the Roman world. Not content with official acceptance, Ambrosius believed the Church's authority was higher than the emperor's: he came into conflict with Emperor Theodosius several times – and generally he got his way. In AD 390 Ambrosius threatened the emperor with excommunication (exclusion from the Church) for a massacre of his political opponents. Theodosius was compelled to do public penance.

Ambrosius was just the first of a series of strong personalities who helped to propel the early Christian church into the historic limelight. Another was his protégé, St Augustine of Hippo (modern-day Annaba, in Algeria). Augustine's mother, St Monica, was a long-standing friend of Ambrosius, so he was delighted when her son came to him to be baptised in 387. Augustine had led a wild life until then, as described in his classic memoir,

The Confessions, but he became a staunch defender of the reputation of the Church. After the sack of Rome by the Visigoths in 410, Christianity was blamed for Rome's decline. St Augustine's defence, in *The City of God*, was destined to become one of the classic studies of the philosophy of history. Yet it was no mere academic tome: in its day it was truly inspirational in its vision of a Church arising, flawed but ceaselessly striving, out of the ashes of earthly glory and temporal power.

Central to the Christian religion were the writings of the Bible, which now included not only the Old Testament of the Jews but the New Testament made up of the Gospels, the Acts of the Apostles (the lives of saints Peter and Paul), St Paul's epistles and other associated writings. These had been translated into Greek, Latin, Syrian and Coptic.

In 387 Hieronymus (St Jerome) produced his retranslation of the entire Bible, known as the *Vulgata* or Vulgate, since Latin was the empire's 'vulgar' or common tongue. Eventually, of course, familiarity with Latin would become limited to the clergy, and the Vulgate's status as official scripture give the Church hierarchy a monopoly over the under-standing and interpretation of the Word; by the time of the Reformation in the 16th century, this was a matter of profound contention. But for now, Latin was clearly the best possible medium for the dissemination of Jesus' teachings, and Jerome became revered as one of the founding fathers of the Church.

Leo the Great and the papacy

If Christianity had flourished under the patronage of the Roman emperors, how would it fare as their empire went into decline? Especially as the Church had established its centre in the west, in Rome itself – a capital seemingly left behind by history and increasingly at the mercy of barbarian raiders?

One man deserves much of the credit for the Church's survival through these dark times: Pope Leo I, known as 'the Great', who did much to build the power of the papacy. Born around 400, he became Bishop of Rome in September 440, at a time when the disintegration of the Western Roman Empire was already palpable. His first objective was to ensure the unity of the Church and the integrity of its institutions, and he was unashamedly dictatorial in his dealings.

Leo carried the idea of the apostolic succession farther than it had ever been taken before, invoking the authority invested in his early predecessor, the Apostle Peter, by Christ himself. 'Whatever you bind on earth shall be bound in heaven; whatever you loose on earth shall be loosed in heaven,' the Saviour had said. Those awesome powers, said Leo, now resided with the Pope.

Wherever he derived his authority, Leo was undoubtedly a man of presence and persuasive powers: in 452 he talked Attila the Hun into abandoning his invasion of northern Italy. He had less luck three years later with Gaiseric, the Vandal leader, who continued with his attack and looting of Rome, but did refrain from destroying the city's fabric.

Rome's continuing decline was now inevitable: the Western Empire came to an ignominious end in 476 when Flavius Odoacer, chief of the Germanic Heruls, deposed the helpless Emperor Romulus Augustulus. Thanks to Leo, though, the Church not only survived but grew in power, rising from the ruins like Augustine's City of God. It had come a long way from its Jewish origins, and from the scattered communities visited by Paul: in time many Christians would come to feel it had travelled much too far. But it is reasonable to ask whether,

without the official patronage of the Roman emperors and the works of the Church fathers, Christianity would ever have made it into modernity at all. Whatever its faults, the Church of these times laid the foundations for an important strand in modern history, with an impact on everything from philosophy and law to literature and art.

Constantine the Great
The emperor on his throne, holding up Christian symbols.

The spread of Hellenism – the influence of Greek culture

By the standards of antiquity, Greek culture was global: it left its mark across an area extending from Spain to India. The Greeks had colonised the west coast of Asia Minor as early as 1000 BC, then a second phase of expansion took place between 750 and 550 BC, with colonists setting out from their home cities in several waves. This period saw Greek settlements springing up in Sicily, southern Italy, the south of France and Spain, and also around the coast of the Black Sea.

Campaigns of conquest

In the 4th century BC, Alexander the Great carried the Greek influence much farther eastward into Asia – an ironic outcome, as the Greeks themselves regarded him as Macedonian, not Greek. Alexander took less than ten years to conquer the mighty Persian Empire before advancing as far as the River Indus, driven by his desire to reach the ends of the Earth. After his death – and a lengthy series of conflicts as his generals fought over the succession – three main Hellenistic kingdoms emerged. The heirs of Antigonus ruled Greece, the Balkans and much of Asia Minor; the Ptolemies reigned in Egypt; and the Seleucids held the lion's share of western Asia. During this period, Greeks left the motherland in droves and emigrated to the newly conquered areas.

When the Romans began to conquer Greece and the Hellenistic kingdoms after 200 BC they were quick to adopt the culture they encountered there, acknowledging it as superior to their own. Thus, the Hellenisation of the ancient world continued long after Greece itself was reduced to a Roman province, and Greek imperial power had come to an end.

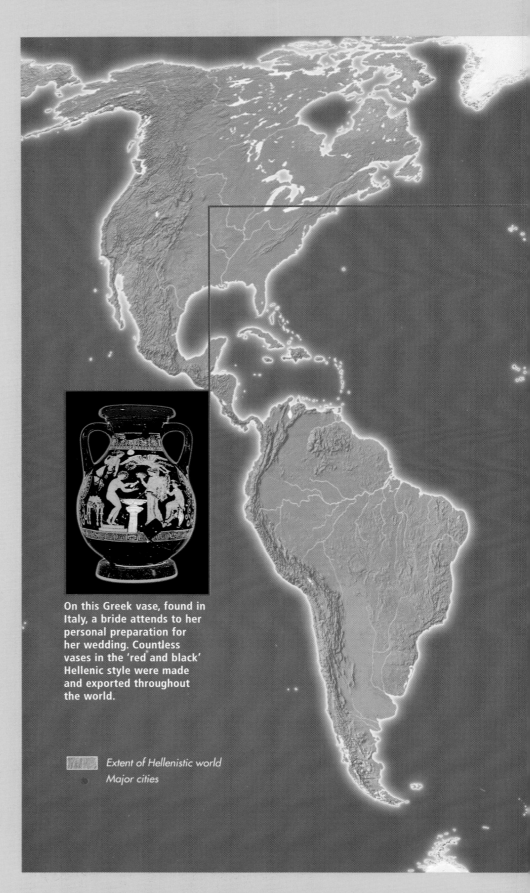

On this Greek vase, found in Italy, a bride attends to her personal preparation for her wedding. Countless vases in the 'red and black' Hellenic style were made and exported throughout the world.

▨▨▨ Extent of Hellenistic world
● Major cities

Greek ships resembling this clay model ruled the waves of the Mediterranean.

Even in desert towns like Petra in modern-day Jordan, buildings were constructed in the Hellenic style.

ANTIGONID KINGDOM

Rome

Athens   Pergamon

SELEUCID KINGDOM

Bactra

Alexandria   Seleucia

PTOLEMAIC KINGDOM

Alexandria Opiana

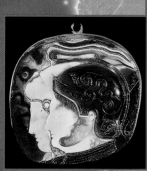

This cameo shows Ptolemy II and his wife Arsinoë, Hellenistic rulers of Egypt.

Alexander the Great helped to spread the cultural influence of Greece through his military campaigns. This coin showing Alexander's image was found in the far east of his realm.

The influence of Greek architecture can be seen from Spain to India. Corinthian capitals like this one topped countless carved stone columns.

Town and city planning

Below: The city of Athens grew organically over the centuries with houses arranged in haphazard fashion in the shadow of the Acropolis, unlike the planned and ordered new cities of the Hellenic world, such as Alexandria and Antioch.

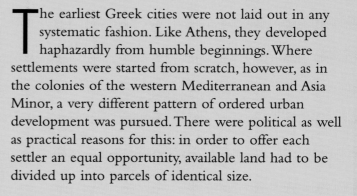

Right: Family life was central to Greek society. This sculpted relief shows a communal family meal.

Above: Elements of Greek architecture can clearly be seen in the oasis town of Hatra in modern-day Iraq.

Right: This statue of Artemis, covered with luxuriant fertility symbols, was found at Ephesus in Asia Minor.

Far left: Craftsmanship and trade were equally vital to the Greek economy. The decoration around this dish depicts workers in a bronze foundry.

The earliest Greek cities were not laid out in any systematic fashion. Like Athens, they developed haphazardly from humble beginnings. Where settlements were started from scratch, however, as in the colonies of the western Mediterranean and Asia Minor, a very different pattern of ordered urban development was pursued. There were political as well as practical reasons for this: in order to offer each settler an equal opportunity, available land had to be divided up into parcels of identical size.

A new type of town

This principle was perfected in the 5th century BC by the renowned town planner Hippodamos of Miletus. In accordance with his plans, all new Greek cities were to be laid out with streets following a right-angled grid, after the fashion of a chessboard, and with identically configured residential quarters. The city centres were reserved for public buildings such as the city hall and the temple, and for open squares where citizens could meet and mingle.

Greek town planning reached its zenith in the Hellenistic period. Whereas, prior to this, towns had usually had no more than 2000–3000 inhabitants, the various Hellenistic rulers now competed to create appropriately monumental settlements. Their model was the city of Alexandria, built on strict Hippo-damian principles on the orders of Alexander the Great in 331 BC. Under the rule of his Ptolemaic successors, the Egyptian seaport became the great metropolis of the Hellenistic world, with a million inhabitants. Just as impressive, in its own way, was the Seleucid capital of Antioch, in Syria, where the people even had the luxury of street lighting.

Template for the future

The layout of such cities was also to influence the Romans. The Hippodamian imprint is clearly discernible in the square street-plans and regular blocks of the cities that they established both in Italy and throughout their empire.

Science and philosophy

Right: The face of Plato, one of the greatest of the Greek philosophers and a major influence on Western thought.

Below: This medieval map of the world was based on the work of the Greek astronomer Ptolemy, who lived in Alexandria in the 2nd century BC.

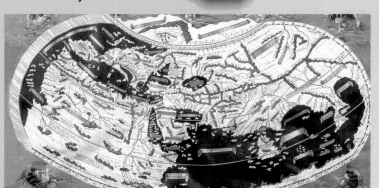

No civilisation has contributed more in the realms of science and philosophy than the Greeks. Their scholars have bequeathed us innumerable ideas and skills, and have long been revered as founders of the 'western' intellectual tradition. Yet they did not do it alone: the stimulus the Greeks received from the East was crucial to their achievements. It is no coincidence that the founding father of Greek philosophy is reckoned to be Thales, from the city of Miletus in Asia Minor. Thales also created a stir in the fields of mathematics and astronomy, and his research is now known to have been inspired in large measure by the findings of Mesopotamian scholars.

The Greeks built on these influences. Intellectual giants like Plato and Aristotle studied the workings of the state, while Hellenistic philosophers pondered the nature of happiness and the individual. Greek scholars made a pioneering contribution to the field of geography, too: having travelled widely – as far as the known world at the time – they were in the forefront of early cartography. Hippocrates, the mentor of physicians, revolutionised medicine in the 5th century BC.

Supporters and patrons

These innovators were helped immeasurably by a generous system of state support. The Great Library (the *Museion*) of Alexandria, for example, founded by the Ptolemaic rulers of Egypt, was a fantastic research institute and resource for all fields of learning.

Archimedes, the most famous mathematician and engineer of antiquity, lived in Sicily in the 3rd century BC. It was the protection and patronage of the king of Syracuse that enabled him to pursue his studies and make his great inventions.

Left: This marble relief shows Greek physicians visiting patients at home.

Below: This Roman mosaic uncovered near Pompeii shows a teacher with his students. It was in academic discussion groups like this that the Greek philosophers developed many of their ideas.

Right: The 'Tower of the Winds' in Athens was built in the 1st century BC. It combined the functions of sundial, weather-vane and water clock.

Art and culture

Every self-respecting Greek city had a theatre, of course, but the cultural metropolis of the Greek world was undoubtedly Athens. Plays were much more than entertainment – they formed a vital part of the city's ritual life and were a major social event.

Plays were almost always performed as part of a festival, and were organised as competitions between the playwrights. Tragedians such as Aeschylus, Sophocles and Euripides presented serious subjects in lofty rhetoric, while comic writers like Aristophanes aimed to amuse the wider public. A jury decided on the winner, who was assured a glittering position in cultural life thereafter.

The actors were exclusively male. They wore masks that denoted differences in rank and character, and also helped to amplify the actors' voices. Great fun was had with comic plays; men sometimes played women whom the plot then required to dress up as men. In addition to full-scale drama, poetic recitations were also popular: these took place in a smaller theatre called the Odeon.

Painting, sculpture and music

Greek artists also made a marvellous contribution to the arts of painting, sculpture and music. The huge number of decorative vases which have survived testify to their painting skills. They also produced larger-scale pictures and frescoes, and they developed the art of mosaic – later taken up enthusiastically by the Romans. Sculptors like the Athenian Phidias from the 5th century BC became extremely famous. His statue of Zeus at Olympia came to be regarded as one of the Seven Wonders of the World.

Greek music was also renowned. The Roman emperor Nero (ruled AD 54–68), a keen composer, made a point of performing his music in Greece, for only there, he thought, would he find a worthy audience.

Top: Both comic and tragic drama made favourite subjects for vase-painters. This detail shows a scene from the play 'Amphitryon'.

Above and right: Many artworks depicted musicians and dancers. This mosaic, found in the ruins of Pompeii, was the work of a Greek artist from Samos. The statue of a female lyre-player was found on the island of Aegina.

The great theatre at Ephesus could seat an audience of 25,000 and was famous for its acoustics.

During performances, Greek actors wore masks such as this, which helped to amplify the voice as well as representing the character.

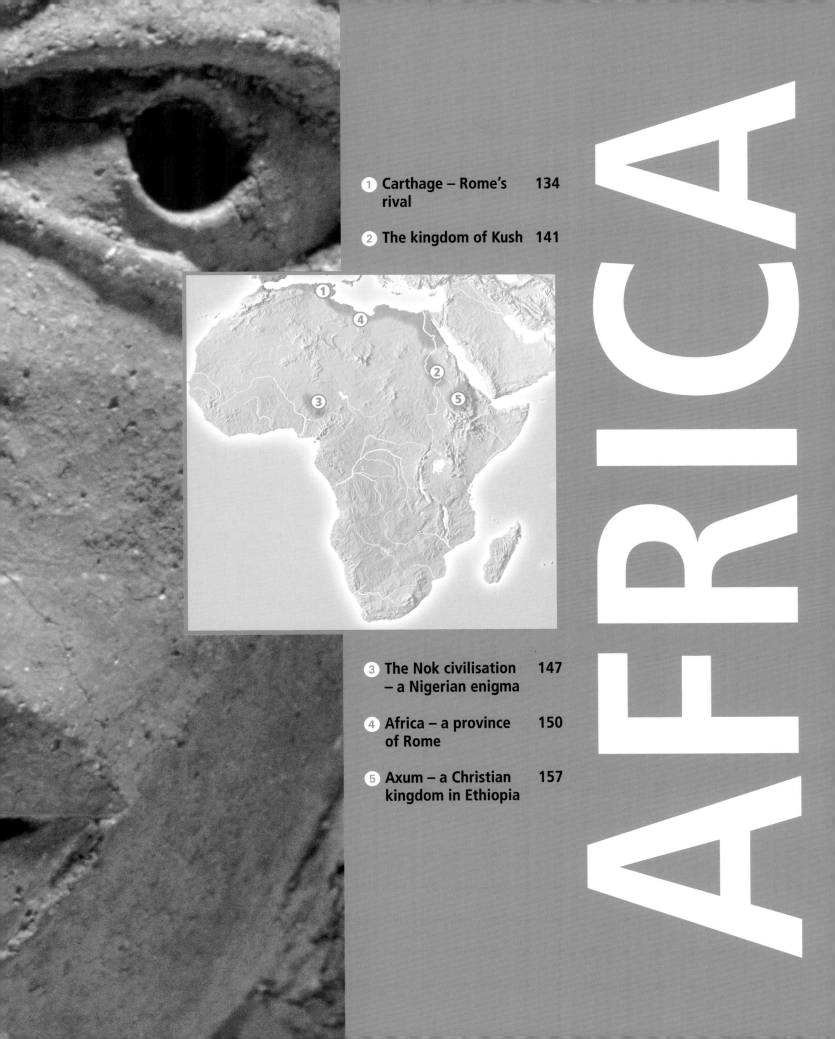

AFRICA

Carthage – Rome's rival

As the Mediterranean's leading maritime power from the 6th century BC onwards, Carthage inevitably came into conflict with the rising Roman state. Their increasingly bitter rivalry sparked off a series of wars, which became a mutual struggle for survival.

The Phoenicians founded Carthage as their 'new city', Qart Hadasht. It was to be a centre for their activities in the western Mediterranean, where they were opening up a thriving trade in metal ores: silver mainly, but also copper, tin and even gold. Hailing originally from coastal Lebanon, where their main cities were Sidon and Tyre, the Phoenicians had been prospecting for possibilities as far afield as Spain and southern France since around 1000 BC. Towards the end of the 9th century BC they were sufficiently involved to need a permanent base in the region, so around 800 BC – traditionally 814 – they established a port city on the north African coast, just to the north of modern-day Tunis.

The site they chose was perfect, with two sheltered harbours that they would deepen and connect with a canal. The city itself stood on an outcrop between the harbours and, once impregnable walls and ramparts had been built to landward, was readily defensible on every side. Qart Hadasht lay near enough halfway between the port of Tyre and the orefields of Spain, and was convenient, too, for trade with the African interior. So well-situated was the city that it grew rapidly in wealth and size, and soon surpassed its 'mother' port of Tyre.

The idea that so illustrious a city as Carthage was becoming should have been built on so mundane a foundation as overseas trade clearly sat uneasily with the chroniclers of ancient times. Soon a more romantic account of the city's origins had been conjured up. Carthage, it was said, had been established by a beautiful Phoenician princess, named Elissa or Dido, who was forced to flee from her homeland when her husband was murdered by her avaricious brother Pygmalion, king of Tyre. As befits the founder of a merchant city, though, Elissa was as canny as she was attractive. Arriving in North Africa, the story goes, she asked the local king Iarbas to sell her the site for a settlement: he sneeringly said he would give her as much land as she could cover with an ox's hide. Elissa agreed, then cut the hide into long thin strips, and enclosed an area large enough to build the city.

Expanding influence

Hard facts about Carthage are more difficult to find, but it seems clear that it grew as a regional power through its early centuries, making subjects of the Libyan and Numidian Berber tribes who lived along that stretch of the North African coast. It also extended its reach farther afield, taking advantage of older-established Phoenician

cities to the east along the North African coast, then setting up its own outposts to the west, not only in North Africa but also to the north in the Balearics, Sardinia and Sicily.

By the end of the 6th century BC, these expansive ambitions had brought the Carthaginians into conflict with the Greeks, upon whose Sicilian colonies they were now encroaching. The rise of Carthage cannot be described as irresistible, because in 540 BC, in alliance with the Etruscans, they fought and lost a major naval battle against the Greeks

Hannibal
The history of the Western world could have been very different had luck gone Hannibal's way. In 216 BC the Carthaginian general came within a whisker of destroying Rome.

near Corsica. They did succeed, however, in thwarting Greek plans to establish new colonies on the island. Some 60 years later, as the Athenians fought off the threat from Persia, Greek colonists on Sicily scored a further victory over the Carthaginians. Despite such setbacks, however, Carthage was slowly but surely building its influence as the western Mediterranean's major maritime power. By the end of the 5th century BC, it had dislodged the Greeks from Sicily.

Economic might

Carthage's driving force was trade, which was thriving. The Carthaginians' interests extended far beyond the famous trade in metal ores. Like their Phoenician forebears, they knew the secrets of making glass beads and the famous 'royal' purple dye from crushed murex seashells. They traded in other luxuries, too: amber and furs from Celtic Europe; spices such as cinnamon, frankincense and myrrh, imported via Egypt and the Middle East. More mundane – but just as lucrative – was the city's trade in salt, brought by Berbers from the mines of the western Sahara. Along the same cross-desert caravan route came other products from West Africa, including gold, ivory and ebony wood. Carthage became the main

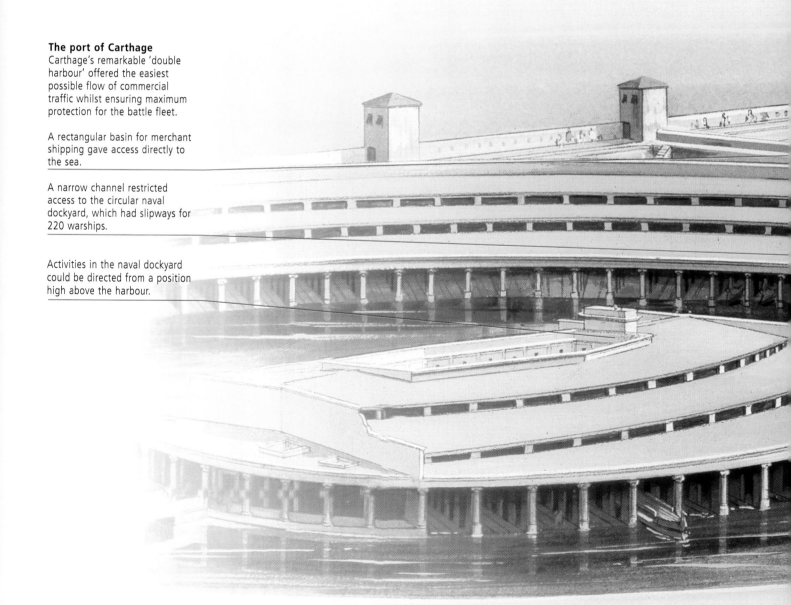

The port of Carthage
Carthage's remarkable 'double harbour' offered the easiest possible flow of commercial traffic whilst ensuring maximum protection for the battle fleet.

A rectangular basin for merchant shipping gave access directly to the sea.

A narrow channel restricted access to the circular naval dockyard, which had slipways for 220 warships.

Activities in the naval dockyard could be directed from a position high above the harbour.

Mediterranean outlet for trade from the African interior. Carthaginians were busy closer to home as well: timber was produced locally, in the Atlas mountains, while the fields and vineyards of the north African coastal strip yielded grain, fruit, nuts, wine and olive oil.

Seaport and citadel

Based on all this commerce, a great city soon arose, home to perhaps as many as half a million people – around the same size as Athens. Extended and developed by its engineers, Carthage's harbour, the *Cothon*, was really two harbours in one: a bustling merchant port and a major naval base. The outer-most harbour, its mouth protected by a bank or mole, was rectangular in shape with an entrance 20m (70ft) across, according to the Roman historian, Polybius, writing at the start of the 1st century BC. This entrance could be closed with iron chains if necessary.

Beyond the merchant port was a circular inner harbour around which were secure slipways for 220 warships, both around the outer structure and the harbour's central island. The harbour-master's house stood high up on this island: from here all activity in the inner harbour could be supervised. Both harbours had to be deep: Carthaginian

merchant ships could carry over 100 tonnes of cargo, and military triremes were up to 40m (120ft) long and 6m (19ft) wide. Vast amounts of earth and rock were excavated from the natural harbour to create this vast facility. High above the harbour rose a hill called the Byrsa, on which stood a mighty citadel. The city was shielded by 35km (22 miles) of defensive walls. Their construction was not, perhaps, as much of an undertaking as it may sound; for much of their length they lay along the coast, and could be relatively insubstantial. On the landward side, however, gigantic walls were built, in places more than 13m (40ft) high and almost 10m (30ft) thick. Within these fortifications were barracks for a garrison more than 20,000 strong, as well as stabling for some 4000 horses and 300 elephants.

Bearded man
This enamelled face mask demonstrates the high standard of Carthaginian artistry.

▬ Carthaginian territories

➡ Carthaginian expansion

The main commercial centre of the city lay between the Byrsa and the harbour: here were busy streets, bustling markets and, toward the harbour, extensive warehousing. A little to the south lay the residential area, whose narrow streets and alleys were lined with towering tenements up to six storeys high.

The business of Carthage was business: the vast majority of its people got on with their lives with no thought of political influence of the sort their plebeian equivalents might hope for through the tribunes of republican Rome, let alone the rights of citizens under the laws of democratic Athens. In that respect, Carthage was more typical of its time. Its rulers did make some concessions to popular government: the early power of the kings seems to have ebbed away until the monarchy was removed altogether, power being invested, instead, in a ruling council of nobles. Also, generals returning from campaigns had to report to a supreme court with 104 members. Though neither of these bodies could have represented more than the very highest echelons of Carthaginian society, it seems to have worked well enough, for around 340 BC no less an authority than Aristotle lavished praises on what he considered to be Carthage's 'excellent' system. The Greek philosopher admitted that it might fall well short of Athenian standards in terms of accountability but pointed out that this injustice was balanced by the ruling oligarchy's generosity in dealing out opportunities for enrichment in the city's many colonies.

Beside the citadel, at the top of the Byrsa, stood the Temple of Eshmun, god of healing. He was one of the crucial triad of Phoenician deities, the others being

Baal Hammon, lord of the universe, and Tanit, the mother goddess, queen of good fortune, the harvest and the moon. Though descended from the Phoenician earth-goddess Astarte, Tanit is uniquely Carthaginian. The city held her in special veneration: she appears both on grave-stones and coins unearthed by modern archaeology, and seems to have taken precedence even over Baal Hammon. Both deities had splendid temples on the Tophet, a sacred precinct situated to the west of the port, beside the necropolis where the dead were laid to rest.

Epic voyages

The Carthaginians (or Phoenicians) were the first Mediterranean seafarers known to brave the Atlantic. A man called Himilco is supposed to have lead a voyage to the 'tin islands'. English tradition has it that Phoenician merchants came to Cornwall to trade for tin, but how realistic are such claims? There is no doubt that the seafaring skills of the Phoenicians and their Carthaginian kinsfolk were up to it, honed as they were by generations of experience. Their ships were well-designed and large, and certainly robust enough for ocean-going trade. Yet while they could realistically have ventured as far afield as Britain, there is no hard evidence that they actually did.

The Greek historian Herodotus claimed that the Phoenicians had circum-navigated Africa all the way to the Red Sea, a claim that seems to be backed up by an account left by Hanno, a Carthaginian sea-captain. Hanno describes a voyage 'to the Libyan regions of the earth beyond the Pillars of Hercules' and, it seems, some considerable way down the Atlantic coast of Africa. On the coast of what is now Mauritania, he reports, the expedition found 'a marsh lying no great way from the sea, thickly grown with tall reeds. Here were elephants and other wild beasts feeding in great numbers.' Where the soil beneath grew firmer, the Carthaginians founded colonies, before the main body of

the expedition pushed on southward. A few days further on they attempted to land at the mouth of a great river but were prevented by stone-throwing natives dressed in skins. They soon passed another river, 'very great and broad, which was full of crocodiles and hippopotami'.

Sailing on for another fortnight, they saw tribes on shore with whom they attempted to speak, but their tongues were incomprehensible to the expedition's African guides – and in any case the natives fled. Yet farther on, Hanno's party put ashore on a large island, but as night fell they saw fires burning through the forest all around, and heard a terrifying uproar of chanting, pipes and drums. Almost as frightening was a volcano – 'a lofty fire … which seemed to touch the stars'. Torrents of fire – clearly molten lava – ran down to a boiling sea; the earth appeared to be on fire for miles around. It took them several days to leave this burning waste behind and find safe anchorage in another sheltered bay. In the recess of this bay there was an island, like the former one, having a lake in which was another island, full of savage men. There were women too, in even greater number. They had hairy bodies, and the interpreters called them Gorillae.

At this point, 'provisions failing us', the expedition turned and made its way back home to Carthage. Hanno left his account of the voyage on a plaque in the Temple of Baal. Modern scholars can only speculate on where his narrative corresponds with real places. The volcano may have been Mount

Grinning mask
Masks such as this, from the 6th century BC, are among the few artefacts to have survived the destruction of Carthage. The exaggerated grotesque may have been intended to scare away evil spirits.

Did the Carthaginians sacrifice their children?

After a grave military defeat towards the end of the 4th century BC, reported the Greek-born Roman historian Diodorus Siculus two centuries later, Carthage was seized by a convulsion of anxiety. The people were 'filled with superstitious dread' that they had neglected their religious duties. In their zeal to make amends for their omission, they selected 200 of the noblest children and sacrificed them publicly.

Based on colourful accounts such as this by writers of antiquity, it was long assumed that the Carthaginians had indulged in the gruesome practice of sacrificing their own children, particularly in times of crisis. The discovery by archaeologists of children's remains in a special cemetery known as the tophet was taken as confirmation of these revolting acts.

Today, however, another interpretation is favoured by many historians: that the tophet was a perfectly normal cemetery, specially for children who had died of disease. The tales of child sacrifice reported with such revulsion were written by Carthage's enemies, and are therefore suspect as propaganda.

Sacred cemetery
The tophet was the city's cemetery, but was it also a place of ritual and sacrifice?

Cameroon, and if the explorers had really found gorillas, they must have reached the forests of the Congo. Other interpreters have suggested that the gorillas were chimpanzees, which would mean that Hanno's expedition may have only got as far as Sierra Leone. Either way, it had been a memorable adventure.

A fatal weakness?

It was the great strength of Carthage as a state that it looked outward to the wider world, a single city with contacts far and wide and with influence out of all proportion to its size. Yet that strength masked its weakness: Carthage never had a population big enough to sustain the protracted large-scale struggle that lay in store with the other power in the region.

Rome, though also a single city, was annexing other communities around it as it grew, absorbing them into a common political system. Carthage, founded as a trading colony, remained an isolated city, its relationship with its hinterland essentially commercial. From as early as the 6th century BC, Carthage was hiring mercenaries, or negotiating assistance from trading allies. The army had a Carthaginian core, a special force of elite loyal soldiers, but this unit was only 2500 strong. A huge standing army would have been a liability for a state such as Carthage, and as yet there had been no call for military strength in depth.

The emergence of Rome would test Carthaginian military might as never before, and Carthage's reserves would ultimately be found wanting. Carthage began the First Punic War (264–241 BC) in what should have been an unassailable position: a great maritime power against naval novices. The Romans improvised their way into the war, copying Carthaginian ships, then inventing their own improbable-looking boarding device, the corvus. Though it took them over 20 years, they secured victory in the end.

Rome was fortunate not to be erased from history in the Second Punic War (218–202 BC). Hannibal, a Carthaginian general from the colony of New Carthage in Spain, had Rome at his mercy. But without the wholehearted backing of his countrymen in Carthage, he became seriously overstretched. Though never defeated in battle in Italy, Hannibal was eventually recalled to Carthage to resist a Roman invasion – and lost.

By the middle of the 2nd century BC, Carthage was a spent force, but to many in Rome its continued existence – worse still, something of a revival in its trading fortunes – represented 'unfinished business'. So when the Carthaginians retaliated to a Numidian incursion into their territory, the Romans chose to regard it as an act of war. In 149 BC a great Roman army crossed to Africa and besieged the city. Carthage held out doggedly for two years, but in 146 the attackers broke through. They enslaved the people, ransacked the city and razed it to the ground. Carthage was no more.

The kingdom of Kush

In Egypt's southern colony of Nubia there arose the independent kingdom of Kush, whose lords would take over Egypt itself and rule there as pharaohs.

The rough waters of the First Cataract marked a natural boundary in the valley of the Nile: as far as the pharaohs were concerned, civilisation ended here. Downriver, to the north, lay the lush and fertile fields of Egypt, kept productive by irrigated agriculture on an impressive scale. But to the south, in its middle reaches, the river flowed across stony semi-desert – even on its banks, there was little greenery to be seen. For countless centuries, the people of Nubia or 'Kush' had scratched a living from

Silent attendants
These statues, found in the tomb of one of the black pharaohs at el-Kurru, would have been his servants in the life beyond.

Egyptian-style tombs
Like other pharaohs, the Kushite kings had the walls of their tombs adorned with hieroglyphs and frescoes acclaiming the great achievements of their reign.

Pyramids of Kush
A corner of the Sudanese desert which will be for ever Egypt: the pyramids of the Kushite kings and queens at Meroë.

little plots of land around impoverished villages, or lived as nomadic herdsmen, roaming far afield in search of grazing. The contrast in lifestyles could hardly have been greater, and it was underlined by differences in race and colour.

The exact racial make-up of the ancient Egyptians is not known, and has been a matter of heated dispute in recent years (although it is unlikely to have caused them much anxiety in their own time). There can be no doubt that racism, conscious or not, underlay the long-prevalent assumption that the great achievements of the Egyptians meant that they must have been in some sense 'honorary whites'. Some recent scholars, in reaction, have attempted to prove that

they were black Africans, but there seems to be little scientific support for such theories. In fact, the peoples of this time do not seem to have been too conscious of racial distinctions as we understand them, and there certainly seems to have been a degree of inter-marriage between the Egyptians and their neighbours. The fact remains, however, that while the Nubians were black, like the peoples of sub-Saharan Africa, the Egyptians were on the whole much lighter-skinned.

An imitation Egypt

Egyptian relations with the Nubians foreshadowed those of the much later European colonial powers with black Africa: the 'miserable peoples of Kush', as the Egyptians called them, were there to be exploited. During the time of the New Kingdom, in the 2nd millennium BC, Nubia had become a colonial possession of the pharaohs. They had developed riverside agriculture along Egyptian lines, and opened mine workings for

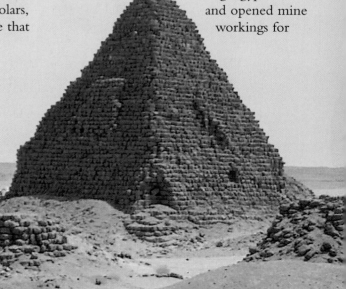

mineral extraction. There were profits to be made from commerce, too: the people may have been 'miserable', according to the Egyptians, but Kush was a gateway to the south, with its untold riches.

Nomadic peoples criss-crossed the desert and came over the mountains bringing all manner of treasures to trade in Kush: incense, ebony, ostrich feathers, precious stones and spices, ivory and gold. A handful of local magnates, acting as plantation-managers or go-betweens for trade, became as wealthy as any Egyptian lords. They lived like the grandees downriver, and when they died they were buried like them, too – lavish tombs like those of the pharaohs themselves have been discovered.

The Nubians worshipped the Egyptian sun-god Amun-Re at a splendid sanctuary which would came to rival that of Thebes. The shrine was at the foot of Gebel Barkal, a great rocky outcrop near the Nubian capital Napata, above the Nile's fourth cataract. Further down the social scale, the 'Egyptianisation' of Nubian society was inexorable: many served as mercenaries in the pharaoh's armies.

The glamour that Egyptian civilisation held for previously impoverished Nubians is understandable, and the replication of Egyptian structures must have made sense to the colonial power, but this creation of an alter-Egypt would prove dangerous in the longer term. When the pharaohs were strong, it mattered little, but when they were weak, it was perhaps not helpful that the Kingdom of Kush felt quite so

thoroughly at ease with Egyptian ways. In fact, Nubia's prosperity would slump with Egypt's when the great days of the New Kingdom came to an end in the middle of the 11th century BC, and the age of uncertainty and periodic conflict known to scholars under the bland title of 'Third Intermediate Period' began. But the memory of greatness seems to have endured, and in the middle of the 8th century BC, the former colony took over a country weakened by centuries of struggle with Libyan invaders.

The black pharaohs

The first of the Nubian pharaohs about whom there is any direct knowledge is Kashata, who reigned from around 760 BC: an inscribed stone proclaims him to be 'King of Upper and Lower Egypt'. How far this assertion of authority actually applied in reality is not clear, but in the reign of Kashata's son Piy (ruled 747–716 BC) there is firm evidence of a Kushite conquest of Egypt as a whole.

Piy came down 'like a cloud-burst', enthused an inscription at Gebel Barkal, 'raging like a panther' at his enemies. His diplomatic cunning seems to have at least equalled his generalship: in what appears to have been a calculated 'charm offensive' he sent his wives and sisters to foster good relations with the families of his defeated foes. Strikingly modern in his concern with self-presentation, he made a major display of his magnanimity in allowing

Nubian woman
This carved figure dates from the 7th century BC. Originally, it would have formed part of a piece of furniture.

Temple of Amun
Broken statues of rams line the route to what is left of the Amun Temple at Gebel Barkal, just outside Napata, the original Kushite capital.

Pharaoh Taharqo
Taharqo's reign (690–664 BC) saw Kush reach its zenith – and the start of its precipitous fall.

his enemies to keep their titles, provided they swore allegiance. The very model of mercy, he told them he forgave them their wrongs. But tender-hearted as he may have been, he was more concerned that the siege of Hermopolis had caused problems in the royal stables: 'It is more grievous in my heart that my horses have suffered hunger than any evil deed that thou hast done in the prosecution of thy desire.' How was so adept a politician to be stopped?

Piy's title as pharaoh was assured and his status as son of Amun was universally acknowledged. Although he later withdrew to his native Nubia, he ruled his realms after the fashion of the pharaohs, and would be buried in a tomb of the

Egyptian style at el-Kurru. His arm's length attitude towards Egypt had consequences, however, as far downriver local rulers grew in strength and restiveness. Piy's younger brother and successor Shabaqo (ruled 716–702 BC) had to journey north to reconquer the northern territories for Kush.

The key to Kushite power, for all Piy's earlier blandishments, was military strength: the black pharaohs were warriors, heroes to their armies, whose central role in the life of the kingdom was acknowledged. Inscriptions dwell approvingly on the amount of time and energy devoted to training, and celebrate the valour of the future-pharaoh, Taharqo, in action against Assyrian invaders at the Battle of Eltekeh (701 BC).

Yet despite coming as conquerors, the Kushites unreservedly adopted Egyptian ways. This was a longstanding habit among Nubia's native kings, but now their enthusiasm was redoubled: they seem to have seen the extent to which their own culture was modified to take on Egyptian characteristics almost as a measure of the legitimacy of their rule. With the zeal of converts, they did their best to become 'more Egyptian than the Egyptians', re-inaugurating the ancient cult of Amun.

Shrewd politics went along with piety in the adoption of successive princesses in the office of 'god's wife of Amun' at the sun-god's shrine at Thebes, a tradition which began with Amerdinis, sister of Piy. This practice allowed divine authority to be concentrated still further in the pharaonic family, whilst providing what amounted to female viceroys in a proud and, all too often, wayward city. Amun's great shrines at Thebes were rebuilt and extended in the Kushite era, and a new temple was built by Taharqo at Karnak. The reign of the Kushite kings also saw a revival of long-discarded New and even Old Kingdom

architectural and artistic forms, a conscious imitation of archaic styles, which must have represented some sort of reaching back to pharaonic roots.

It became routine for the black pharaohs to be buried in pyramids; they created their own sphinxes, too, and had their seat at Memphis, the capital of Old Kingdom Egypt 2000 years earlier. Shabaqo, says one inscription, took great pains to have old and damaged documents transcribed: the Kushites were careful custodians of the Egyptian heritage.

On the move

Shabaqo died in 702 BC; twelve years later he was succeeded by his younger brother, Taharqo, whose rule would be the longest of all the black pharaohs. When the Assyrians invaded again, however – under Esarhaddon in 674 BC – Taharqo fared less well than at the Battle of Eltekeh. The Kushite pharaoh was defeated, but inconclusively, and succeeded in re-taking power. Then, in 667 BC, the Assyrians were back with an army led by Esarhaddon's son Ashurbanipal. Taharqo's troops were routed and the pharaoh was forced to flee. From then on, the Kushite rulers were confined to their ancestral homeland in Nubia. Several attempts were made to reconquer Egypt, but all were beaten back by the puppet pharaohs installed by the Assyrians. In 591 BC one of these, Psamtik II, dealt what was to prove the death-blow to Kushite hopes: his forces, it was claimed, 'waded in Kushite blood as if it were water'.

Golden brooch
This memento of old Egypt was pinned to the mummy of Meroitic king Natakamani. It shows the winged goddess, Isis.

The Kushite kings now bowed to the inevitable and moved their capital to Meroë, a site between the 5th and 6th cataracts of the Nile, around 480km (300 miles) upriver from Napata. There, by the 4th century BC, they had built a modestly successful civilisation. Rumours of untold wealth were probably exaggerated, although the Meroitic rulers did still have control of the lucrative trade route from the heart of Africa down the Nile Valley to the Mediterranean, a traffic now revitalised by the introduction of the camel from Arabia. The importance of this cannot be over-estimated: forbidding tracts of desert now became accessible highways. Merchants from Meroë could trade not only up and down the Nile but across the country to the Red Sea ports.

Men of iron

There was no bonanza, however: for the most part, the people of Meroë had to work hard for their living, and fight hard with neighbouring peoples for their survival. Along with agriculture (mainly millet and barley) and the herding of cattle, they felled forests for the smelting of the region's abundant iron ore.

The Meroitic rulers continued to live like Egyptians in exile. They were still buried in pyramids, decorated with art and hieroglyphics clearly descended from Egyptian forms (though the informal script of Kush eventually left these origins behind, and has never been deciphered by modern scholars). In something of a departure from Egyptian ways, however, they did embrace iron-age technology. Though aware of iron, the strongly conservative Egyptians had refused to adopt it – most likely a factor in their eventual decline. The transplanted kings of Kush disregarded this near-taboo, and for a while it stood them in good stead, both economically and militarily.

Almost imperceptibly, Meroë took on other aspects of black African, as opposed to Egyptian, culture: the decorative scarring of the face described by several visitors is one example of this. The matrilineal transmission of royal rank and property, while perhaps reflecting the prominence given earlier by the Kushite pharaohs to the office of 'god's wife to Amun', represents another departure from Egyptian norms. Queens loom large – literally – in Meroitic art. Massively plump though by no means matronly figures, they tower terrifyingly over the prostrate forms of vanquished foes.

Meroitic civilisation would ultimately turn out to create its own downfall – ironically, through their iron industry. The relentless demand for charcoal for smelting led first to deforestation and then to drought. If the great slagheaps around the old city testify to the scale of the iron industry, the barrenness of what was once a fruitful landscape bears witness to the environmental damage done. By the 2nd century AD, Meroë was in steep economic decline. By the mid-4th century, it had been conquered by Axum.

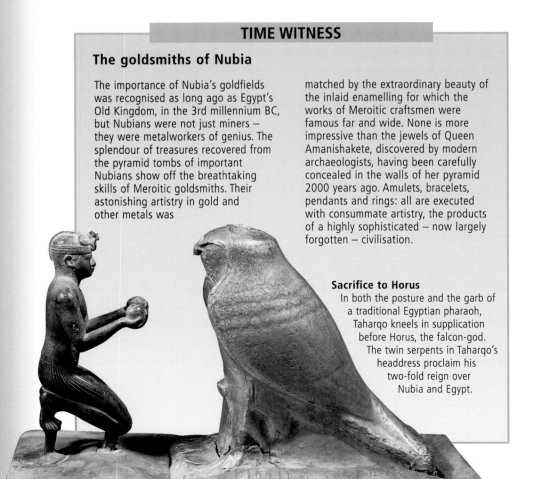

TIME WITNESS

The goldsmiths of Nubia

The importance of Nubia's goldfields was recognised as long ago as Egypt's Old Kingdom, in the 3rd millennium BC, but Nubians were not just miners – they were metalworkers of genius. The splendour of treasures recovered from the pyramid tombs of important Nubians show off the breathtaking skills of Meroitic goldsmiths. Their astonishing artistry in gold and other metals was matched by the extraordinary beauty of the inlaid enamelling for which the works of Meroitic craftsmen were famous far and wide. None is more impressive than the jewels of Queen Amanishakete, discovered by modern archaeologists, having been carefully concealed in the walls of her pyramid 2000 years ago. Amulets, bracelets, pendants and rings: all are executed with consummate artistry, the products of a highly sophisticated – now largely forgotten – civilisation.

Sacrifice to Horus
In both the posture and the garb of a traditional Egyptian pharaoh, Taharqo kneels in supplication before Horus, the falcon-god. The twin serpents in Taharqo's headdress proclaim his two-fold reign over Nubia and Egypt.

The Nok civilisation – a Nigerian enigma

Terracotta heads and other forms unearthed in northeastern Nigeria offer a tantalizing glimpse of a remarkable iron-age culture. Their origins are mysterious, but their expressiveness is captivating.

In the early 1940s, the Jos Plateau of northeastern Nigeria was a centre for open-cast tin mining. The miners had learned by experience that the best places to concentrate on were the ancient watercourses, filled in by erosion centuries before. Here, they would find deposits carried down by long-gone streams. Along with the tin, however, they found lumps of iron slag, stone tools and some surprisingly fine terracotta forms – remnants of a former metalworking civilisation.

In 1943 a ceramic head was turned up near the village of Nok, and was brought to the attention of Bernard Fagg, Nigeria's British-born Director of Antiquities. His enquiries among local people revealed that odds and ends of this sort had been turning up for as long as anyone could remember: one especially handsome head was being used as a scarecrow. But if it was old news to the locals, the 'Nok civilisation' was a revelation to the world: the first fully developed iron-age culture known to have existed in Black Africa.

Intrigued, Bernard Fagg pursued further investigations into the lost culture, and found undisturbed village sites in the nearby Taruga Valley. Radiocarbon dating suggested that the civilisation had flourished from around 2500 years ago, in the second half of the 1st millennium BC. Along with fragments of ornamental terracotta and domestic pottery, they uncovered grindstones, tools and weapons with iron blades, as well as evidence of iron-smelting on a considerable scale. There were heaps of iron slag, as well as the remains of furnaces. These were cylindrical in form, with two chambers: one would have contained wood or charcoal fuel, gathered from the wooded slopes of the valley; the other would have contained the metal ore. Open pipes of clay would have run through the furnace wall, allowing men standing round the outside to blow into the fire in concert, raising the temperature. (A similar system of smelting was used elsewhere in Africa into comparatively recent times: although labour-intensive, it yields high-quality iron.) Once the molten iron was ready, it was poured into stone moulds of whatever shape was required – axe-heads, tools, weapon-blades.

This Nok terracotta head of a woman was created around 500 BC.

Female finery
Crowned by an extravagant coiffure and bedecked with jewellery, this female sculpture cuts an impressive figure.

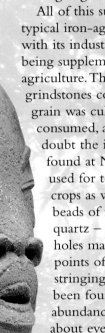

Then it would simply be a matter of fitting a wooden handle and sharpening the cutting edge ready for use.

All of this suggests a fairly typical iron-age culture, with its industrial activities being supplemented by agriculture. The discovery of grindstones confirms that grain was cultivated and consumed, although no doubt the iron hoes found at Nok sites were used for tending other crops as well. Beautiful beads of finely ground quartz – pierced with holes made by tiny points of iron for stringing – have also been found in abundance. Like just about every other culture in the history of the world, it seems the people of the Nok civilisation had a taste for personal ornamentation.

Talking heads?

The terracotta pieces that have been found are stunningly beautiful work: this was a culture with a highly developed aesthetic sense. It also had craftsmen of considerable skill – although if we judge by the traditions of later civilisations in the region, these figures may well have been made by women. The artisans used local clay, building up the forms by piling up the moist clay in a series of coils, a structure implicitly echoed in the bead armlets and necklaces

VIEWPOINT

Wood first?

It has been suggested that such advanced artistic skills as are evident in the Nok figures are not to be found at the start of any artistic tradition: they must have been honed and perfected over generations. Where, then, did they originate?

Some scholars argue that the terracotta heads are probably modelled on earlier wooden carvings. That, they say, would explain certain unusual features of the terracotta figures: the teeth and lips are often incised, for example, where they might have been expected to be moulded, and the mouth or beard usually forms a single block protruding from the face.

Carved wooden originals seem improbable, since the rain forest does not extend anywhere near the Nok region – but it may have done so 2000 years ago.

and in the swirling hairstyles on many of the sculptures. There is evidence, too, that after building up the figures the artists then stripped them down – they piled on excess clay that was then pared away as though carving wood. The pieces may well have been finished off with some sort of protective coating, but if so, this always seems to have been washed away.

And what of the men and women the figures apparently depict? There is a danger of reading too much into a few ornamental or perhaps ritual figures, which may not have captured the actual appearances or lifestyles of the people who made them. In the case of the Nok, however, the absence of other evidence means there is little choice. Some 200 forms have been found, the majority of them fragments rather than complete figures; most represent humans, but there have been elephants, monkeys, snakes and other animals too.

The prevalence of heads may be misleading: this does not seem to have been a 'headhunting' culture like, say, the European Celts; those heads which have been found seem to have broken off larger statues. Judging by the size of the heads, which can be anything from 10–40cm (4–16in) high, the full statues could have been anything up to 1.4m (4½ft) tall. All have the same distinctive 'triangular' eyes, which are pierced in the middle to indicate pupils. The male heads have pronounced masculine features – pointed beards, for instance, or moustaches. Both male and female figures have elaborate hairstyles, with buns and cascading layers of braids – bravura work by the potters who created them, but revealing too, perhaps, of how the Nok people wore their hair. The holes in these hairdos may have been for the insertion of decorative feathers and shells; in many cases strings of beads or pearls are threaded through the hair. The full-length figures which have been found suggest that personal adornment did not stop there: multiple bead necklaces and amulets are worn.

Realistic or ritual figures?

The extent to which the figures realistically represent the men and women of the Nok culture is a matter of speculation. Some faces seem to have been scarified, a practice followed by some – but by no means all – later West African cultures. Some are so misshapen that scholars have wondered whether disfiguring illnesses were being represented; others have suggested that they are caricatures.

The faces express a range of emotions, which often seem to be exaggerated. Pantomime puzzlement, anger, anxiety, glumness and many other moods are shown: the obvious accomplishment of the artists indicates that the stylisation with which emotions are depicted is deliberate. Were the expressions meant to amuse? Were the figures intended to satirise individuals? Or were they designed to ward off demons? This prompts a further question over whether the figures were ever meant to be human at all: were they actually devils themselves? Or deities? In contrast with the human forms, the figures of animals are much more restrained – even naturalistic.

The answers to such questions are at best elusive, and can only be offered with the utmost caution, based on what little is known of later Nigerian cultures. In later civilisations, where figures of a similar sort have been found, they have generally been placed in special shrines in the courtyards of family homes. They may have been a physical embodiment of the spirits of tribal ancestors, to which ritual offerings would be made. Far from being intended to deride any particular individual for the

purposes of satire or mischief, the distortion of the faces and features was more likely designed to ensure that no similarity with a living person might be perceived. That these craftsmen could produce accurate depictions of living beings was quite clear from their superb animal figures: in their human forms, in contrast, they made great play of the lack of realism. A possible explanation for this explicit distortion could lie in the fact that so many West African societies lived in fear of witchcraft. Any thought that life-like effigies of individuals were being made for the purposes of inflicting harm would have been very badly received by the community at large.

Iron-age decline

As with many iron-age cultures, the greatest harm to Nok society seems ultimately to have been self-inflicted: no ancestor could protect against the damage resulting from generations of deforestation and over-cultivation. The constant demand for fuel for smelting seems to have left large areas increasingly denuded of brushwood and timber, leaving topsoils exposed and highly vulnerable to erosion. Dried to a powder in times of drought, the soil simply washed away when the rains came down. Crumbling banks collapsed into streams, along with the fragments of a ruined civilisation, which might account for the presence of the terracotta heads in long empty watercourses in what is now an arid grassland.

All male
A fine moustache and phallic tube emphasise the masculinity of this kneeling figure.

Africa – a province of Rome

The Romans fought a long series of wars in order to conquer North Africa. Once they had, it became the most vital province of the Empire.

Cleopatra VII
A portrait bust of the famous Ptolemaic Queen of Egypt (69–30 BC), made after her death.

Cato the Elder ended every one of his speeches in the Roman Senate with a ringing exhortation: *Delenda est Carthago* – 'Carthage must be destroyed'. Eventually, in 146 BC, he got his way and more than a hundred years of enmity was brought to a bitter end.

Carthage, a rich trading city in North Africa, had been the arch-rival to the up-and-coming power of Rome. They had clashed in two long wars, so Cato was by no means alone in believing that Carthage should be obliterated once and for all. After the Roman victory in the Third Punic War (the word comes from Punici, the Roman name for the Carthaginians) their legions reduced the city to rubble.

The Romans fully understood the implications of what they had done. The general Scipio – who after his final victory over Carthage was accorded the honour of using the title 'Africanus' – shed real tears at the thought of Carthage burning to the ground. It wasn't just the fate of the city that saddened him, but the reminder it offered of the frailty of human achievement, the transience of empire. For the moment, though, Rome was on the up: its victory over Carthage not only made the Romans masters of the Mediterranean but also brought them a new province – Africa.

Caesar and Cleopatra

North Africa remained a focal point throughout the Roman period. Some of the Roman civil wars of the 1st century BC were actually played out on African soil. It was at Thapsus in modern Tunisia that, in 46 BC, Julius Caesar overcame the Pompeians to become Rome's sole ruler. As dictator, he imposed a strict regime on the region and the hitherto independent kingdom of Numidia was merged with the old province of Africa to form a new province of Proconsular Africa.

Egypt had been in Caesar's sights since 48 BC, when he had pursued his rival Pompey into the northeast of Africa. Illustrious as its ancient history might be, Egypt had long since lost its political significance. In 332 BC it had become a minor part of Alexander's empire. Ptolemy, one of his generals, seized the territory after the great conqueror's death, and he and his descendants ruled it as their kingdom.

The last queen of the Ptolemaic dynasty, Cleopatra VII, used her charm and political adroitness to win over the great Caesar. With his backing, she defeated her brother Ptolemy XIII to take the Egyptian throne. She did not have long to savour her triumph, however. In the power struggle that followed Julius Caesar's assassination in 44 BC, Cleopatra supported Mark Antony against Caesar's adopted son, Octavian.

Nile scenes like this one were a favourite subject for Roman mosaics.

Imperial family
Septimius Severus, the first African-born emperor, pictured with his family. The head of one of his sons, Geta (on left), has been deliberately obscured; when Severus's other son, Caracalla (on right) came to power, he murdered his brother and had all images of him destroyed.

On 2 September, 31 BC, Cleopatra's forces were decisively beaten at the naval battle of Actium. Unable to endure the ignominy of defeat, she committed suicide.

Now Egypt, too, was a territory of Rome, but Octavian – elevated to the title of Emperor Augustus – never forgot the haven it had provided for his greatest enemy, Mark Antony. The immeasurable agricultural abundance of the Nile Valley had enabled Antony and his army to hold out for a protracted period: Augustus was resolved to prevent any possible repetition of such resistance. Egypt was accordingly given a special administrative status which placed it under the Emperor's direct command.

A thriving province

During Rome's imperial period, Africa was one of the richest parts of the Roman Empire. The fertility of the coastal strip to the north of the Sahara quickly became the stuff of legend, and ships set out from its ports every day laden with grain bound for Roman bakeries. Yet Africa was more than a granary: it was rich in produce of just about every kind, from fruit and olive oil to wine and gold. In the reign of the Emperor Hadrian (AD 117–138) it was said that you could travel the entire distance from Carthage to Alexandria without once having to leave the shadow of the palm trees.

Not only were Africa's Roman overlords delighted with their colonial possession, but the inhabitants of the region also thrived. To begin with, the Romans garrisoned soldiers here in ever greater numbers to keep an eye on the nomadic tribes and impose a stable lifestyle. As time went on increasing numbers of

civilian settlements were established – some 500 in all, connected by a dense network of roads.

Indigenous landowners were not slow in responding to the needs of the new Roman ruling class. Estates once given over to the cultivation of wheat destined for the empire's capital city were put to other uses as the astute North Africans saw possibilities in more lucrative commodities such as wine, figs and, above all, olives. The oil pressed from olives had a wide variety of uses in Roman households, not only in cooking, but also as a beauty treatment. It was used in the preparation of soaps, perfumes and face creams. And, perhaps most important of all, it provided the fuel for lamps.

Huge profits were to be made from olives, a fact not lost on the Emperor Domitian, who reigned from AD 81 to 96. The strength of the competition coming from Africa prompted his crude intervention to create an Italian monopoly in the production of wine and olives. Domitian ordered that half of all the vines and olive trees planted in the provinces should be destroyed and cereals planted in their place. The ruling was rescinded under his successors, leaving African producers free to devote themselves to the full-scale production of wine and olives once more.

EVERYDAY LIFE

How North Africans became Romans – a new era and a new way of life

The advent of Roman rule brought a new way of life for North Africa's peoples, the vast majority of whom had until then followed a nomadic, pastoral lifestyle. Although urban settlements had been introduced on the coast several centuries earlier in the form of Phoenician trading posts – most notably Carthage – life in the interior proceeded much as before. The establishment of cities by the Romans allowed the garrisoning of troops to ensure order, and the acclimatisation of the native nomads to more settled modes of living.

The culture shock must have been profound, with changes touching every aspect of daily existence. Aqueducts brought fresh water direct to the new towns, for instance, and those who could afford it even had a supply piped directly into their houses. There was abundant water, too, at the hot-spring bath houses where the inhabitants of the African provinces could indulge what quickly became a passion for bathing. Marketplaces were laid out where all the produce of the region could be bought. Residents and visitors could while away their time under the shady colonnades, discussing business with the city's movers and shakers.

There was a cultural transformation, too. Tragedies and comedies by famous writers were staged in stunning theatres. Gladiators fought to the death before roaring crowds in spacious amphitheatres, and in circus arenas charioteers raced for victory.

It was the rich, in particular, who loved to imitate the Roman lifestyle. They built their houses in the Roman manner, wore the toga, learnt Latin, and sent their sons to the best schools. In this way, North Africans became almost more Roman than the Romans. In the process, they contributed considerably to the consolidation of Roman rule in the province, in return for the pleasures and the rewards of 'civilisation'.

An archaeological El Dorado

The prosperity of Roman Africa is evident to this day, its cities and villas impressive even in a ruined state. Wealthy citizens and emperors alike sought to immortalise themselves in lavish building projects. Very few of the countries once under Roman rule can boast as many magnificent buildings as modern-day Tunisia and Libya. Climatic conditions have played their part; after the cities were abandoned, the dry desert sand covered them, helping to preserve them.

Near the tiny settlement of El Djem, Tunisia, a significant city once stood: Thysdus had a three-tiered amphitheatre in which wild animal baiting and

The praetorium at Lambaesis
The ruins of the governor's residence hint at its former glory. Lambaesis (Tazoult, in modern Algeria), was the capital of the province of Numidia from the reign of Emperor Septimius Severus onward.

Loss of learning

Before the Romans came to Egypt, thousands of papyrus rolls had been stored in the library at Alexandria, the largest such institution in existence at that time. The collected learning of all the scholars of the ancient world was deposited here – a treasure truly beyond price. In 48 BC, it all went up in smoke.

Cleopatra's struggle with her brother for control of Egypt had brought Julius Caesar onto the scene, but his battles with Ptolemy XIII's forces had been fiercer and incurred heavier losses than he had anticipated. A fire broke out on one of Caesar's ships moored in Alexandria; it quickly spread to others then to the nearby quayside. The library, with the scholarship of centuries, was engulfed in the flames.

Images of the dead
In Roman Egypt, portraits of the dead were painted on wood panels and placed on mummified corpses (background image). This hauntingly beautiful portrait (right) comes from a mummy in Al-Faiyum in Upper Egypt.

gladiatorial shows could be staged for crowds of up to 30,000. Timgad, in Libya, was founded by Emperor Trajan in AD 100. Originally no more than a garrison town for the Third Legion, over time it grew into a considerable city with all the proper amenities from theatres to thermal baths, from libraries to temples.

The most magnificent ruins by far, however, are those to be seen at Leptis Magna, in Libya. The forum, which formed the political and economic heart of the city, rivalled even that of Rome in size and splendour, and the city's theatre is one of the best preserved of all antiquity. The majesty of Leptis Magna was not a matter of mere chance: the city was the birthplace of Rome's first African-born Emperor.

An African becomes Emperor

Such a career rise was by no means uncommon in a Roman world, which demanded cultural conformity but was largely free of what we would today call 'racism'. All inhabitants of the Empire, irrespective of whether they came from Syria, Britain or North Africa, had the chance of attaining Roman citizenship, after which the way was open to even the very highest offices of state. This meant that there were phenomenal possibilities for self-advancement in the administration, or in military or political life.

The inhabitants of the province of Africa eagerly took advantage of these great opportunities – so much so that, by the 3rd century AD, fully 12 per cent of all Roman senators were of African origin. By that time, the office of Emperor was no longer reserved for those of Italian birth. The first 'foreigner' had become Emperor in AD 98, when Spanish-born Trajan ascended the throne. His successor, Hadrian, had also been born on the Iberian Peninsula. Many of Hadrian's contemporaries scathingly remarked that his command of Latin was less than perfect, but this had not presented a serious obstacle to his career.

Septimius Severus, born in Leptis Magna in AD 146, was the first Roman Emperor not to come from Europe.

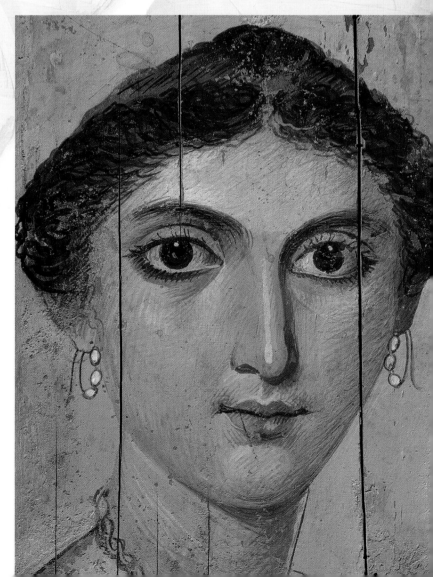

His path to success would be smoothed by the fact that his father was a large landowner. In Rome, Severus first won acclaim as a lawyer, then climbed relentlessly upwards through the imperial bureaucracy. No one ever dreamt he would rise to become Emperor, but in AD 193 fortune came to his aid when Emperor Pertinax was murdered by his bodyguard. Pertinax left no legal heir to take his place, and the military – who made the decisions in such cases – could not agree on a suitable successor.

Simultaneously, several different candidates were put forward in different provinces. Septimius Severus was then the regional legate in Pannonia, the province beyond the Danube, and his legions selected him as their candidate. He arrived in Rome ahead of his rivals and by the simple rule of 'first come, first served', he was duly elected by the Senate. His opponents, predictably enough, refused to accept his authority, and it was a few years before his position was secure. Over time, however, he built an unassailable power-base in Rome, and with his African wife Paccia Marciana, he brought a definite hint of the exotic to the Empire's capital. After Paccia's death a decade later, he married Julia Domna: she too was a foreigner, from Emesa (Homs), in Syria.

After a life of constant warring, it was fitting, perhaps, that Septimius Severus should have been away on campaign when he met his end: he died in AD 211, fighting the Scots at Hadrian's Wall. The military had been the decisive factor in his rule, yet he had not neglected other aspects of imperial life: the economy in particular had experienced a resurgence during his reign. And the lavish buildings he commissioned in his home province ensured that Leptis Magna became a jewel among the cities of North Africa.

End of the glory days

Building and investment continued apace in Roman Africa, but the Empire as a whole was living on borrowed time.

With hindsight, it is clear that the power of Rome had reached a crucial turning-point: increasingly, there were signs of the onset of decline. The sense of crisis became ever more palpable throughout the Roman world, with inflation and civil war. Eventually it became unmistakeable even in North Africa, where specifically local problems compounded the crisis. Climate change had a profound impact – the Sahara Desert expanded slowly but inexorably northward, nibbling away at the fertile coastal strip, despite irrigation schemes, aqueducts and wells. The whole basis of the region's prosperity was slipping away and the borders of the Empire, once so secure, were increasingly subject to attacks by desert nomads. A defensive wall erected along the edge of the Sahara no longer presented any real barrier to these onslaughts.

A new religion takes root

By the 2nd century AD, the new faith of Christianity was taking hold. Christian missionaries proved most successful in Egypt, where they formed their own community, the Copts, who still exist today. At about the same time, a bishop is recorded for the first time in

Exotic slaves
Romans were particularly fascinated by African slaves. Their exotic origins and dark skin colour appealed to wealthy buyers.

Carthage – the old Phoenician city had been re-established by the Romans and had prospered impressively. By the 3rd century, the whole north of the continent was largely Christianised. Even the notorious persecutions under the Emperors Decius (AD 249–251) and Diocletian (284–305) could not prevent Christianity's spread. Quite the contrary, in fact: Africa was becoming a Christian stronghold.

Two of the early Church's most influential figures were North African in origin. Tertullian, who was born in Carthage in around AD 160, was the first Christian philosopher to write in Latin, thereby making his ideas widely accessible to large areas of the Roman world. This North African thinker was familiar with Christianity long before most people in the Empire's capital of Rome, and was influential in promoting the new faith to an initially sceptical Roman public.

Arguably of more lasting significance, however, was the life and work of St Augustine of Hippo, the most important Christian theologian of late Antiquity. Like Tertullian, this Father of the early Church came from Carthage, but he discovered his vocation much later in life than his predecessor. The ebullient young Augustine was baptized in Milan in AD 387, at the age of 33, and thereafter adopted a completely different way of life. Ordained a priest, he shunned worldly things and led a life of monastic solitude, dedicating himself largely to Bible study.

On his return to his homeland, Augustine was appointed bishop in the North African city of Hippo Regius. His long life, which finally ended on 28 August, 430, was occupied by writing prolific texts on the Christian faith. The sack of Rome by the Visigoths in AD 410 stimulated his greatest work, *The City of God*, which remained one of the key texts of Christian theology until the Late Middle Ages.

Arrival of the Vandals

Five hundred years earlier, Scipio had gazed into the flames of a ransacked Carthage and pondered the fragility of human power. Now the same fate had duly overtaken his own city of Rome. As things turned out, Roman North Africa held out longer than the tottering imperial centre, but even so its fate was firmly sealed.

In AD 429, the Vandal leader Genseric crossed from Italy with 80,000 troops and began his conquest of what had been such a thriving province. It is an irony of history that Carthage was to hold out longest, the last outpost of Roman rule in North Africa, yet on 19 October, 439, this city, too, fell to the Vandals.

Citizens at play
The Romans introduced the game of dice to Africa. This Tunisian mosaic shows players indulging in this favourite of pastimes.

Axum – a Christian kingdom in Ethiopia

At its height, the kingdom of Axum extended from the Upper Nile to southern Arabia. Its rulers founded a tradition of Christianity that has continued to this day.

Around AD 50 an Alexandrian merchant, of whom nothing else is known, kept a record of a trip down the Erythraean Sea (now called the Red Sea) to the Indian Ocean. 'After several days' sailing,' he reports, 'the seafarer comes to Adulis, a fair-sized village, from which there is a three days' journey to Coloe, an inland town and the first market for ivory. From that place to the city of the people called the Axumites there is a five days' journey more; to that place all the ivory is brought from the country beyond the Nile … and thence to Adulis.'

This is the first written reference we have to the existence of a city which was set to dominate this corner of north-eastern Africa in the centuries to follow. The Axumite kingdom was centred on what is now northern Ethiopia and Eritrea, but at its height it reached considerably farther, including even Yemen, in the southwestern part of the Arabian peninsula. Its mercantile contacts spread farther still; links with the Roman world were well established, and it traded, too, with Persia and India. The conversion of its kings to Christianity in the 4th century gave Axum a unique place among the indigenous empires of Africa. It would find itself increasingly isolated as time went on and the influence of Islam extended through the region as a whole.

Soaring stone
The highest stele left standing in the ruins of the ancient city of Axum is some 21m (69ft) tall. Its chiselled doors and windows echo the architecture of the royal palaces.

Coptic connections

The Greek name for Egypt, Aegyptos, was rendered in Arabic as *qubt* – hence the name 'Copts' which became attached to Egyptian Christians. When Frumentius, a Syrian adviser to King Ezana, was seeking help in completing the conversion of the Axumite people in the 4th century, it was in Alexandria that he found his missionaries. After a series of theological disputes with both the Roman and Eastern Orthodox Churches, the Copts went their own way in the 5th century, but the link with the Ethiopian Church has endured to this day.

Apostolic succession
Bishop Petros is backed by St Peter in this fresco from the Sudanese cathedral of Faras.

An entrepreneurial empire

Modern archaeologists can shed little light on Axum's origins, but the findings they have made tend to confirm the account of our ancient merchant-adventurer. The Axumites seem to have been set apart from the beginning to some extent by the semitic origins of their ancestors, who were one of a number of tribes who crossed over from the Arabian Peninsula around 500 BC. Like the other peoples of pre-Islamic Arabia they worshipped the sun, moon and a range of other divinities; of special importance seem to have been Astar, the goddess of love, and Mahrem, the god of war.

Founded in the 1st century AD, Axum is thought to have developed as a trading centre, mediating between the African interior and what was already becoming a thriving Red Sea trade. From the heart of Africa came caravans bringing gold, ivory and slaves; incense, glass and ironware would have been among goods carried the other way. It seems likely that several cities must have vied at first for the lucrative role of middleman-state: Axum absorbed its competitors, or made them tributaries. Already in decline, the neighbouring Meroitic civilisation of the Kushite kings seems ultimately to have been another casualty of Axum's inex- orable rise to power in the region.

By the 3rd century AD, Axum was already powerful and wealthy enough to start minting coins on its own account – a crucial stage in self-definition for any state, and a bonus to historians. The coins of this era have given us a far clearer sense of the Axumite kings than we have of other African rulers of the time.

Christian kings

One king in particular seems to have been important: Ezana, who reigned from AD 320–350, and who is believed to have been the first Ethiopian king to embrace Christianity. It appears that he was converted by a Syrian, St Frumentius – called Salama by the Axumites themselves. According to ancient Byzantine accounts, Frumentius was born in Syria but was Greek in origin: as a boy he was either shipwrecked or taken hostage on the Red Sea coast. Either way, in around AD 316 he wound up at Axum, becoming a trusted adviser to the king, and companion to the crown prince Ezana. He stayed at Ezana's side as the new king began his reign. Ezana marked his conversion to Christianity by striking a new set of coins, replacing the old Arabian sun-disc and crescent-moon with the cross of Christianity. To begin with, the new creed was confined to the ruling elite, but Frumentius sent for missionaries from Alexandria.

A brief heyday

The majesty of Axum at its height is evident in the lofty granite stelae or standing stones which can still be seen amid the ruins of the city: these marked the sites of subterranean tombs. Today the tallest – a single slab carved into the shape of a slim and graceful 10-storey building, complete with ground-level door – rises to an awesome 21m (69ft). Originally there were 199 such monuments, the tallest over 33m (108ft) high, a masterpiece both of sculpture and engineering.

The stelae monuments span the whole history of Axum: in earlier days they were surmounted with crescent signs and suns; later on they were topped by Christian

crosses. But the kingdom was living on borrowed time. Long-term climatic changes were beginning to make Ethiopian agriculture less productive – crops were at the mercy of flash floods and unpredictable droughts. The impact was worsened by the effects of over-cultivation in a region whose population had risen dramatically in a comparatively short space of time.

More important still, however, were events unfolding over the water in Arabia, where in the 7th century the prophet Muhammad was inspired with the words of Allah. The early expansion of Islam was an extraordinary phenom-enon, involving military and mercantile invasions of enormous territories. By the beginning of the 8th century, the kingdom of Axum was vulnerable to both.

In 702, it is said, the Axumites rashly attacked Arab shipping in the Red Sea off Jeddah, and that it was in retaliation for this that the Arabs attacked Axumite outlets along the coast. Whatever the reason, the loss of its access to the sea left Axum economically high and dry. Culturally, too, it was now marooned, a Christian enclave in what had become a Muslim region.

The cathedral of Maria Sion
According to one legend, the Israelite Ark of the Covenant is concealed in Axum's ancient cathedral of Maria Sion.

AMERICA

In the valleys of Peru – the Paracas civilisation

The highly developed Paracas civilisation existed in Peru two millennia before the Incas. Its achievements in medicine, in art and especially in textiles were truly remarkable.

Confidently, the surgeon positioned his knife on the patient's head, then deftly opened up a small portion of the cranium, drilled along a circular line and removed a piece of bone. Afterwards, everything was closed up again with professional skill. This brain operation did not take place in a specialised modern hospital, but some 2500 years ago in ancient Peru, on the Paracas Peninsula of the desert coast west of the Andes. Here, long before the Incas appeared, one of the first advanced civilisations of South America flourished. The actual name of its people is lost in time, since they left no written records. What is known of them today is based entirely on the painstaking work of archaeologists. Through this we have learnt that members of the Paracas civilisation were already familiar with the complex surgical technique of trephination or trepanning.

Dressing the dead
In the Paracas culture, rulers and other important personages were carried to their graves wrapped in elaborately woven fabrics, so that their status would be clearly apparent in the afterlife.

Researchers investigating Paracas graves found that almost half of the bodies exhibited curious deformations of the skull which pointed to this type of treatment. Sometimes, it seems, the ancient Peruvian doctors used an alternative method – instead of drilling, the skull covering was scraped away, leaving a characteristic oval-shaped deformation of the head. Why such difficult operations should have been undertaken so extensively can only be guessed at: other early human civilisations used trephination to treat chronic headaches or epilepsy – illnesses usually attributed to evil spirits, which the operation could be seen as releasing, a ritual rationalisation of what we now see as a medical procedure.

A hierarchy in death

Because there are so few remains of settlements, our most important source of information on the Paracas civilisation are its graves. It seems clear that they believed in an afterlife. The dead were buried with gifts which might be of practical use to them, or reinforce their social status, in the realm of the dead. A sense of hierarchy is

Dancing warriors
Stunning textiles like this one were made from camelid wool from llamas, alpacas or vicunas. Unique decorative patterns were characteristic of the Paracas weavers.

evident: those who had been poor in this life were given just a few provisions to take with them on their journey, while the rich entered the afterlife laden with ceramics and golden jewellery.

Two extensive cemeteries have been found by archaeologists on the Paracas Peninsula, both on the slopes of the Cerro Colorado range. Some of the graves had already been robbed, but many had survived intact. Thanks to the intense aridity of the climate, they were in a remarkably good state of preservation.

In the older of the two cemeteries, which was in use from around 550 BC, bottle-shaped burial shafts (cavernas) were arranged in terraces along the slope. Here, researchers uncovered some 40 corpses of men, women and children. Later, a second, larger necropolis was built. Here, in an extensive complex of vaults grouped round underground courtyards, 429 mummies were found, all males, crouched in foetal positions and bundled up in multilayered wrappings. The richness of the textiles used, and of the other grave goods found with the bodies, suggests that this must have been a cemetery for prominent figures.

Exporters of pottery

The quality of the ceramics found in these graves is astonishing, and underlines the awesome artistic level of the Paracas civilisation. Such magnificent pottery was clearly not manufactured solely for personal use, but for export. The design of the pottery was sophisticated and original. Researchers concluded that the coloured pictorial motifs – mostly big cats, birds and other animals – were painted onto the clay after firing, in a procedure characteristic of the Paracas people.

Pioneer weavers

Impressive as Paracas achievements in ceramics may have been, the civilisation is especially famous for its textiles – arguably unsurpassed by any culture before or since. They pioneered weaving in South America, producing high-quality products and mastering every known needlework technique, from knitting and embroidery to lace and brocade. Again, it is from the offerings buried in their tombs that we have learned that many of the dead – the richest, presumably – were wrapped in lengths of elaborately woven or embroidered fabric. These were decorated with fantastic figures that partly resembled humans, and partly animals. Some display figures that might be interpreted as flying shamans or deities, including a distinctive, goggle-eyed 'oculate being' – perhaps a sun-god. Ordinary citizens who could not afford such luxurious trappings were dispatched into the hereafter clad in simple woollen capes.

The extraordinary skills of its weavers were among the most important factors in the rise of the Paracas civilisation to economic and cultural dominance in the region. Fabrics were not only used for clothing the dead, but also for protecting the living from the elements and for showing off social status. As money was still unknown, fabrics played a key role as a valuable bartering commodity, and thanks to the superlative quality of their products, the Paracas started out with a huge advantage.

A life in textiles
The elaborately decorated figure above holds a knife and trophy heads, perhaps indicating that its owner was a warrior.

EVERYDAY LIFE

Master weavers of varied colours and fabrics

The weavers of Paracas had mastered every technique of hand weaving and decoration, from knitting to tapestry. They used cotton for simple textiles, but for something more impressive they used the wool of the llama or alpaca. In its untreated state, this ranged across a spectrum of white, grey, brown and black, but the Paracas people developed an impressive palette of over 190 often brightly-coloured dyes. These were made out of a range of substances, from minerals and plants to insects and shellfish – blue was made from indigo, for example, and the cochineal insect produced a rich red colour. The most sumptuous fabrics also incorporated hummingbird feathers, shimmering spondyllus shells, or interwoven gold and silver threads.

Gradual decline

So arresting are the sumptuous
Paracas ceramics and fabrics, it
is easy to forget how little we
know of the social and political
organisation of the people who
produced them. Was there a single
king at the head of the state?
Did several influential figures rule
independently of one another? Was
this even a unified realm?

Archaeologists are unsure. There are
some clear signs of a state organisation
directed from above. At those settlements
which have been excavated, building and
living arrangements give the impression of
having been guided by an intelligent plan.
In the largest settlement, dubbed Animas
Altas, the mounds on which the houses
were sited all face north, for instance;
there were also arenas for public meetings
and sheds for storing merchandise.

Animas Altas also appears to have been
the scene of a tragedy during a later phase
of the Paracas civilisation. Around 100 BC
the city was destroyed, most probably by a
hostile attack – yet by whom cannot be
known for sure. Inevitably, however, the
prosperity of this people must have
aroused envy and ambition among their
neighbours. The catastrophe at Animas
Altas must have been a heavy blow for
these artists in the shadows of the Andes.
The decline of Paracas from this time on
appears to have been gradual but relentless. Other settlements had to be
abandoned, possibly also under pressure
from powerful conquerors.

In the 1st century AD, the Paracas
civilisation came to an end and the
populace withdrew to scattered villages in
the southern valleys of Peru. In their place
new civilisations arose, first and foremost
the Nazca. However, since the start of
archaeological excavations in the early
years of the 20th century, the sensational
Paracas discoveries have ensured that
this mysterious people hold a special place
in the history of early civilisations in
South America.

Distorted beauty
The skulls of the Paracas people
had flattened foreheads, as in
the example above, probably
resulting from their ideal of
physical human beauty. The
flattening of the forehead
would begin in early infancy,
when the skull is still pliable.
Today, we can appreciate the
brilliant colours of the textiles
found in the Paracas graves
(left and background) thanks to
the near-perfect preservation
conditions of the desert. Much
of the mythology represented
by the designs, however,
remains a mystery.

The early Maya of Central America

Near the end of the 1st millennium BC, Mesoamerica was in transition. As the culture of the Olmecs slowly died, the spectacular civilisation of the Maya was being born.

In the far south of Chiapas, Mexico's southernmost state by the border with Guatemala, stand the ruins of Izapa, which around 2500 years ago became an early centre for the civilisation of the Maya. Much of the site is now overgrown, several of its ancient platforms and plazas no more than undulations in the ground. Even in its heyday, around 300 BC, Izapa lacked the spectacular vistas of the classic Maya sites, such as Tikal and Palenque.

Some archaeologists refer to the Izapa monuments as 'platform mounds', withholding the title of 'pyramid' because they were raised up with earth and only clad with cobbles from the nearby river. Yet a certain grandeur still remains: the largest pyramid is 20m (65ft) high, and over 80 stelae or standing stones are to be seen. Many are ornately carved, in a style plainly reminiscent of the Olmecs, yet more crowded and apparently chaotic – almost cluttered. There is an unmistakeable dynamism in these forms suggestive of a civilisation on the rise.

Naturally affluent

Eventually, the more famous Mayan cities grew up in the lowlands of the Yucatán peninsula to the north, but these centres would not become significant until much later. The Olmec heartlands had been farther north still, around Veracruz on Mexico's Atlantic coast, although the cultural reach of that civilisation had been long. Yet it was here on the Pacific coast of Chiapas, and in the upland rainforest region of Guatemala, that the Maya culture appears to have had its origins.

Warm, wet weather all year round and rich rainforest soils made the region just about ideal for agriculture. Crops needed no encouragement to grow here; even basic methods produced bountiful harvests of maize, manioc, beans, gourds, cacao (cocoa), cotton and tobacco. Fruit, from pawpaws to guava, grew wild in the rainforest. There was good hunting: from wild turkeys and iguanas in wooded country, to deer and jackrabbits in the coastal scrub. From the sea came fish in abundance, while inland-dwellers took a catch from rivers and streams. Coastal communities also caught

Temple of the gods
Spectacular stone pyramids, like this one at Tikal in Guatemala (right), had their origins in structures created in the early Mayan cities of Izapa and Kaminaljuyú. All were built to honour the Mayan gods (background).

turtles and gathered their eggs, along with a range of seafood. What a village could not produce for itself, it could obtain by barter from its neighbours.

By any standards, this was a generous country. It was abundant in building materials, too: huts were wooden, roofed over with layers of palm leaves. Though built close to rivers and streams for convenience, they were elevated on platforms of stones and firmly stamped earth; in larger settlements, they were arranged around a central courtyard. Simple ceramic vessels were made for storing and serving food, as well as clay figurines that represented the gods or the ancestors of the community.

Upwardly mobile

Civilisation thrives where there is plenty: surpluses can be stored for future security, or accumulated as wealth which can be traded for luxuries. And commerce also involves cultural exchange – of ideas, influences, aesthetic judgments, lifestyles. Disparities of property and rank are always features of developed societies, and so it was when, early in the 1st millennium BC, Mayan village communities began to come together around larger, more prestigious ceremonial centres. Izapa appears to have been among the first of these. Here, an emergent aristocracy and priesthood established themselves, exacting tribute from the people in return for military and mystical protection. They traded the produce they received for luxury goods, and a regional traffic was soon flourishing.

Izapa had a head-start in commerce and more general development because the forests of the Pacific seaboard produced the best, most abundant crops of cacao. Among the peoples of Central America, cacao was king. It was so valued that, in time, some civilisations in the region used it as a form of money. For the fortunate Izapans, it literally grew on trees.

The Izapans were thus in a position to trade for beautifully painted ceramics and fine jewellery fashioned in gold – or, even better, a green stone known universally (though incorrectly) as 'jade'. True jade, or nephrite, does not occur in the Americas, but there are fine green-blue stones, most notably a variety of sodium aluminium silicate which takes its greenish tinge from a mixture of iron and copper. Central America may have lacked genuine jade, but it can claim exclusive ownership of the fantastic quetzal bird, whose gorgeous tail feathers were much sought after for headdresses.

As the wealth of a community grew, labour could readily be spared from agriculture for more specialised work. Whether producing high-status ceramics, lavish jewellery or clothing, or building fantastic pyramids and stelae, this non-essential labour proclaimed the prosperity and power of the community as a whole. The new ruling class had most to gain. Like the elites of other ages and countries, they led lives of leisure. Hunting was a popular pastime: the jaguar of the jungle was considered a particularly noble prize. Spear and arrowheads for hunting – or war, of course, for developed states must compete with one another – were made from flint or, in some cases, obsidian. A type of black volcanic glass, extremely hard and capable of being sharpened, obsidian was highly prized in what was, for all its sophistication, a stone-age culture.

The city of Kaminaljuyú

Today it has largely been lost in the suburban sprawl of Guatemala City, but in its day Kaminaljuyú's own expansion must have seemed prodigious. It was founded a century or so later than Izapa, on a site just over 100 miles to the southeast, but it soon dwarfed the earlier city in size and grandeur. Large areas of marshland were drained around the city to open up cultivable land to feed a rapidly growing population, believed to have doubled between 700 and 400 BC. By 200 BC, Kaminaljuyú boasted over 200 stone-clad pyramids or platform mounds, grouped around long rectangular plazas.

The forms of the Kaminaljuyú mounds clearly show how stepped-pyramid construction would have flowed logically from building practices already long established among the early Maya. They had always raised platforms on which to build their homes; now a series of these were simply set one on top of the other. In time – in the 'classic' Maya age – towering pyramids of solid stone would be erected, but the basic principle had been worked out centuries before.

The largest example at Kaminaljuyú is 20m (65ft) high, with a base measuring 90 x 70m (295 x 230ft). Like later Mayan pyramids, it was presumably topped by a temple, a house for the gods, but being built from wood this did not survive. Within the mound, in close proximity so they could be looked after by their divine ancestors, were the tombs of two wealthy rulers. Their burial chambers were packed

with rich funerary offerings including an abundance of fine ceramic vessels, 'jade' beads, quartz crystals, stingray spines, sheets of shimmering mica and painted gourds, as well as valuable tools of obsidian, bone and soapstone.

Obsidian was treasured by tribes throughout the region and was of great importance in Kaminaljuyú: the city itself was virtually equidistant between two important sources – Jilotepeque and El Chayal, both some 35km (20 miles) away. The city controlled the extraction of obsidian at both places, and perhaps, too, the traffic in 'jade' from Motagua, about 75km (50 miles) away, although this monopoly may not have been won until a later stage in the city's history.

Kaminaljuyú's other great advantage as a commercial centre was its geographical position astride a line where the watersheds of the Atlantic and Pacific oceans met. This meant it could be accessed with equal ease by peoples from both sides of the isthmus, and thus be a meeting place for the cultures of either coast. It seems to have been from Kaminaljuyú that Mayan civilisation began to spread slowly but

Double jug
The coati in this ingenious Mayan drinking jug doubles the vessel's carrying capacity. A relative of the raccoon, the coati is an omniverous mammal indigenous to Central and South America.

steadily northwards across the Petén lowlands and eventually into Yucatán. Right out in the middle of the Petén plain, the city of El Mirador would undergo an extraordinary expansion under Mayan influence. By around AD 100 it covered an area of over 16km² (6sq miles) and its population numbered in the tens of thousands.

This Mayan metropolis was connected to the nearby city of Nakbé by a causeway across swampy ground. Although Nakbé was much older (founded around 1000 BC) it was soon the junior partner. El Mirador had paved streets and plazas and an artificial reservoir for water. Its tallest pyramid, now known as the Danta, rose an awesome 70m (230ft), and another, the Tigre, was only a little shorter at 55m (180ft) – on a par with the great monuments of the classic Mayan era.

Another way in which El Mirador prefigured the later Mayan era is in the first appearance of an inscribed script, which has been found on pottery fragments and on some stone sculptures. Eventually, the Mayans would have the first fully developed written script in the Americas; prior to this, although some stelae seem to suggest the existence of a stock of recognisable symbols, there is nothing that could really be described as 'writing'.

A study in stelae

The erection of upright stones, or stelae, often richly carved, was a feature of Mayan culture throughout its history – one inherited from the earlier Olmecs. Those at Izapa and Kaminaljuyú, though far

Sad ceramic
This doleful-looking storage jar is from the early Mayan period. It was found at Kaminaljuyú, Guatemala.

more ornate in their design than Olmec examples, clearly show the influence of the earlier civilisation. They reflect a close bond with nature: a god grins baring jaguar fangs; a man stands before what appears to be a tree of life; a snake slithers from a man's ear, a fish from another. There are also scenes from the Popul Voh, the great foundation myth of the Maya that celebrates the eternal cycle of death and rebirth in the tale of the Heroic Twins, sons of the all-nourishing maize god. Highly stylised yet still recognisable divinities and heroes twist and cavort, their attitudes tortured but their tautness and energy unmistakeable.

Similar qualities are evident in later Mayan stelae, too, but archaeologists have been struck by a certain loss of innocence in the later periods. Across the Mayan lands in the classic phase and after, scenes of the same heroic deeds by the same heroic princes are endlessly repeated, pointing to the encouragement of dynastic cults through ideology. The art may be extraordinarily beautiful, but it is what could be called 'propagandist' – created to promote the authority of the state.

Not that earlier Mayan communities lacked the capacity for ruthlessness. Some stelae from the early 'formation' period show the ritual of human sacrifice: the victim, dressed as a god, was decapitated before a watching ruler. It is assumed that the sacrifice re-enacted, on some symbolic level, the nightly death of the sun deity which was necessary for the return of day, and the interment of the seed which would later spring up as maize. Later cultures in the region, notably the Aztecs, would carry out such sacrifices on a massive scale, but it seems to have been a tradition of great antiquity.

As Mayan culture developed, it steadily expanded and its centre drifted to the north and west. In time, it would illustrate perfectly the cyclical pattern that was so central to the Mayan vision of the world. As one civilisation grew up, so another was born that would eventually eclipse it.

The Adena and Hopewell – master mound-builders

From the middle of the 1st millennium BC into the early centuries AD, these two early cultures of North America developed elaborate burial cults, culminating in the construction of enormous earth mounds.

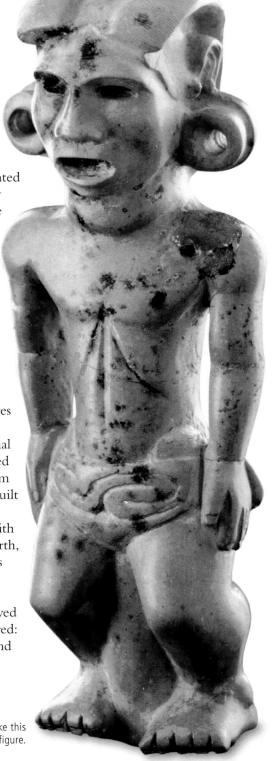

Since the end of the Ice Age, small groups and tribes had been roaming North America's so-called Eastern Woodlands, living by hunting, catching fish and gathering wild plants and fruits. From the beginning of the 1st millennium BC, these groups started to move increasingly towards the cultivation of edible plants and they began to settle in villages which they occupied for protracted periods.

Their basic agricultural understanding and skills had originated in Mexico, spreading slowly into what is now the southern United States, then from there to the lands farther north. The people created clearings in the forests, where they established small village communities. Adopting a kind of market gardening, they grew a range of plants including squashes, wild rice and sunflowers, as well as a wide variety of roots and herbs.

Maize, which would later play such a key role in the agrarian economy, was not grown at this stage. In any case, agriculture was still no more than a secondary activity: plant foods – whether gathered from the wild or purposely grown – were eaten to supplement the spoils of hunting and fishing, which were still the staple of the North American diet.

Another important innovation was the firing of pottery vessels, which allowed food to be stored efficiently and prepared more easily. These vessels could be hung over an open fire, or placed in the embers, so that relatively sophisticated and tasty meals could be cooked. They could also be used to hold maple juice as it slowly thickened into a syrup.

Around 500 BC, tribes whose lifestyles were characterised by an extremely elaborate cult of the dead, started to settle in the Ohio River valley. They have become known to us as the 'Adena' people, after the archaeological site where the first main finds were made.

Village communities

The Adena people lived in small villages which only rarely had more than ten dwellings, though these were communal roundhouses which held large extended families. Measuring between 6 and 24m (20–80 ft) across, the dwellings were built from thick wooden poles, with wattle walls between; the roofs were made with poles covered over with bark. The hearth, situated at the centre of the house, was the focus of life for the household: up to 40 people would have lived in the largest of these buildings. How they lived from day to day can only be conjectured: what we know of the Adena people and their handicrafts, like so many early cultures, has been gleaned from the offerings they left with their dead.

Pipes were popular offerings in Adena mound-graves, like this one carved in the form of a human figure.

Adena culture
Hopewell culture
Hopewell influence

Lake Michigan
Lake Huron
Lake Erie
Peebles
Missouri
Ohio
Appalachian Mts
Mississippi
Marksville

GULF OF MEXICO

Hopewell shaman
The guardian spirits of the tribe frequently took the form of a totemic animal. The skin covering the shaman in this sculpure is that of a bear.

Elaborate burial rites

Most Adena artefacts have been uncovered in burial mounds, of which an estimated 500 may have been built in their heartland in the Midwest. Up to the end of the 1st millennium BC, graves were little more than oval-shaped pits lined with bark, in which only a single person was interred. After the funerary rites had been conducted, the graves were covered over with a flat layer of earth.

The dead were handled in different ways, with some corpses being buried and others cremated. In some cases, the body was left exposed on a platform; the bones buried once the flesh had either been taken by animals or rotted away. One ritual which seems to confirm a belief in the continuation of existence after death was the painting of the corpse or the bones with red ochre or some other red

pigment. A range of everyday objects have been found placed with the bodies as grave goods, including flint blades, stone axes, combs and bodkins made from bone, as well as jewellery fashioned from bone, mussel shells or even copper beads.

From around the 1st century AD, the Adena began to build bigger, more elaborate tombs, placing their dead in spacious burial vaults or wooden mausoleums, which were then covered by mounds of earth, often huge in scale. The largest in West Virginia's Grave Creek Mound, which measures an impressive 21m (70ft) in height and 73m (240ft) in diameter. Some 72,000 tonnes of earth were shifted to create it. Important Adena burial mounds were surrounded by walls in the shape of a circle or a pentagon, within which funeral services and rituals for the dead were presumably held.

Shamans' graves

The power of the great Adena priests and chieftains is evident not only in the impressive scale of such burial complexes but in the rich furnishings amidst which they were laid to rest. Finds have included intricately decorated earthenware jars and magnificent stone handles from spear slings, along with diadems, breastplates and rings made out of valuable copper. Realistically, the copper could only have originated in the Great Lakes area, well to the north of the Adena heartland, which suggests an extensive trading network. Alongside these have been found stone stamps, which were used to decorate clothes or the naked skin with fantastical motifs depicting mythical animals.

The dead were also often given soapstone pipes in the form of human figures or animals. These were probably for smoking sacred drugs during the ritual ceremonies – a mixture of bark and leaves from the killikillick or bearberry bush. (Tobacco arrived relatively late in the region, being brought from South America by traders after AD 250.)

Especially remarkable among the grave goods were engraved skulls of humans – trophies, perhaps, from headhunting expeditions. Shamans or priests were sometimes buried with imitation antlers made of copper, deer skulls complete with antlers, and in one case the remains of a mask made from the upper jaw of a wolf, which the dead person was holding in his mouth. These were part of ritual shaman garb; although the Adena were increasingly turning towards agriculture for food, they still looked to the forests for their religious totems.

For the most part, the Adena people remain unfathomable and Ohio's Great Serpent Mound is a monument to that mystery. This extraordinary earthwork, formed in the shape of a snake devouring an egg, serves to remind us how little we understand of this remarkable civilisation.

The enterprising Hopewell tribes

From about 100 BC, other native tribes began to encroach on Adena territory from the west; by AD 100, they were more or less in control of the entire region. Named, once again, after an archaeological site in Ohio, these tribes are known collectively as the Hopewell people. Apart from more refined forms of stoneworking, pottery and textile making, their civilisation was not unlike that of the Adena, but their cult of the dead was conducted on an altogether larger scale.

The same is true of their geographical expansion: Hopewell communities were concentrated in the Ohio and Missouri

Valleys, but their cultural influence is clearly apparent through an area stretching from the Great Lakes down the Mississippi Valley to the Gulf of Mexico. Their trading networks extended still farther afield – artefacts of obvious Hopewell manufacture have turned up at sites throughout much of North America.

Such far-reaching contacts supplied them with exotic goods as prestige possessions and grave goods. Mussel shells came from the coast of Florida, as did the teeth of sharks and alligators. Copper and silver were transported from the Great Lakes area, while obsidian and grizzly-bear teeth were brought all the way from the Rocky Mountains. The major rivers acted as arteries for communications, allowing bulk quantities to be moved comparatively swiftly and safely by canoe.

Indian cities of the dead

The monumental cemeteries of the Hopewell are even more impressive than those of the Adena people. Sometimes

The Great Serpent Mound
This famous and rather beautiful Adena burial mound is at Brush Creek in Ohio. Uncoiled, it would stretch almost 400m (1300ft) in length.

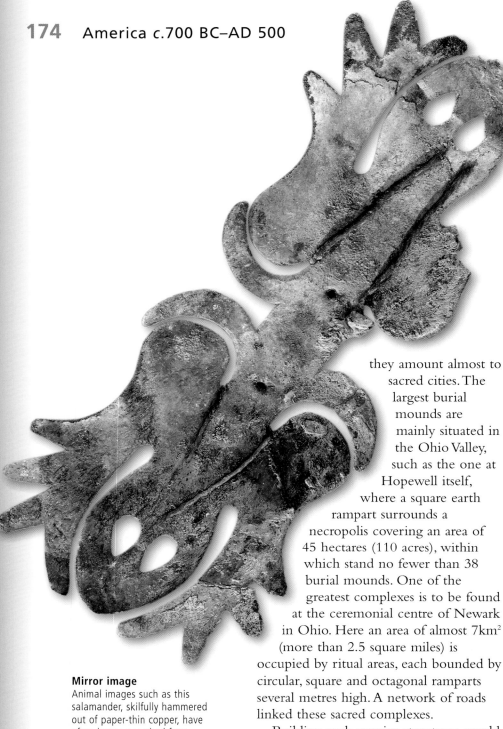

Mirror image
Animal images such as this salamander, skilfully hammered out of paper-thin copper, have often been unearthed from Hopewell tombs. Their presence seems to indicate the prominent role animals played in the worldview of the peoples of this time.

they amount almost to sacred cities. The largest burial mounds are mainly situated in the Ohio Valley, such as the one at Hopewell itself, where a square earth rampart surrounds a necropolis covering an area of 45 hectares (110 acres), within which stand no fewer than 38 burial mounds. One of the greatest complexes is to be found at the ceremonial centre of Newark in Ohio. Here an area of almost 7km² (more than 2.5 square miles) is occupied by ritual areas, each bounded by circular, square and octagonal ramparts several metres high. A network of roads linked these sacred complexes.

Building such massive structures would have required a workforce of hundreds. Simple stone tools and wicker baskets were used to shift earth by the tens of thousands of cubic metres. Though larger than the Adena settlements, Hopewell communities must still have been tiny by any modern standards, so such labour-intensive undertakings must have taken many years to complete.

In addition, the Hopewell people – in the upper Mississippi region especially – constructed several so-called 'picture mounds' along the lines of the Great

Serpent Mound of the Adena. Many have been ploughed up by modern farmers, but some have been preserved. They take the form of figures resembling human beings or stylised animals such as birds, turtles, bears, deer and dogs, and in some cases they are several hundred metres in length.

These monuments must have been intimately bound up with a cult of the dead. Their particular forms may symbolise guardian spirits in the shape of totemic animals, which played a key role in the visions of the ancient priests or shamans and in the life of the tribes. The intention was, perhaps, to place the departed, himself maybe a shaman, under the protection of the particular guiding spirit in whose form the mound was made.

The end of Hopewell splendour
The grave goods of the Hopewell elite were far more magnificent than those of the Adena. Among the gifts found in their richly appointed graves are thousands of freshwater pearls, copper breastplates, copper implements and jewellery, mica tablets, galena crystals and necklaces made of grizzly bear claws. From textile fragments recovered from the mounds, we also have some idea of how the Hopewell people dressed. At warmer times of the year, the women would have worn wraparound knee-length skirts and gone naked above the waist; the men wore simple loincloths.

The Hopewell way of life remained stable for three centuries or more but then, some time around AD 400, a number of key changes occurred. Within the space of just a few generations, hunting and warfare were revolutionised by the bow and arrow, and food production was transformed by the introduction of maize. How these affected the Hopewell is not fully understood, but overpopulation may have contributed to the destabilisation of the culture, which by AD 500 was in steep – and ultimately terminal – decline.

The Nazca of Peru – reading between the lines

The Nazca people have gained renown through the mysterious images that they inscribed on the deserts of Peru, but these were not their only remarkable accomplishments.

The extraordinary Nazca lines and figures were discovered by the modern world around 80 years ago, when the first airline passenger services began to fly over the South American continent. As the planes crossed the Cordillera and headed westward over the arid coastal lowlands of Peru, passengers and crew must have been amazed by what they saw far below them on the desert floor. Images on an enormous scale stood out clearly against the ground in which they had been inscribed. Spirals, squares, trapezoids and straight lines could be discerned, quite staggering in size and inexplicable in formation. Other figures unambiguously showed animals – apes, birds, dolphins and spiders, for example – all so gigantic they could be clearly seen even from a great height.

As researchers got to work on these strange earthworks at ground-level, it quickly became apparent that they could barely be made out: sightseers who flocked to the region were in for a disappointment. These images could only

Earth etchings
The famous Nazca hieroglyphs have resisted all our attempts to interpret their symbolism and define them. This unusual example is on a sloping coastal cliff and is therefore visible from out at sea; most can only be seen from the air.

be seen clearly from a great height. Basing their operations at the nondescript settlement of Nazca, archaeologists set out to examine the designs which spread across several square miles of the southern Peruvian desert or pampas. Bounded to the north by the Pisco Valley and to the south by the Yauca and Acarí Valleys, the area looked from the air like a blackboard full of a giant's doodlings. On the ground, however, only extended scratches could be seen.

Enduring symbols in the earth

The researchers called these scrapings on the earth 'geoglyphs', recalling the concept of the ancient Egyptian 'hieroglyph' – literally, a 'carved sacred symbol'. By analogy, these geoglyphs were signs that had been carved into the earth, and they had been created in a very special way. Their unknown makers began by scraping off the reddish-brown topsoil to expose the yellowy hue of the layer below: it was this colour-contrast that formed the basis for their designs.

The scholars were truly astonished by the scale of the figures, which in some cases were over 100m (300ft) in length. One exotic-looking bird measured an impressive 120m (400ft) from beak to tail-tip. The experts calculated that to create just the bird figure, its makers must have removed no less than 10 million square metres of rubble, a backbreaking task in the heat and aridity of the desert. But who were these people? When did they live? And why did they do it?

There is no doubt that the images are of great antiquity. It is only thanks to the extreme climatic conditions in the Peruvian desert that they are still to be seen at all: anywhere else they would have been washed away long since. This is a region where it hardly ever rains, but the earth is softened by moisture at night, which allows the stones to sink deeper into the clay-and-

Irrigation basins
In the dry Peruvian desert, every drop of water is precious. These spiral-shaped basins, located south of the River Ica, collected rainwater.

gypsum groundsoil; the mixture then sets hard, like cement, in the sunlight.

Ceramic skills

That advanced cultures had emerged in southern Peru at an early date was not news to archaeologists. The people of the Paracas civilisation were already known to have achieved a consummate mastery of ceramics and textile manufacture. Named after the village around which the remains had been found, the Nazca civilisation was also not unknown to the researchers. This culture was in its heyday between 200 BC and AD 600. When valuable pottery from ancient Peru had come onto the market in Europe in the mid-18th century, antiquarians had set out in search of traces of this mysterious people.

They had concentrated their efforts first and foremost on the Nazca graves. Where grave robbers had not beaten them to it, they made exciting finds. In common with other Andean peoples, the Nazca were accustomed to giving their dead all sorts of everyday objects to accompany them on their journey into the

Pan-pipe player
Pottery finds show that music played an important role for the Nazca. This ceramic flute player is banging a drum at the same time.

afterlife. In many of the larger graves, the archaeologists also found mummified bodies – these were buried in a squatting position, like those of the Paracas. And, similarly, their clothing and accoutrements announced their social status. Pottery proved a particularly rich seam: it was both plentiful and stunningly made, and its design and decoration offered insights into the minds of the Nazca people. Nature evidently held a special allure for them, hence depictions of animals appeared with remarkably frequency on their pottery. The Nazca were especially fond of portraying killer whales, condors, cats and snakes. No doubt, these animals would all have had specific religious significance, but in the absence of other evidence, what these were cannot be determined.

Magic and religion

One ritual that we do know of strikes the modern observer as impossibly cruel. Like the Paracas, the Nazca were in the habit of decapitating conquered adversaries. Excavations brought more than a hundred such heads to light, and these findings are corroborated by vase-paintings which show

Killer whale in clay
A key figure in Nazca mythology, the orca or killer whale was often represented in colourful pottery.

Nazca warriors holding severed heads up in triumph. Yet that was not all. Heads were often preserved – the brain was removed through a hole bored in the base of the skull, and the lips were sealed with needles or thorns. Then a hole was made in the forehead, so that the head could be carried around on a cord. These trophies were probably valued as marks of military prowess, but may also have represented the

banishment of the evil spirits which had inhabited their dead enemy.

Religion was generally important for the Nazca, just as it was for most other early peoples. Their ritual centre was probably the temple city of Cahuachi, which was located in the vicinity of the geoglyphs. The priests there led a comfortable life: recent excavations in the ruins revealed impressive textiles, possibly the ceremonial garb worn by the cult's officials. Another remarkable feature of this site is the large number of temples, among them a pyramid 30m (almost 100ft) high. So was it the Nazca who drew the famous images on the desert floor in the shadow of the Andes? Much evidence has come to light since their discovery to support this theory. One of the most compelling arguments came with the discovery of a line linking Cahuachi with a Nazca settlement on the edge of the desert.

Behind the symbols

Yet the crucial question still remains: what exactly was the purpose of the geoglyphs? Why, many centuries ago, did the Nazca put themselves to so much hard work – and significant technical effort – to create these astounding lines and figures in the unyielding earth of a desert landscape? Countless theories have been advanced – all are ultimately unprovable, since the Nazca themselves are so thoroughly shrouded in silence.

The absence of any written records to provide insights into Nazca thinking has left endless scope for speculation. For a long time, an astronomical explanation was popular, according to which the images in the earth represented constellations, and were used to chart the course of celestial bodies across the sky. Scientific interest would not have been the only factor in play here: the Nazca might also, by these means, have been able to establish the rhythm of their yearly farming activities by the stars.

Other experts, influenced by the highly developed textile industry of the Nazca, believed the lines represented gigantic weaving frames for the production of magnificent mystic fabrics. Such scholars point to the striking resemblance between the motifs scratched out on the ground in the geoglyphs and those woven into the textiles of the Nazca. Still others are of the opinion that the patterns on the ground marked the processional routes of the Nazca; on festival days, religious ceremonies would have been held here. Another theory that attracted considerable support was that the lines and figures were laid out to show the course of underground streams.

The Nazca were indeed confronted by a fundamental difficulty in this regard: the lack of water was a constant threat to their existence. The ways they found of surmounting this problem are testimony to their energy and inventiveness. They had already devised basins for the purpose of collecting precious moisture; they also built extensive systems of underground canals to bring water from the mountain foothills to make the barren land fertile. Ultimately, however, all their efforts were to be in vain. And herein may lie the real key to the riddle of the Nazca lines.

Devastating climate change

An advance in our understanding was made not by archaeologists, but by geographers engaged in the scientific study of long-term environmental vulnerability and climate change. Their researches suggested that by the time the Nazca began drawing their famous figures on the ground, the climate, having worsened over generations, had gone beyond being merely difficult and had become almost impossible.

Despite all the ingenious measures they had devised, it seems the Nazca were suffering a drought that was turning out to be not only severe but also painfully

prolonged. The discovery of tiny deposits of loess led the scientists to the conclusion that this region had not always been the desert it is today: there must once have been an abundance of vegetation. This view was confirmed by the discovery of snails' shells – another unmistakable sign of watered, fertile soil.

This fecundity had withered away, however, and with it the whole basis for human habitation in the region; the Nazca must have struggled against their fate with mounting anxiety. But to no avail: however cunning their canal systems, however resourceful their irrigation methods, there was nothing anyone could do to turn around the long-term trends of climate change. This, runs the argument, was the crisis in which the great geoglyphs were conceived. What, the people asked themselves, were the gods for? Had generations of Nazca not been brought up to believe that the earth, the sea, the sky and the waters – all the powers of nature – were under direct

VIEWPOINT

Hot-air balloons and UFO landing strips

The lively debate surrounding the mystery of the Nazca geoglyphs has occasionally given rise to many fantastic hypotheses – vehemently rebutted by serious researchers but picked up by the media all the more eagerly as a result.

For a time, there was the theory that the Nazca had been history's first balloonists. How else could figures indistinguishable at ground-level have been drawn so accurately? In order to 'prove' this theory, a flight was even made in a balloon made of cotton carefully manufactured according to known Nazca techniques. By then, however, the scientific speculation was already taking the Nazca out of their supposed balloons and installing them in spaceships. For the Austrian writer and mystic Erich von Däniken, the Peruvian geoglyphs confirmed his idea that the Earth had been visited by extra-terrestrial beings in prehistoric times. Von Däniken believed the images in the desert sands of Peru simply marked the sites where the space ships

had landed. This view won little support in the scientific and archaeological communities, though there is no doubt that, as a pseudoscientific fad, it caught the popular imagination.

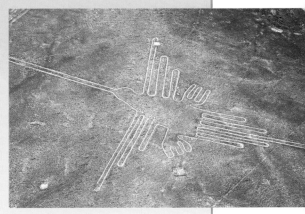

Giant hummingbird
One of the most distinctive and unusual of the Nazca line figures.

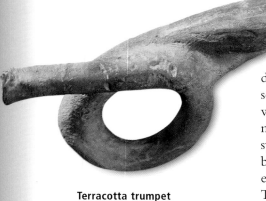

Terracotta trumpet
This clay trumpet, decorated with a human figure, would have been played at religious festivals.

divine control? Pressed to provide a solution, their priests perhaps came up with a way of sending out a desperate message to the gods to enlist their sympathy and support. With a courage born of desperation, the Nazca now embarked on their monumental task. Thousands of people dug sand and stone from the earth according to very precise plans. They could only make out the vaguest outlines of the figures and lines that they were excavating. Yet that wasn't really the point; the key thing was that the gods, from their lofty heights, should receive the earthly plea for assistance loud and clear. For the divinities to recognise what the Nazca wanted, the symbols had to be clearly intelligible: the lines marked out the courses of streams and movements of water in the ground. The animal figures were specially selected to reinforce the same message: in the Andean region, apes, birds and fish were traditionally associated with rain and fertility.

Last traces

After the Nazca had completed their laborious work, they could only wait. Yet the rains they had hoped for never came. On the contrary, the drought grew deeper, approaching ever more closely the conditions of near-rainlessness that prevail in the region today. Unheeded by the gods, the Nazca could no longer continue to eke out an existence in such arid conditions, and so they left their homeland, vanishing without trace from the historical record. They left behind them their grand designs, mute witnesses to a vain attempt to communicate with their gods all those centuries ago.

Perhaps this was something like the scene that played out in southern Peru some 1500 years ago. We shall, of course, never know for certain, but interestingly, researchers have since found similar geoglyphs in other parts of South America. In ancient Chile, in particular, it seems that peasants placed exactly the same hopes in the gods, creating scrapings in the earth to plead for water during a period of drought. It seems possible that they, at least, were more successful in their plea, but of the final fate of the Nazca, who can say?

Wounded knee
The Nazca often depicted everyday scenes in their art. This intricately painted ceramic figure shows a man with a scraped knee.

Teotihuacán – city of the gods

At its height some 1500 years ago, Teotihuacán, in what is now Mexico, was one of the greatest cities in the world. The gods had come here, the Aztecs later said, to create the Sun.

During the day, services leave the Terminal de Autobuses del Norte every half hour to travel the 50km (30 mile) route to the ruins of Teotihuacán. The journey takes an hour and most of that time is spent crawling through the congested streets of Mexico City. The modern city has a population of over 30 million, and sometimes it seems that every one of them has a car. All automobile life is here, engaged in the struggle to get from A to B. Battered lorries belch and roar; local buses lurch over potholes; little taxis dart between; casual pedestrians weave in and out, dodging the bumpers.

The Pyramid of the Sun
From the Temple of Quetzalcoatl, with its dynamic serpent sculptures, there is a superb view northwards towards the colossal Pyramid of the Sun.

Every stop–start inch is a little drama, accompanied by a fanfare of honking horns and angry shouting in the shimmering heat. Finally the traffic thins and the bus is leaving the city. Almost immediately, it is time to get off: we have arrived.

Obsidian – a highly valued natural resource

A kind of volcanic glass, fired and compressed within the Earth itself, obsidian was much prized in the ancient Americas for its hardness and its beauty. It was especially important for making tools and weaponry in societies which as yet lacked iron, as it could hold a superb cutting edge. Complete blades could be struck off from an obsidian core with a single stroke, without the laborious flaking required to make other kinds of stone blades. And the quality was of the highest order: as the Spanish Conquistadors would discover in due course, an obsidian blade could decapitate a horse.

Obsidian monkey
Though vital for tools and weaponry, obsidian was also valued for its beauty. It was fashioned into jewellery and fine ornaments like this monkey-pot.

The sudden sense of peace is astonishing. Within moments it is replaced by overwhelming awe as we look up at the ruins. Even today, Teotihuacán is a stupendous sight, its two vast pyramids rising high above an atmospheric 'Avenue of the Dead'. A city ruled by an elite of priests, the place still has an air of dread solemnity.

Yet there were two Teotihuacáns, and if one was indeed the sacred city of the gods, the other was the sprawling, teeming megalopolis of its day. This second Teotihuacán extended over 2000 hectares (5000 acres), had a population of at least 150,000 and must have felt as crowded and cosmopolitan as modern Mexico City.

The place where time began

The sacred city came first. It was founded in the 1st century BC, 50 years or so before the birth of Christ, and centred on a cave revered as the womb of all creation. This natural grotto in the volcanic rock opened very slightly to the west, at a point directly facing where the sun set on two days of the year – around 13 August and 29 April. These were about 260 days apart, which was the length of the divinatory year used by the region's shamanic priests. Over 1500 years later, the Spanish priest Fr Bernardino de Sahagún wrote down an Aztec legend describing how the gods had 'had their beginning … there in Teotihuacán':

'The time was when there still was darkness. There all the gods assembled among themselves to decide who would bear upon his back the burden of rule, who would be the sun.'

The founders of Teotihuacán may or may not have told the same story, but a sense of their own majestic destiny – and the importance of time – is seen in every

stone of the ancient city. It was astronomically orientated and built to a grid plan along a north–south axis, just to the west of the cavern shrine. In modern times, this straight and spacious processional way would become known as the 'Avenue of the Dead', though it was lined with temples rather than with tombs. The sheer scale of the undertaking is awesome: this central processional way is 5km (3 miles) long. From its conception, the city was envisaged in gigantic terms.

At the beginning of the 1st century AD, work began on building the mighty Pyramid of the Sun, which was raised up directly on top of the sacred cave. Rising in five stages and climbed by means of a gigantic staircase, this stepped pyramid is 65m (210ft) high – originally it was topped by a wooden temple that would have made it even higher. Each side of this massive structure – the biggest ever built in pre-Columbian America – is 215m (700ft) in length. Curiously, if this figure is translated into varas, an old Latin American unit based on an average arm's

The Avenue of the Dead
Seen from the steps of the Pyramid of the Moon, this processional way forms the main north–south axis of the city; to the left is the Pyramid of the Sun.

The Plumed Serpent
Feathered serpent heads gape
and glare from all around the
Pyramid of Quetzalcoatl – the
god of creativity, life, leadership
and power.

length (about 0.83m, or 32 inches), it
comes out at 260 – again, the number of
days in the divinatory year. In all its
rugged grandeur, the Pyramid of the Sun
as it is today can only hint at
its former magnificence. In
the heyday of Teotihuacán,
it is believed, it would have
been covered in white lime
plaster and brightly painted,
as resplendent as the sun
itself whose rays it reflected
so gloriously.

A smaller but still
impressive Pyramid of the
Moon was built a few
decades later, marking the
northern limit of the sacred
precinct in spectacular style.
From its position at the
northern end of the great
processional way, one might
have expected it to be the
larger of the two great
pyramids, yet somehow its
lesser scale makes the effect
still more striking. The
reason is that it echoes the

shape of the massive mountain, the *Cerro
gordo* ('Fat Hill'), which stands in the
distance behind it. The unexpectedly small
size of the Pyramid of the Moon makes
the volcanic mass appear to crowd forward
into the view, as though it too were a part
of the Teotihuacán complex.

Pyramid-building in antiquity was
undertaken for different reasons in
different places and at different times. For
example, the ancient Egyptians may have
conceived the early step-pyramid as a
literal staircase for the dead Pharaoh to
ascend to heaven, whereas later straight-
edged pyramids suggested the rays of the
sun. In cultures in the Americas, on the
other hand, their religious beliefs were
closely tied in to the topography of the
countries in which they lived; pyramids
were stylised mountains, even portraits of
nearby peaks. Known by its pre-Spanish
name of *Tenan*, 'Mother of Waters', *Cerro
gordo* was revered by Teotihuacanos as the
source of their city's all-important water
supply. The temple on top of the Pyramid
of the Moon was quite possibly not
dedicated to the moon at
all, but to an early version of
the Aztec goddess of fresh
water, Chalchiuhtlicue.

Governing principles
The Avenue of the Dead is
intersected 3km (2 miles)
to the south by another
avenue running from east to
west, and dividing the city
into four square sections.
The southeasterly section
was dominated by a
ciudadela or citadel more
than 400m (1300ft) square.
Within its walls, the temple
of Quetzalcoatl topped a
seven-tiered pyramid all of
its own, beneath which have
been found the graves of
over 200 (most probably
260) young men, offered in
sacrifice to the feathered

serpent – god of creativity and life. The bodies had been interred in groups of 18, the number of days in each of the 20 months of the solar year: time was built into the growing city.

Glowering snakeheads of sculpted stone protrude from the walls of Quetzalcoatl's pyramid: alternate heads are ringed with feathers – which also suggest the rays of the sun – or wear the squared headdress of military leadership and civic authority. At the foot of the temple pyramid was an enormous esplanade, large enough for 100,000 people to have assembled. And this still left room in the *ciudadela* for extensive administration blocks, as well as residential compounds for the city's rulers.

Ordinary Teotihuacanos lived less luxuriously and less centrally, though they too seem to have lived in separate high-walled compounds, each some 50–60m (160–190ft) square. The poor were crammed in together in some squalor – excavations suggest their tiny one-roomed homes were separated by only the very narrowest of alleys – but the neatness of the overall grid-plan was preserved.

Such a layout was comparatively unusual in the ancient world, where towns and cities tended to grow more haphazardly. The early cities of the Indus had followed a grid-like plan; more recently the Greeks and Romans had adopted them – for them (as for modern planners) the grid represented the imposition of human order on natural anarchy. In the ancient Americas, however, almost the converse seems to apply. Teotihuacán seems to have been intended as the architectural expression of an overarching cosmological order, in which the works of humanity conformed to a wider divine plan. The city was both ordered and energised by its place at the centre of a set of geographical relations and astronomical rhythms: in form and function alike it was truly the 'city of the gods'.

The commercial quarter

Directly across from the *ciudadela*, in the city's southwestern quadrant, is an area known to archaeologists as the Great Complex. With its hundreds of workshops and warehouses and a large open area which has every appearance of a market

An inner life
This extraordinary ceramic figure has a moveable head and arms, and its chest opens up to reveal another figure within – perhaps a representation of the heart or soul.

Water of life
Butterflies dance and men wave
burgeoning vegetation in this partially
restored wall painting in praise of the
rain god, Tlaloc.

square, this has been taken to be the
commercial quarter of the ancient city.
It is certain that commodities came and
went here in great quantities, and there is
no doubt that many of the city's artisans
set up here, including skilled craftsmen
working in everything from gold and
silver to ceramics and obsidian. But it is
unclear whether anything resembling
what we would understand as exchange or
trade took place, or whether this was the
centre of the sort of 'temple economy'
seen, for example, in Minoan Crete.

There, agricultural production was
organised and recorded – and any surplus
collected centrally as a sort of taxation –
by a powerful priesthood operating in the
capital. If shortages existed locally, they
could be made up from central stocks;
anything remaining could be stored or
sold abroad. The priests supervised imports
and exports, and coordinated the work of
the hundreds of craftsmen whose

workshops were housed within the temple
precincts. Some of the luxury items they
made would be kept in Crete, others
traded through the eastern Mediterranean
and beyond, part of an extensive and
profitable network of external trade.

Despite much archaeological evidence,
it is not known if such a system was used
in Teotihuacán. It would not be at all
surprising, though, given the obvious
pre-eminence of the priesthood in a city
where the monumental sculptures, though
impressive, are oddly impersonal, giving
no hint of the existence of individualised
monarchs or ruling dynasties.

A wider empire

Whether it came as trade, was collected
as tax or tribute by an earthly empire, or
was given as offerings to a priesthood
which claimed to represent the deities,
it is certain that wealth poured into
Teotihuacán. It came from communities

up and down the Valley of Mexico, in which the city seems to have been the centre of a wider state covering some 26,000km² (10,000sq miles). The main basis of its wealth was agricultural: large areas of land were reclaimed from the valley's lakes, and the resulting *chinampas* proved highly productive. Drier areas were irrigated with canals, and they too were marvellously fertile, in many cases yielding several crops (of maize, beans and squashes) in a year.

The region was also well-endowed with mineral wealth, especially obsidian: traces of over 100 specialist obsidian workshops have been found in Teotihuacán itself. Otumba, to the north, had long been valued as a source of high-quality black obsidian, but deposits found farther east at Pachuca, with their superb quality and beautiful green colour, were also prized throughout Mexico and Central America. Obsidian and fine ceramics seem to have been traded throughout the region: in return, tropical products of all kinds, including the quetzal feathers in demand for headdresses, were imported from the Mayan regions of southern Mexico and Guatemala; ornamental seashells came from the Pacific and Atlantic coasts.

Trade was so important to Teotihuacán that it may have had colonies in these places. Conversely, there seem to have been *barrios* or quarters in Teotihuacán which were populated by communities of craftsmen and traders from Oaxaca (southern Mexico), Veracruz (the Atlantic coast) and Michoacán (on the Pacific).

Decline and fall

By the middle of the 1st millennium AD, Teotihuacán was the region's pre-eminent power, the greatest city the Americas had ever seen. From about AD 650, though, it

seems it started to decline. The reasons for this are far from clear. Maybe large-scale deforestation was responsible: the Teotihuacanos had felled vast areas for timber for construction and for burning to make the special plaster for their pyramids. This had left the Valley of Mexico vulnerable to erosion, with calamitous effects on agriculture. Perhaps invasions were to blame: nomadic tribes moved into the region from the north, encroached on their territory and inter-rupted trade. Most historians agree that, whatever the problems faced, they would have been dealt with more effectively had the ruling hierarchy been more flexible. Art and sculpture from late-period Teoti-huacán has led some to suspect a rise of militarism, at a time when adaptation rather than aggression was required.

By the end of the 8th century, decline had turned into calamitous fall: unknown invaders attacked the city and seem to have razed it to the ground. The myth of the 'city of the gods' lived on – even the Aztecs would hold its memory in reverence – but the actual city of Teotihuacán was dead and gone.

Death mask
This painted terracotta mask adorned a censer in which incense was burned – in the hope, it is thought, of communicating with the ancestor depicted. The large earrings and nose ornament are indicators of high rank.

Abbreviations: t = top, c = centre, b = below, l = left, r = right, T = Timeline, B = background.

akg   = akg-images
BPK = Bildarchiv Preußischer Kulturbesitz
BAL = Bridgeman Art Library
TAA = The Art Archive

Front cover: Kunsthistorisches Museum Wien
Back cover, top to bottom: The Detroit Institute of Arts, USA/Bridgeman Giraudon; Erich Lessing/akg; Werner Forman/akg; Erich Lessing/akg.

1: Pirozzi/akg; 2/3: Anders Blomqvist/Lonely Planet Images; 4/5: The Detroit Institute of Arts, USA/ Bridgeman Giraudon; 6: akg/E. Lessing; 6/7: Z. Radovan, Jerusalem; B: akg; 7 t: Z. Radovan, Jerusalem; 8 t and T: akg/E. Lessing; 8/9: akg; 10 t: BPK; b: akg/ E. Lessing; 11 and T: akg/E. Lessing; 12: AP Photo/HO; 13: BPK; 14 and T: akg/E. Lessing; 14/15 B: Gérard Degeorge/akg; 15: akg; 16: akg; 17: akg/W. Forman; 18: bpk/P. Stüning; 19: akg; 20 t, b and T: Corbis/Royal Ontario Museum; 21: Corbis/B. Burstein; 22: akg; 23: TAA/Dagli Orti; 24: BPK/J. Liepe; 25: BPK/ J. Zimmermann; 26: akg/E. Lessing; 27 t: Corbis/C. North; b: Bildarchiv Steffens/H. Stierlin; 28: Bildarchiv Steffens/BAL; 29: Corbis/C. Lisle; 30: Bildarchiv Steffens/BAL; 31: Corbis/Burstein Collection; 32 and T: akg/J.-L. Nou; 33: akg/E. Lessing; 34: BPK; 35 t: TAA/ Dagli Orti; b and T: BPK; 36: TAA/Dagli Orti; 36/37: TAA/Dagli Orti; 38: Bildarchiv Steffens/ BAL; 39: BPK/I. Geske-Heiden; 40/41 and T: BPK/ L. Braun; 42: akg/E. Lessing; 43 t: TAA/Dagli Orti; b: akg/E. Lessing; 44/45: akg/E. Lessing; B: Gilles Mermet/akg; 46: akg/W. Forman; 47: Corbis/K. Su; 48: akg/E. Lessing; 49: rmn/T. Ollivier; 50/51: Mauritius/ Steve Bloom Images; 51 t: Privatsammlung/ Paul Freeman/Bridgeman Giraudon; 52 t: TAA/Musée Cernuschi Paris/Dagli Orti; b and T: akg/E. Lessing; 53 t: TAA; b: Corbis/ Christie's Images; 54: National Museums of Scotland/ Bridgeman Giraudon; 55: JAPAN-PHOTO-ARCHIV; 56: akg/E. Lessing; 57: akg/E. Lessing; 58 and 58/59 B: akg/E. Lessing; 59 and T: akg; 60 and T: akg/J.-L. Nou; 61: akg/J.-L. Nou; 62/63 t: Corbis/L. Hebberd; 63 b: Bildarchiv Steffens/BAL; 64/65: Erich Lessing/akg; 66 and T: akg; 67: akg/R. O'Dea; 68 t: akg/J. Hios; b: Bildarchiv Steffens/BAL; 69 t: BPK/J. Liepe; r: akg/J. Hios; 70: TAA/Dagli Orti; 71: akg/Nimatallah; 72: TAA/ Dagli Orti; 72/73 and T: akg/E. Lessing; 74: akg; 75: akg; 76: TAA/Dagli Orti; 77 and T: BPK/F. Faillet; 78 t: TAA/Dagli Orti; 78/79: akg/P. Connolly; 80 and T: akg/Naumachie; 80/81 B: S. Yamashita/ CORBIS; 81: Bildarchiv Steffens/L. Janicek; 82: TAA/ Dagli Orti; 83 and 84/85 B: Bildarchiv Steffens/BAL; 84: BPK/J. Laurentius; 85 t: TAA/Dagli Orti; b: TAA/ Dagli Orti; 86: TAA/Naturwissenschaftliche Akademie Kiew/Dagli Orti; 87 B: BPK/J. Liepe; b and T: Paul Maeyaert/Bridgeman Giraudon; 88: akg; 88/89 B: Erich Lessing/akg; 89: BPK/G. Le Gall; 90 t: akg/E. Lessing; b: akg/E. Lessing; 91: BPK/J. Laurentius; 92: TAA/Dagli Orti; 92/93 B: akg; 93 l: BPK/A. Dagli Orti; r: akg/E. Lessing; 94: TAA/Museo Archeologico Nazionale, Neapel/Dagli Orti; 95: akg/E. Lessing; 96: akg/E. Lessing; 97: Bildarchiv Steffens/BAL; 98 c and t: akg/E. Lessing; b: Corbis/W. Forman; 99 and T: akg; 100 and T: TAA/British Museum; 101: akg; 102: Bildarchiv Steffens/BAL; 102/103 B: Corbis; 103: akg/Rabatti-Dominge; 104: TAA/Dagli Orti; 105 t: akg; b: Musée Denon, Chalon-sur-Saone/ Bridgeman Giraudon; 106 and T: akg/A. Lorenzini; 106/107: C. Kozycki-Deppe, Bielefeld-Jöllenbeck; 107: akg; 108 b: BPK/Kraft; t: akg/W. Forman;

108/109: Mauritius/ Knöll; 109: BPK; 110: Basilica di San Giovanni Battista, Monza/Bridgeman Giraudon; 111 and T: akg; B: akg/E. Lessing; 112 t: C. M. Dixon, Kingston Canterbury Kent; b: Corbis/S. Sexton; 113, 114: akg/Pirozzi; 114/115 B: akg/W. Forman; 115 t: Louvre, Paris/Bridgeman Giraudon; b: akg; 116: akg; 116/117 B: Mauritius/ Rossenbach; 117: TAA/Dagli Orti; 118: TAA/Basilica San Giusto Triest/Dagli Orti; 119: TAA/Archäol. Museum El-Jem Tunesien/Dagli Orti; 120: TAA/Dagli Orti; 120/121 B: TAA/Museo della Civiltà Romana Rom/Dagli Orti; 121: TAA/ Kloster Humor Rumänien/ Dagli Orti; 122 and T: akg/J.-L. Nou; 123 and T: TAA/ Archäol. Museum Split/Dagli Orti; 122/123 B: akg/E. Lessing; 124: Ashmolean Museum, University of Oxford/Bridgeman Giraudon; 125 t r: akg; c l: BPK; t l: akg/E. Lessing; c r: akg; b: F. Teichmann, Stuttgart; 126 t: BPK/I. Geske; 126/127: T. Daley; 127 b l: Corbis/N. Wheeler; t l: akg/E. Lessing; c l: akg/E. Lessing; b: TAA/ Ephesos Museum Türkei/Dagli Orti; 128 c: TAA/Marine Museum Lissabon/Dagli Orti; t and T: TAA/Staatl. Glyptothek München/Dagli Orti; b: TAA/Archäol. Nationalmuseum Athen/Dagli Orti; 128/129: BPK; 129 t: TAA/Dagli Orti; 130 t: Foto Scala; b: TAA/Museo Archeologico Nazionale, Neapel/Dagli Orti; c:. akg/ E. Lessing; 131 b: TAA/Museo Nazionale Taranto/ Dagli Orti; 132/133: Werner Forman/akg; 134/135 B: Privatsammlung/Bridgeman Giraudon; 135 and T: Museo Archeologico Nazionale, Neapel/ Alinari/ Bridgeman Giraudon; 136/137: akg/P. Connolly; 138 t: akg/E. Lessing; b: akg/E. Lessing; 139: akg/ E. Lessing; 140: akg/E. Lessing; 141: Agentur Focus/ E. Ferorelli; 142/143: Corbis/J. Blair; 142 t: Agentur Focus/E. Ferorelli; 143 r: TAA/Musée du Louvre Paris/Dagli Orti; 144 t: Corbis/J. Blair; b: akg/ A. Jemolo; 145: Agentur Focus/ E. Ferorelli; 146: TAA/ Musée du Louvre Paris/Dagli Orti; 147: akg/W. Forman; 148 and T: Museum of Fine Arts, Houston, Texas/Bridgeman Giraudon; 148/149 B: Mauritius; 149 l: Privatsammlung/Heini Schneebeli/Bridgeman Giraudon; 150: BPK, J. Congetius; 151 and T: TAA/ Museo Prenestino Palestrina/Dagli Orti; 152: BPK; 152/153: Corbis/R. Wood; 154: TAA/Musée du Louvre Paris/Dagli Orti; 154/155 B: akg/E. Lessing; 155: akg/E. Lessing; 156: TAA/Bardo Museum Tunis/Dagli Orti; 157 and T: agk/W. Forman; 158: Muzeum Narodowe, Warschau/Bridgeman Giraudon; 159: Corbis/D. Bartruff; 160/161: Erich Lessing/akg; 162: TAA/Archäol. Museum Lima/Album/ J. E. Molina; 163: TAA/Museo de Arte Municipal Lima/Dagli Orti; 164 and T: TAA/Archäol. Museum Lima/Dagli Orti; 165 b and B: akg/W. Forman; t: TAA/Archäol. Museum Lima/Dagli Orti; 166/167: TAA/Dagli Orti; 167 B: Corbis/G. B. Vanni; 168 l: TAA/Anthropol. Museum Mexiko; r: TAA/Dagli Orti; 169: akg/A. Baguzzi; 170 and T: Privatsammlung/ Bridgeman Giraudon; 171, 172 and T: Ohio Historical Society; 173: Corbis/R. A. Cooke; 174: Ohio Historical Society; 175: Corbis/ R. Soumar; 176/177: Corbis/Y. Arthus-Bertrand; 177: TAA/ Archäol. Museum Lima/Dagli Orti; 178: Museum of Fine Arts, Houston, Texas/Bridgeman Giraudon; 179: Agentur Focus/ Science Photo Library; 180 t: TAA/ Ethnografisches Museum Göteborg/Dagli Orti; b and T: TAA/Archäol. Museum Lima/Dagli Orti; 181 and T: TAA/Dagli Orti; 182 t: E. Thiem/Lotos-Film Kaufbeuren; 182/183: Corbis/A. Hornak; 184: Corbis; 185: TAA/Archäol. Museum Teotihuacán Mexiko/ Dagli Orti; 186: akg/W. Forman; 187: TAA/Anthropol. Museum Mexiko/Dagli Orti

The Illustrated History of the World:
THE ANCIENT WORLD was published
by The Reader's Digest Association Ltd, London.

First English edition copyright © 2004
The Reader's Digest Association Ltd
11 Westferry Circus, Canary Wharf, London E14 4HE
www.readersdigest.co.uk

Reprinted with amendments 2005

Reader's Digest English Edition
Series editor: Christine Noble
Writer: Michael Kerrigan
Translated from German by: JMS Books, Peter Lewis
Design: Jane McKenna
Copy editor: Jill Steed
Proofreader: Ron Pankhurst
Index: Hilary Bird, Marie Lorimer
Prepress account manager: Penelope Grose
Production controller: Katherine Bunn
Colour proofing: Colour Systems Ltd, London
Printed and bound by: Arvato Iberia, Europe

Reader's Digest, General Books
Editorial director: Julian Browne
Art director: Nick Clark

We are committed to both the quality of our products and the service we provide to our customers. We value your comments, so please free to contact us on 08705 113366, or via our website at: www.readersdigest.co.uk

If you have any comments or suggestions about the content of our books, you can email us at:
gbeditorial@readersdigest.co.uk

First published as *Reader's Digest Illustrierte Weltgeschichte: DIE WELT DER ANTIKE* © 2004 Reader's Digest – Deutschland, Schweiz, Österreich Verlag Das Beste GmbH – Stuttgart, Zürich, Vienna

Reader's Digest, German Edition
Writers: Karin Feuerstein-Praßer, Marion Jung, Dr. Wolfgang Lotz, Karin Prager, Otto Schertler, Karin Schneider-Ferber, Dr. Holger Sonnabend
Editing and design: Media Compact Service
Colour separations: Meyle + Müller GmbH + Co., Pforzheim.

ISBN: 0 276 42987 7
CONCEPT CODE: GR 0081/G/S
BOOK CODE: 632-002-2
ORACLE CODE: 351600009H.00.24